LIBRARY CONSORTIA
A Complete Handbook

LIBRARY CONSORTIA
A Complete Handbook

By
DR. ANIL KUMAR DHIMAN
Information Scientist
Gurukul Kangri University, Haridwar
Uttarakhand (India)

Ess Ess Publications
New Delhi

LIBRARY CONSORTIA
A Complete Handbook

ISBN : 978-81-947398-2-1
Price : Rs. 1650/-

First Published 2021

Published by:
Ess Ess Publications
4831/24, Ansari Road,
Darya Ganj,
New Delhi-110 002.
INDIA
Phones: 23260807, 41563444
Fax: 41563334
E-mail: info@essessreference.com
www.essessreference.com

Cover Design by Patch Creative Unit

Printed and bound in India

Dedicated to

MY LATE PARENTS

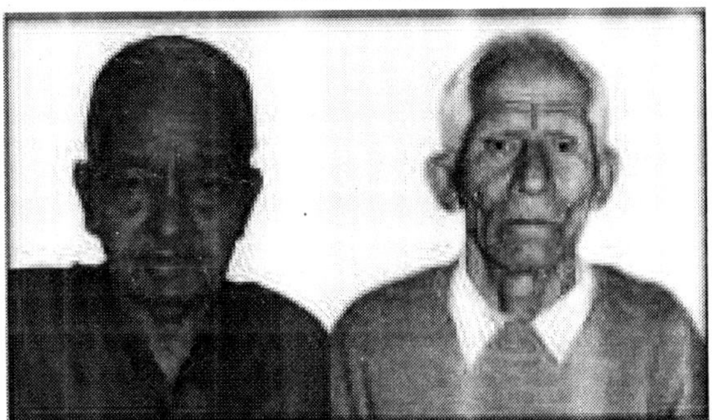

Smt. Kamla Devi and Shri Ram Lal Dhiman

Contents

Preface

It is seen that advancement in information & communication technology has led to the sharing of electronic resources in digital era which ultimate lead to the formation of Library Consortia worldwide. Though library consortia seem to appear almost hundred year back in USA in the form of library cooperation in modern sense but as they are seen today have appeared only in the last decade of 20th century. Further, two decades of present century witnessed a tremendous growth in their formation. Thus, keeping in view the importance of Library Consortia in present environment, this book is written to make aware the users about the advancement in the field of Library Consortia.

Introduction as usual is the 1st chapter which deals with the concept of library cooperation and its types that has led to the formation of library networks. Further, their role is described in brief with their contribution in the development of library services and automation activities etc. Major library networks at the international and national level are also discussed.

Chapter 2nd is on the "Library Consortium: An Overview" which provides an overview on the library consortia. Later, aims and objectives, purpose and benefits of forming library consortia are also discussed well. Further, the needs for forming library consortia, factors responsible and challenges of library consortia are explained in this chapter.

"Consortia: Types and Models" is the 3rd chapter where the types and models of library consortia based on many factors and characteristics are detailed out. Further, the characteristics of committed leadership, formal governing structure, staff participation, trained staff, sufficient funds and a mutually agreed collection development and assessment framework with the methodology for a successful consortium, are discussed.

Chapter 4th is about "Library Consortia: Components and Benefits" where various components of the library consortia such as stakeholders– users, publishers and the library documents covering e-journals and e-books, are detailed out and discussed. It is seen that the journals are the major source of communication of nascent thought among sources of information, but they are the note chord of any library's collection. Nowadays, the presence of other form of e-publications such as the e-books and e-databases etc. are emerging; thus, other forms of e-publications are discussed. This chapter ends with the advantages, disadvantages, and criteria for the success of library consortia, and the collective strength of members which provides it the power to bargain with the publishers for better subscription rates and terms of licenses.

Chapter 5th is on the "Governance, Structure and Funding of Library Consortia" which provides detailed information on the governance, organization structure and financial management of the library consortium. There are found many substantial committees which provide the opportunities for managerial and operational staff of member libraries to share knowledge with others. These all are discussed in this chapter. Further, the funding pattern for consortia and collection management for journals based on the use studies are detailed out.

"Negotiations and Licensing" is the 6th chapter where

various pricing models of information sources, factors influencing pricing models, license agreements for the consortia are dealt in details. Further, negotiation process is discussed alongwith the method of conducting the negotiations and skills required are detailed out.

7th chapter is on "Management Issues and Challenges" where the management issues and several challenges which authorities face in managing the library consortia are discussed along with static budget provisions, identification of information resources useful to users, rapidly changing technology and infrastructure. Further, issues regarding pricing of information resources, access- and archival-related issues regarding information resources, problems in licensing the resources and uses, and usability of information resources subscribed to/ purchased by the library consortia, are discussed.

8th chapter is on "Nationwide Single Library Consortium: the Merging" which discusses about the concept of nation-wide single library consortium. It is seen that there are two ways of formation of new consortium: migration into new consortium that takes place where existing consortia members, not satisfied with resources made available will see requirements elsewhere; and secondly is the merging where two or more than two consortia are merged to form a new consortium. Both of them are discussed very well. Besides, national site licensing is also discussed with the examples from international and national levels. Further, a frame of reference for the development of nationwide library consortia and details on a universal life cycle at the inter-organizational level of analysis are also given.

9th chapter is on the "Evolving Roles of Library Consortia" that discusses the evolving roles of library consortia. It starts with the mission, and further expands with the role of Library Consortia in open access initiatives. For archiving of the e-resources, various initiatives of Digital Preservation System (DPS), like PORTICO, LOCKSS etc. are also briefly described. The chapter ends with the role of library consortia in knowledge management and the comments on the future of the library consortia.

Last chapter is 10th chapter which emphasizes over the "Important Library Consortia" exist worldwide to provide information to their users with an edge over the normal routes of accessibility. However, there is an urgent drive to pay attention for induction and the motivation of the library communities towards the technology driven opportunities and to orient with the challenges of the current environment.

It is seen that a lot of literature available on library consortia but it is scattered and a very few consolidate books are available on this subject. However, present book is basically based on the work of Y.M. Patil on "Consortium Approach to Resource Sharing in an E-Environment"; and that Aditya Tripathi and Jawahar Lal on "Library Consortia: Practical Guide for Library Managers", but lot of information is taken and supplemented from other sources, especially the journals. Thus, this book consolidates the scattered literature in the field of library consortia, its development and presents their status all over the world with main emphasis on India. I thankfully acknowledge all the authors whose works have been consulted / are used or from which the help is taken in compiling this book.

I dedicate this book to my parents who are no more to see this work in present form but their blessings will be remained with me. I also would like to thank my better half, Dr. Yashoda Rani and my son Mr. Aman Kumar Jagdev, who is studying in B.Tech. (CS) – both of them helped me during various phases of completion of this work. In the last but least, I also thank Mr. Sumit Sethi, the owner of Ess Ess Publications, New Delhi for publishing this book on the right time.

Although, the care has been taken in providing

correct and update information in this book yet the readers are requested to point out the mistakes of the books to me so that they could be rectified in next edition of the book. However, it is hoped that this book will be useful not only for the working professionals but also the teachers of library & information science will find it worthy.

— **Dr. Anil Kumar Dhiman**
Information Scientist
Gurukul Kangri University
Haridwar (Uttarakhand) India

List of Abbreviations

AACR-II	Anglo American Cataloguing Rules – II
AARLIN	Australian Academic and Research Library Network
ADS	Astrophysics Data System
ADR	Alliance Digital Repository
ADSUG	ADS Users Group
AICTE	All India Council on Technical Education
AIIMS	All India Institute of Medical Sciences
ALA	American Library Association
ALIS	Access to Libraries in Northamptonshire
ALPSP	Association of Learned and Professional Society Publishers
ANKOS	Anatolian University Libraries Consortium
ANSI	American National Standards Institute
ARL	Association of Research Libraries
ASCII	American Standard Code for Information Interchange
ATUNET	Asia Technological University Network
BALNET	Bangalore Library Network
BARC	Bhabha Atomic Research Centre
BNB	British National Bibliography
BONET	Bombay Library Network

CALIBNET	Calcutta Library Network
CALICO	Cape Libraries Co-operative/Cape Library Consortium
CALIM	Consortium of Academic Libraries in Manchester
CALIS	China Academic Library & Information System
CALIS	China Academic Library Consortium
CARL	Canadian Association of Research Libraries
CARLI	Consortium of Academic and Research Libraries in Illinois
CASHL	China Academic Humanities and Social Science Library
CASS	Collaborative Academic Store for Scotland
CAVAL	Co-operative Action by Victorian Academic Libraries
CC	Carolina Consortium
CCF	Common Communication Format
CCLC	Community College Library Consortium
CDAC	Centre for Development of Advanced Computing
CDOT	Centre for Development of Telematic
CD-ROM	Compact Disc – Read Only Memory
CERA	Consortium for e-Resources in Agriculture
CFTRI	Central Food Technological Research Institute
CIC	Committee on Institutional Cooperation
CIP	Cataloguing in Publication
CISTI	Canada Institute for Scientific and Technical Information
CLIR	Council on Library and Information Resources (US)

COC	Consortium of Consortia
CONCERT	Consortium on Core Electronic Resources in Taiwan
COUNTER	Counting Online Usage of Networked Electronic Resources
CRL	Centre for Research Libraries
CSIR	Council of Scientific and Industrial Research
CSIRO	Commonwealth Scientific and Industrial Research Organization
CUCOLIS	Current Content for Library and Information Science
CURL	Consortium for University Research Libraries
DAE	Department of Atomic Energy
DBMS	Database Management System
DDS	Document Delivery System
DELCON	DBT's Electronic Library Consortium
DELNET	Developing Library Network
DESIDOC	Defense Scientific Information & Documentation Centre
DIALOG	An Online Information Service owned by ProQuest
DIT	Department of Information Technology
DLF	Digital Library Federation
DOAJ	Directory of Open Access Journals
DOP	Department of Posts
DOT	Department of Telecommunication
DPS	Digital Preservation Systems
DRDO	Defense Research and Development Organization
DSIR	Department of Scientific and Industrial Research

DST	Department of Science & Technology
EASEL	Eastern Seaboard Libraries
EBSCO	Elton B. Stephens Company
EIFL	Electronic Information for Libraries
EPIC	Electronic Purchasing in Collaboration
E-RAMS	E-Resources Access Management
ERIC	Education Resources Information Centre
ERMED	Electronic Resources in Medicine
ERNET	Education and Research Network
FORSA	Forum for Resource Sharing in Astronomy and Astrophysics
FRELICO	Free State Library Cooperative
FTE	Full Time Equivalent
GAELIC	Gauteng and Environs Library Consortium
GALILEO	Georgia Library Learning Office
GST	Goods and Services Tax
HELINET	Health Science Library and Information Network
HTML	Hyper Text Markup Language
IARI	Indian Agriculture and Research Institute
ICAR	Indian Council of Agricultural Research
ICCMP	Illinois Cooperative Collection Management Programme
ICCPC	Iowa Community College Online Consortium
ICMR	Indian Council of Medical Research
ICOLC	International Coalition of Library Consortia
ICT	Information & Communication Technology
IDAL	Illinois Digital Academic Library
IEL	IEEE'S Electronic Library
IFLA	International Federation of Library Associations and Institutions

IGCAR	Indira Gandhi Centre for Atomic Research
IIA	Indian Institute of Astrophysics
IIM	Indian Institute of Management
ILL	Inter-Library Loan
ILLINET	Illinois Library and Information Network
INDEST	Indian National Digital Library in Science & Technology
INDONET	India's First Computer and Data Network
INFER	Italian National Forum on Electronic Information Resources
INFLIBNET	Information & Library Network
INSDOC	Indian National Scientific Documentation Centre
IR	Information Retrieval
ISI	Indian Statistical Institute
ISO	Indian Standard Organization
IUCAA	Inter University Centre for Astronomy and Astro-Physics
IULC	Inter University Library Committee
JANET	Joint Academic Network (UK)
JCCC	J-Gate Custom Content for Consortium
JCS	Joint Customer Service
JISC	Joint Information System Committee
JSTOR	Journal Storage
KESLI Consortium	Korean Electronic Site License Initiative Consortium
KM	Knowledge Management
KRLDC	Kansas Regents Library Database Consortium
LC	Library of Congress
LCSH	Library of Congress Subject Headings
LISA	Library and Information Science Abstract

LOC	Library of Congress
LOUIS	Louisiana Library Network
MALIBNET	Madras Library Network
MARC	Machine Readable Cataloguing
MCIT	Ministry of Communication and Information Technology
MEDLINE	Medical Literature Analysis and Retrieval System Online
MIRACL	Missouri Research and Academic Consortium of Libraries
MOBIUS	Consortium of Libraries in Missouri
MYLIBNET	Mysore Library Network
NAL	National Aerospace Laboratory
NARS	National Agricultural Research System
NASA	National Aeronautics and Space Administration
NASSDOC	National Social Science Documentation Centre
NBHM	National Board of Higher Mathematics
NCBS	National Centre for Biological Sciences
NCL	National Chemical Laboratory
NCLIS	National Commission of Libraries and Information Science
NCRA	National Centre for Radio Astrophysics
NEICON	National Electronic Information Consortium
NELINET	New England Library and Information Services Network
NERL	Northeast Research Libraries Consortium
NESLI	National Electronic Site Licensing
NIC	National Informatics Centre
NICNET	National Informatics Centre Network

NILRC	Network of Illinois Learning Resources in Community Colleges
NISCAIR	National Institute of Science Communication and Information Resource
NISCOM	National Institute of Science Communication
NISO	National Information Standards Organization
NISSAT	National Information System for Science & Technology
NIT	National Institute of Technology
NKRC	National Knowledge Resource Consortium
NLIST	National Library and Information services Infrastructure for Scholarly Content
NML	National Medical Library
NSTL	National Science and Technology Library (China)
NULIC	Nigerian University Libraries Consortium
OA	Open Access
OAIster	Online Combined Bibliographic Catalogue of Open Access Material aggregated using OAI-PMH
OCLC	Online Computer Library Centre
ODLIS	Online Dictionary of Library & Information Science
OhioLINK	Ohio Library and Information Network
OPAC	Online Public Access Catalogue
OUP	Oxford University Press
PALC	Pennsylvania Academic Library Consortium
PCG	Publishers Communication Group
PDF	Portable Document Format
PIRUS	Publishers and Institutional Repository Usage Statistics

PPV	Pay per View
PRL	Physical Research Laboratory
PULINET	Provincial Library Network
PUNENET	Pune Library Network
RLG	Research Libraries Group
ROI	Return on Investment
RRL	Regional Research Laboratory
RTF	Rich Text Format
SAMEER	Society for Applied Microwave Electronics Engineering & Research
SANLIC	South African National Library and Information Consortium
SCELC	State-wide California Electronic Library Consortium
SCONUL	Standing Conference of National and University Libraries
SERU	Shared E-Resource Understanding
SGML	Standard Generalized Markup Language
SNDT University	Shreemati Nathibai Damodar Thackeray Women University
SOLINET	Southeastern Library Network
SPARC	Scheme for Promotion of Academic and Research Collaboration
SURF	Samenwerkende Universitaire Reken Faciliteiten (Netherlands)
SUSHI	Standardized Usage Statistics Harvesting Initiative
SWALNET	Swaziland Library and Information Network
TEBNET	Taiwan E-Book Network
THAILNET	Thai Library Network
TIFR	Tata Institute of Fundamental Research

TRAI	Telecom Regulatory Authority of India
TRLN	Triangle Research Libraries Network
UAP	Universal Availability of Publication
UBC	Universal Bibliographic Control
UGC	University Grants Commission
UGC-INFONET	University Grants Commission – Information Network
UKB	Dutch Consortium of the Thirteen University Libraries
UKERNA	United Kingdom Education and Research Networking Association
UKLP	UK Libraries Plus
UNDP	United Nations Development Programme
UNESCO	United Nations Educational, Scientific and Cultural Organization
UNIMARC	Universal Machine-Readable Catalogue
USBE	United States Book Exchange
USMARC	US Machine Readable Catalogue
VALE	Virtual Academic Library Environment of New Jersey
VIVA	Virtual Library of Virginia
WISPALS	Wisconsin Project for Automated Libraries
WRLC	Washington Research Library Consortium
WWW	World Wide Web

ABOUT THE BOOK

The present book "Library Consortia – A Complete Handbook" is primarily written to make aware the users about the concept and development of library consortia that has emerged worldwide as a major mean for resource sharing in digital environment. The book is divided into ten chapter, namely:

- Introduction
- Library Consortium: An Overview
- Consortia: Types and Models
- Library Consortia: Components and Benefits
- Governance, Structure and Funding of Library Consortia
- Negotiations and Licensing
- Management Issues and Challenges
- Nationwide Single Library Consortium: the Merging
- Evolving Roles of Library Consortia
- Important Library Consortia

It is hoped that this book will be useful not only for the working professionals but also the teachers of library & information science will find it worthy.

1
Introduction

The development of information & communication technology has compelled the libraries to adopt new philosophies and technologies for service delivery and also to reduce the cost of information around the world. But maintaining the breath and depths of collections is the single greatest challenge confronting libraries, be it, academic, special, national, or public. However, failure to confront this challenge successfully and fundamentally threatens the library's mission and vision. Libraries have realized that no matter how they are well funded, it is difficult to acquire all the materials needed by their clientele. In view of this fact, partnership and cooperation-local, national and international - have become inevitable for all libraries.

Historically, it is observed that there existed a common form of library cooperation for sharing of union catalogue information, storage facilities, collection development and sharing human resource at local, regional, and national level. In other way, library cooperation has been on inter-library loan wherein libraries agree to enter into reciprocal borrowing and use of other materials from other libraries (Potter, 1997; Kohl,

2003). This form of library cooperation enabled librarians to borrow micro/macro documents which otherwise were not available locally. This was achieved through available means of communication, viz. postal delivery, fax and courier services etc.

1.1. DEFINITION OF COOPERATION

Basically, cooperation is a mode of operation with common goal of sharing available resources held in other organizations. Its goal is to enhance the access to available materials with least spending with minimum time.

Webster's Dictionary defines *cooperative* in part as "given to or marked by working together or by joint effort toward a common end" and *coordinates* as "to bring into a common action, movement or condition; regulate and combine in harmonious action"

Cooperation, coordination and collaboration invariably are used as synonymous terms in resource sharing or consortium approach for resource sharing. Each has a different connotation which can be defined as follows (Evans, 2002):

Cooperation : It is the level with the least interaction between participating organizations but there is no formal common mission, structure or planning effort. The participants share information as needed and retain all authority with virtually no risk. It is easiest level to achieve desired goals. However, there is little stability to such efforts and they tend to be of short duration.

Coordination : It is middle level activity where discussion takes place with generally agreed to missions or goals. These may be written documents with common structure and planning/operation process.

Collaboration : It is the highest-level activity with formal legal structure created by the participants. It involves participants contributing some of their resources like 3Ms -money, matter and materials and physical space, etc. to the programme/projects.

1.2. LIBRARY COOPERATION

Library cooperation is an age-old concept that was evolved as a realization to the fact that no library is an island. It is a social phenomenon by which libraries are mutually engaged to increase the service capabilities of a single library and by which the librarians extend their option to serve clients. It includes sharing of materials or function or services that constitute a library system. A material includes both documentary and non-documentary forms. Its function covers the activities concerning about the acquisition, processing, storage, etc. and services include techniques, activities and procedures employed to establish contact between the document and its consumer i.e. lending, reference, documentation and translation etc.

1.2.1. Library Cooperation - a Formative Stage of Sharing Library Resources

Cooperation is the important feature of public life, where people work together with common interest and intention. This means, they take care to act in ways that nurture each other's interests. When it is not possible to meet everyone's interests, they agree for joint plans of action that aim at sharing the pain on a basis that all regard as fair. Enhanced user services and greater satisfaction of user wants and needs must be a principal rationale for any sort of co-operative activity among libraries. The libraries all over the world recognize that they can no longer endeavour to own all the materials that their users need or want, and that sharing is necessary in order to achieve maximum reader satisfaction. Co-operation in terms of resource sharing and collection development is one way to satisfy the users' demand.

Co-operation thus, is an essential facet of modern library management in most of the countries. Co-operation may occur at many levels; from simple inter-library loan services and reciprocal access for users, to more direct resource sharing and joint storage facilities, to co-operative collection development and joint licensing agreements with vendors and publishers. These co-operative activities are becoming increasingly important for library services primarily because of the rapidly growing data, improvements in telecommunications and rising costs associated with the acquisition of library materials. Evidently, there is a growing body that electronic access leads to greater usage of resources. The motivation for co-operation that might lie embedded in the philosophy of librarianship goes beyond a statement of principle and becomes increasingly realistic as the factors facilitating delivery - technological, organizational, political - improve the common sharing of information through a network is ordinarily consortium.

1.2.2. Historical Perspective of Library Cooperation

Library cooperation seems to develop from sharing of union catalogue information, storage facilities, collection development, and human resources at local, national, and regional levels. Another form of co-operation has been based mainly on inter-library lending services where co-operating libraries agree to enter into reciprocal borrowing and use of materials from other libraries. This form of co-operation enabled libraries to borrow books and periodical articles which were not available locally. Though, there was the need for library cooperation in the past, it was meted out locally with locally available resources and locale network. However, the information revolution that transformed the world into a global village extended the library services to collect and retrieve information available in various forms either in their building or outside.

Library Cooperation among libraries can be traced back to 200 B.C., when materials from the great Alexandria library were borrowed by the library of Pergamum. Libraries over the centuries practiced resource sharing in the form of inter-library loan either formally or informally. Later, planned library cooperation started in Germany around the year 1770 when G.H. Lessing, the Librarian in Wolfenbuttel formulated aplan for the exchange of duplicate materials between libraries (Dhiman and Rani, 2007).

However, the system of library cooperation as we see today began in the second half of the twentieth century with the establishment of Online Computer Library Centre (OCLC), USA in 1967. The interest in resource sharing rose among the libraries around the world in the next decades.

Library cooperation in 20th century was mainly concentrated on the compilation of union catalogues of holdings of participating libraries. With the infusion of information technology into libraries, the mode of cooperation took a new pace. In 21st century, library cooperation took a diversified impetus in the form of cooperative content acquisition, catalogue sharing, continuing education, cooperative digitization and storage, etc. But the advances in internet technologies, the new forms and formats of digital documents and new modes of scholarly communication make a great impact on the activities of libraries round the globe (Jaswal, 2005).

1.2.3. Definitions of Library Cooperation

The term library co-operation, library networking, library linkages, library collaboration, and library consortia are used to describe formal and informal co-operation, partnership and resource sharing activities in libraries (Martey 2002). In the literature dealing with library cooperation, a variety of words are used to define collaborative efforts. Brodie (1996) notes that "some of these are "action" words, such as connect, consult, cooperate, collaborate, collude; and "organization" and others refer to, for example, conference, committee, coalition, consortium, corporation and community.

Inspite of different shades of meaning, such as degree of engagement or social acceptability, these words always suggest the coming together of distinct parties to achieve a common end, where in activities usually limited in time space. In general, the participants in such activities maintain distinct roles and remain "in control" of the situation". Cooperation, as defined by Merriam Webster's Collegiate Dictionary, is "the action of cooperating with common effort; the association of persons for common benefit"(Merriam- Webster's Collegiate Dictionary, n.d.). When it is used in the context of libraries it becomes library cooperation.

Library cooperation in the APT review of 1995 (APT partnership, 1995) is defined as: "the creation and operation of equitable, that is mutually 'fair', collaborative arrangements between libraries and information providers which enhance the common good though making information available to all potential users (without obstacle to access by reason of cost) which is more extensive or more valuable to the user and/or is of lower cost to the collaborating providers".

1.2.4. Major Barriers to Library Co-operation

The logic that co-operation helps us to achieve the key aims of library profession seems incontrovertible, yet there are many who continue to resist the reality. Evans (2002) devotes considerable space to barriers to cooperation under six headings:

- Institutional;
- Legal, political and administrative;
- Technological;
- Physical;
- Human and
- knowledge-based issues.

These impediments present an unrealistically pessimistic view and tend to give minor problems the same level of significance as major barriers. However, there are four major barriers to effective co-operative ventures:

- Desire for autonomy;
- Competitive environment;
- Changing institutional focus; and
- Financial constraints.

Though, these barriers to co-operation are more than matched, by factors that facilitate the development of effective co-operative arrangements but the unending inflationary spiral in the cost of library materials is probably the principal factor in favour of co-operation. This is accompanied by increased output by publishers, and the escalating introduction of new or improved multimedia formats. However, costs and volume, will continue to be the principal motivators that push libraries into co-operative arrangements. These factors favouring co-operation are evident as the co-operative enterprise over the years has evolved from resource sharing to coordinated collection development to coordinated collection management. These have emerged as the principal phases in the history of library co-operation to date.

1.2.5. Types of Library Cooperation

Based on the geographical area covered, library cooperation may be of following tyeps:

- International Level: Universal Availability of Publication (UAP) programme introduced by IFLA, Universal Bibliographic Control (UBC)];
- National Level : National Social Science Documentation Center (NASSDOC);
- Regional Level and
- Local Level.

Further, based on the functional area covered library cooperation may be of following types:

- Sharing of documentary resources, such as the cooperative acquisition, cooperative processing, cooperative storage for the documents which are less used, cooperative delivery system i.e., inter-library lending, development of network, developing consortia.
- Sharing of manpower resources such as the arrangement for the cooperative staff training.
- Sharing of other library facilities or equipment such as the sharing of the computer and reprographic equipment that cannot be afforded by small libraries due to their high cost and sharing of finance.

Besides, based on subject basis, library cooperation may be general or subject based cooperation.

1.2.6. Kinds of Library Cooperation

The following are some of the kinds of library cooperation.

(i) Co-operative Acquisition : The process of acquisition involves selecting, placing orders to vendors, passing of bills, payments, etc. All these activities can be minimized by cooperative acquisition, which will also result in saving the cost, earning of a larger discount, saving time and clerical labour.

INSDOC (Now NISCAIR), New Delhi, initiated Centralized Acquisition of Periodicals (CAP) through which it was acquiring foreign periodicals for about 30 CSIR laboratories.

(ii) Cooperative Processing : If each library, within the network of resources sharing, processes a book through the computer then the job of cataloguing can be shared by all the libraries within the network in the form of-

- ***Printed Catalogue Card Service* :** In this process some libraries, usually of national status, undertake the responsibility of producing printed catalogue cards which are available on a payment basis for other libraries. Library of Congress and BNB are producing printed catalogue card service.

- ***Prenatal Cataloguing / Cataloguing In Publication (CIP)*** : The term prenatal cataloguing was used by Dr. S. R. Ranganathan. Prenatal technical work involves completion of technical work by the national central library of a country on each book before its release by the publisher.

  The Cataloguing in Publication (CIP) programme was initiated by Library of Congress (LOC), USA in 1971 with 27 participating publishers. Here, the process of classification and cataloguing of a publication is done before the book is released. The cataloguing data provided by the LOC is printed on the reverse of the title page which helps the individual libraries in copying down the data on their catalogue card.

- ***Centralized Classification and Cataloguing***: Centralized classification and cataloguing service of Online Computer Library Centre (OCLC), and Machine-Readable Catalogue (MARC) project of the Library of Congress are remarkable in this direction. Online cataloguing, retrospective conversion using databases also lead to economy with quality.

(iii) Cooperative Storage : Every library has limited space for storage of books. So, the old and less used books are weeded out regularly to provide space for new acquisition. Moreover, the maintenance of the unused or little used books not only consume valuable space of the library but also involve money and labour. Hence, by cooperation / resources sharing a centralized cooperative storage of less used books can be achieved.

The material which is not in active use may be stored on a cooperative basis at a central dormitory. With the initiative of NASSDOC (ICSSR), New Delhi and Jawaharlal Nehru University, Delhi an Inter Library Resource Centre

(ILRC) was established in New Delhi in 1975. Some 38 libraries of Delhi deposited their less used serials and government documents at this centre.

(iv) Cooperation through Networking : The term 'network' is synonymously used for 'Resource Sharing' or 'Cooperative System', because of two important reasons – potential improvement of Library and Information operations by inter-connecting individual library systems with the more recently developed facilities for data and information transfer; and the significant role played by the computer telecommunications and new reprographic techniques.

Network implies "Computer and Communication links with each other and to share programmes, facilities, data and knowledge-bases". A network can be local, national or even international, wherein multiple computers are interconnected, which can communicate with each other. The nodes may be computers, terminals, workstations or communication units of various kinds distributed over different locations. Networking is important for all types of libraries in modern times as they enable users to have access to the resources of other libraries.

1.3. LIBRARY NETWORKING

Library networking is an arrangement or a structure that links a group of libraries which have agreed to work together and / or share their resources in an organized basis to a certain degree. It can be defined as a "two or more libraries engaged in a common pattern of information exchange through communication for some functional purposes". It is meant to promote and facilitate the sharing of resources available within a group of participating libraries.

Library networking refers to a "interconnected platform of some group of libraries with certain agreements aims to satisfy and fulfill their users' need. The common objective of a library network is to acquire and develop unique collection of the each and avoiding the duplication of materials to resolve the budgetary problem. Each library performs sharing of resources to each other's on demand basis" (Wikipedia, 2019).

1.3.1. Definitions

The National Commission on Libraries and Information Science (NCLIS, 1975) in its National Programme Document defines a library network as: "two or more libraries and/or other organizations engaged in a common pattern of information exchange, through communications, for some functional purpose".

Jebraj and Devadoss (2005) has described a library network broadly "as a group of libraries coming together with some agreement of understanding to help each other with a view to satisfying the information needs of their clientele".

Thus, a library network usually consists of a formal arrangement whereby materials, information and services provided by a variety of libraries and other organizations are available to all potential users. Libraries may be in different jurisdictions but they agree to serve one another on the same basis as each serves its own constituents. Computer and telecommunications may be among the tools used for facilitating communication among them".

1.3.2. Precondition for Networking

The agreements between library authorities of different libraries, building or developing required infrastructure, maintenance of standardization in terms of classification schemes, cataloguing schemes, uses of some common library management software and so on are some of the preconditions before developing any kind of network. Some other preconditions are (Johnson, Sheeba Zion and Boselin Prabhu, 2019):

(i) Automation of the Member Library : For the success of network in the long run, each of the member libraries must have a policy to automate every function of the library - acquisition, cataloguing, classification, serials control, circulation, SDI, current awareness services etc. - in the shortest possible time. This helps the library to have a computer environment which is required to design, develop, maintain and to operate several databases, to reduce the cost of library operations as well as network operations.

(ii) Hardware and Software : The network should be able to recommend to participating libraries the type of hardware and software they need for their in-house functions and for networking purposes. Hardware should be selected considering the number of entries the participating libraries can generate within the next few years.

(iii) Trained Manpower : Trained staff should be there to look after all activities in member libraries. If there is no adequately trained manpower in each of the member libraries, attempts should be made to train or/ and recruit new skilled library personnel.

(iv) Standardization : It is essential to agree upon a standard for the purpose of creating databases. Thus, all libraries should follow a standard MARC format, AACR-II, a standard thesaurus like Library of Congress Subject Headings (LCSH) etc. uniformly. Although efforts should be made to have one classification scheme for all participating libraries yet the use of different numbers should not become a hurdle as search requests are mostly about authors, titles, editors and subject descriptions.

Besides, it is preferable to have certain communication facilities such as Fax, Telephone, dedicated leased line etc. as a part of the network system in each of the member libraries for the effective working of the network. E-mail and internet facilities should also be made available with the libraries so that they should be able to access international databases, preferably individually or through the network host to begin with.

1.3.3. Advantages of Library Networking

The advantages of library networking are as follows (Johnson, Sheeba and Boselin Prabhu, 2019):

(i) Cooperative Collection Development : In the age of information explosion no individual library, however resourceful, can be self-sufficient in terms of documents. For a library; however, rich it may be impossible to acquire and store all the documents within its four walls. Networking may help to develop collection in terms of books, periodicals, patents, standards, audio visuals, CDs etc. and share those resources.

(ii) Meets Specialized User Demand : User needs are varied and diversified. To meet the specialized need one has to approach such special collection or special service that are available in special libraries. Networking may help in the sharing of experience and expertise of the library personnel.

(iii) Breaks Financial Constraint : It is noted that library budgets are decreasing day by day. Thus, with the provision of library networking a library can arrange for cooperative staff training, can exchange the staff for performing some technical works. Sharing of the finance for cooperative acquisition and collection development, processing, etc. can also be made.

(iv) Reduces Unnecessary Duplication of Work : The networking will remove the efforts in duplication of classification, cataloguing, and such others working.

(v) Barrier Breaker : Library networking is needed to break the barriers of distance and time. Further, it will reduce the physical movement of materials.

(vi) Sharing of Hardware Resources : Expensive computer equipment, microfilming equipment, digitizing devices for newspaper, reprographic systems, etc. can be procured by a networking group for the benefit of all the libraries of the network. Networking is also needed to connect personal computers with the server computer and/or super computer for problem solving.

(vii) Sharing of Software Resources : The software that is too expensive to procure by individual libraries can be procured and shared by the network for solving larger programmes, information retrieval, and so on. The software can be installed in the central computer and all other computers can be used as client, if it is intranet. Otherwise, not required in this direction.

(viii) Development of Union Catalogue : Network helps in developing union catalogue to refer the user to the documents in any of the other participating libraries and it can be consulted by the user in order to know which document is available in which library. For example, Union Catalogue of Social Science Serials was compiled and published by the NASSDOC (ICSSR), New Delhi in 1980s. Inflibnet efforts are also praiseworthy to mention in this direction.

(ix) Development of Database : Library network helps in developing special database to meet out some special need by the participatory libraries. Local information which is available over the network can be controlled locally that satisfies the accuracy using networking. For example, National Union Catalogue of Scientific Serial in India in 1988 was the result of the work of INSDOC in collaboration with several scientific libraries all over India.

(x) Document Delivery Service (DDS) : Networks enable librarians, faced with clients' information needs beyond their local resources, to identify and obtain materials and services for those clients. Inter-library loan, Document Delivery Service (DDS) provides the user the required documents irrespective of its location.

(xi) Humanware : Manpower training and refresher course facilities-stimulating, promoting and coordinating research and training programme for library staff- can be arranged by the network members.

However, the development of library networks can be described under two headings: International level and Institutional level.

1.4. DEVELOPMENT OF LIBRARY NETWORKS AT INTERNATIONAL LEVEL

Library networking as a means of resource sharing has its beginning in late 1970 sand developed during 1980 s. Joint Academic Network (JANET), Online Computer Library Centre (OCLC), etc. at international level joint are functioning properly. However, the examples of library networks in the western countries suggest that all networks based on a fee structure can be maintained without grant and are viable in the long run.

Library networking also took place in other parts of the world, such in Brazil, where Janet Frederik described the national plan for university libraries in Brazil and recommended a centre for co-operative cataloguing a standard format for computerized cataloguing and development of an on-line network, but in 2011 at national level, libraries already connected with the electronic consortium library whether public libraries or university libraries (www.bn.br). National Library of Japan (NLJ), through a by law, holds an advisory role in coordinating libraries in Japan nevertheless, it did not promote or maintain nationwide resource-sharing networks. However, it planned to co-ordinate the distribution of machine-readable data as part of a national shared cataloguing system. NLJ was found to have been providing computer-based current awareness bulletins for general science and technology, social sciences, humanities and the arts. But inspite of technological development, especially in the field of electronics, it appears that Japan has not shown much interest in library networking. In Thailand, at present most of universities has joined networking either to share resource among the different units and faculties within their university by setting up local area networks or among several universities, such as the academic network called PULINET,THAILNET and ATUNET(www.ndl.go.jp/en/cdnlao/meeting/pdf/CR2009_Thailand.pdf). Pakistan Library Network is a research initiative of Planwel Academic and Research Network to build electronic access network of all the regional libraries for furthering research and development; as per the mission statement of PLANWEL for Building Technology Based Communities and Bringing Technology to the People. It is an effort to ensure that all underprivileged communities in the region have equal access to information (http://www.planwel.edu/pln.htm). However, libraries of Bangladesh in the field of science and technology are suffering from scarcity of scientific publications. But in order to enhance the availability of research publication, especially of scientific research in the country, Bangladesh Academy of Sciences (BAS) took initiative to collect electronic resources through the Programme for Enhancement of Research Information (PERI), a programme of International Network for the Availability of Scientific Publications (INASP) and in response to the initiative, several universities and research organizations have taken its membership (Rezaul Islam, 2012).

Some of the important international library networks are briefly discussed below (Based on Patil, 2014; Sevukan and Sharma, 2017):

1.4.1. OCLC (Online Computer Library Centre)

OCLC was founded in 1967 by the presidents of the colleges and universities in the state of Ohio as College Library Center (OCLC) to develop a computerized system in which the libraries of Ohio academic institutions could share resources at reduce costs. It was established under the guidance of library automation pioneer Frederic Kilgour. In 1977, the Ohio members of OCLC adopted changes in the governance structure that enabled libraries outside Ohio to become members and participate in the election of the Board of Trustees; the Ohio College Library Center became OCLC, Inc. In 1981, the legal name of the corporation became Online Computer Library Center, Inc. (http://www.oclc.org/).

Online Computer Library Center, Inc. (OCLC), a non-profit corporation, is a membership-based, service and research organization dedicated to the purpose of furthering access to the world's information at reduced cost. The OCLC members are institutions, primarily libraries, which use OCLC products and services to locate, acquire, catalogue, lend and preserve books and other library materials. Researchers, students, faculty, scholars, professional librarians, and other information seekers use OCLC systems through libraries to obtain bibliographic, abstract, citation, and full-text information. The OCLC cataloguing and resource sharing system is the largest and most heavily used computer library system in the world. The OCLC First Search service ranks among the leaders in the online information industry in terms of connect hours. The OCLC bibliographic database, WorldCat (the OCLC Online Union Catalogue), is one of the most consulted electronic databases in higher education.

(a) Objectives : The objectives of OCLC are to:

(i) Establish, maintain and operate a computerized library network and to promote the evolution of library use, of libraries themselves and of librarianship;

(ii) Provide processes and products for the benefit of library users and libraries;

(iii) Increase the availability of library resources to individual library patrons and to reduce the rate-of-rise of library per-unit costs, and

(iv) Further the ease of access to and the use of the ever-expanding body of worldwide scientific, literary and educational knowledge and information.

(b) Membership : OCLC member libraries make up the world's largest network. More than 53 thousand libraries in 170 countries and territories around the world use OCLC services to locate, acquire, catalogue, lend and preserve library materials.

(c) Services : OCLC offers several products and services; a few of them are described below:

(i) ***WorldCat :*** WorldCat is a worldwide union catalogue created and maintained collectively by more than 72,000 libraries representing hundreds of languages and cultures. It is the largest and most comprehensive database of its kind that is built from the bibliographic and ownership information of contributing libraries. WorldCat is the foundation of many OCLC services that facilitates libraries to process, manage and share information resources.

WorldCat includes catalogue records dating back to thousands of years nearly in every format. Records exist for everything from stone tablets to electronic books, wax recordings to MP3s, DVDs and Web sites. Whether an item is physical or digitally preserved, popular or one-of-a-kind, the integrity of its record is maintained by the input of cataloguing members, OCLC's standards and quality control. As of May 2019, WorldCat contained over 450 million bibliographic records in 484 languages, representing over 2.8 billion physical and digital library assets and the WorldCat person's dataset included over 100 million people. Every 10 seconds a new record is added to the catalogue, and it is searched every second.

(ii) ***NetLibrary*** **:** OCLC's NetLibrary platform provides access to electronic books from a wide range of publishers forming monographs and reference resources on hundreds of subject areas which could be accessed through an intuitive, easy-to-use interface that offered a single point of access. Users can find the latest titles, reference sources, business and economics resources, best-selling fiction, and more. It has been acquired by EBSCO in June 2010.

(iii) ***OCLC's Electronic Collections Online*** **:** OCLC's Electronic Collections Online is a powerful electronic journals service that offers web-based access to a growing collection of more than 5,000 titles in a wide range of subject areas from over 70 publishers. It provides access to 4.2 million records from 1995 onwards. It also provides a robust archiving solution and searching across journals. OCLC has secured archival rights to journal content, subscription to e-journals through the OCLC; thus, it ensures perpetual access to the journals subscribed through OCLC for the paid period of subscription.

(iv) ***OCLC Database Service: FirstSearch*** **:** FirstSearch (FS) is an online service that provides web access to research databases consisting primarily of journals. The service provides seamless electronic access to more than eighty databases containing 258 million full-text and full-image articles via WorldCat in most subject fields. Libraries have an option to select databases based on their needs. Some of the more important databases included in FirstSearch are : Article First; Clase and Periodica; Elcctronic Books; Electronic Collections Online; ERIC; GPO Monthly Catalogue; MEDLINE; OAIster; PapersFirst; ProceedingsFirst; SCIPIO; WorldCat (The OCLC Online Union Catalogue) and WorldCat Dissertations and Theses (WorldCatDissertations).

However, the size and period covered in FirstSearch varies between the individual databases but may include data going back as far 1980. FirstSearch facilitates search across multiple databases through its simple menu-driven search interface. Full-image articles from Electronic Collections Online journals are linked to corresponding citations in databases throughout the FirstSearch service. Subscribers to FirstSearch may also place their orders online for articles that are not accessible tc them.

(v) ***EZ Proxy Authentication and Access Software*** : It is the world's leading access and authentication solution. EZproxy helps to provide users with remote access to Web-based licensed content offered by libraries, and is easy to set up and maintain. More than 2,500 institutions in over 60 countries have purchased EZproxy software. EZproxy is now also available as a hosted solution, giving libraries the option to outsource the set-up and ongoing management of their proxy configuration.

(vi) ***QuestionPoint: Cooperative Virtual Reference Service*** : QuestionPoint is a unique virtual reference service, supported by global network of cooperating libraries worldwide, as well as an infrastructure of software tools and communications. QuestionPoint is also a source of unique centralized knowledge resources built by a collaborative network of member libraries.

(d) Benefits Benefits : Some of its 24x7 cooperative benefits and features24/7 Cooperative benefits and features are as follows:

- ***Meet Users at their Point of Need*** : It provides reference service round the clock with trustworthy, real-time one-on-one reference assistance from professional librarians, right from the library Web page or other Web portal.

- ***Expand your Reference Desk hours without increasing Staff*** **:** Cooperative coverage is provided 24 hours a day, 7 days a week, to the customers as a modest weekly contribution of staffing.
- ***Belong to Several Groups simultaneously*** **:** It can belong to several groups simultaneously, such as a local consortium and a subject-specific group. Any number of librarians may monitor the service at any time within the cooperative, means that an individual customer's library is more likely to be monitoring.
- ***Q & A Knowledge Base*** **:** It is carefully reviewed and maintained by Cooperative contributors.
- ***Subject Referral through the Global Reference Network*** **:** It automatic routes submitted question or chat session to a partner library based on criteria such as subject, language or hours of coverage.
- ***Pricing based on Population*** **:** It means a lower cost for each participating library.

  Besides, its reference management benefits and features may include the following;
- ***Web-based Chat, Cobrowse and Cooperative Reference Tools*** **:** It uses best-in-class technology and require no special software or browser plug-ins. A librarian does not need to use Operating System to do simple chat and page push but a highest-level co-browsing, Internet Explorer browser is required. A streamlined conference process allows librarians to transfer to another librarian smoothly. There is also support for multilingual reference transactions.
- ***Unique Customizable Messages*** **:** Instead of just one list of scripted chat messages for an entire group of libraries, each library can add their own individual scripted messages, which appear when one of their customers comes into the queue.

- ***Expanded Patron Link Views*** : This feature allows patrons, while still in session, to click on previous links sent to them by the librarian.
- ***Administrative Monitoring*** : Administrators can join any of their librarian's chat sessions, to send private notes or suggestions unseen by patrons, or to communicate directly with the patron. In addition, librarians can add notes during or after a session which are visible only to other librarians. These librarian notes assist in question follow up as well as in quality control and other administrative functions.
- ***Customizable Surveys and Reporting Tools*** : Each library can customize its own unique survey for patrons and make it available after the chat session, after a follow up is complete, or after an answer is sent in response to a student email. Surveys also help the libraries to measure user satisfaction levels and make service improvements. Librarians have the flexibility to characterize sessions and retrieve statistical information through descriptive categories such as research, business, instruction, etc. to help them to identify trends and perform usage analysis.
- ***Flexible, Institution-Based Pricing Model*** : Instead of per-seat; even greater savings are possible if you work cooperatively within a group of libraries.
- ***Fully Accessible User Interface*** : It supports users with accessibility needs, including those who use screen readers.
- ***User Customization of Interface*** : Here, the colour scheme and font size and an optional chime for new messages are available.
- ***Customizable Management Reports*** : Various types of the reportscan also be obtained.
- ***Reach Out to Users from Every Web Page*** : Its Qwidget combines the simplicity of a chat widget

(on the user side) with the full features of Question Point's reference management system.

Its virtual reference service is also a well-designed and executed delivering that is expected to benefit to both library staff and patrons. Customize services to fit any size library or group-from a small public library to a group of large academic libraries are also available. However, as part of the Implementation Services package one may receive: a dedicated Implementation Manager, who is single point of contact throughout the project. The Manager partners to set milestones, define key tasks, design workflows and educate library staff; virtual or self-paced training programme can be configured for the staff and their needs. There is also the option to receive further training, including live instruction, for an additional fee; and first-line technical support during and after the implementation is also there to help resolve any technical issues or questions that arise using the Question Point service and participation in the 24/7 Reference Cooperative.

Implementation Managers have superior understanding of the Question Point solution plus an outstanding knowledge of reference services and libraries. Some other servicers may also be there, such as: OCLC's digitization, microfilm and archival services are designed to protect and share collections for their members. OCLC also has infrastructure and skilled staff at their preservation centres. Besides, the OCLC's collection development services can assess the strengths and gaps of collection available in the libraries if a member institution using their analysis tools.

1.4.2. RLG (Research Libraries Group)

Research Libraries Group (RLG), a not-for-profit organization consisting of over 150 research libraries, archives, museums, and other cultural memory institutions was founded in 1974 by the New York Public

Library, Columbia University, Harvard University and Yale University. The reason for the formation of yet another consortium in US when OCLC already existed, was the dissatisfaction of research libraries with OCLC record keeping. Thus, the RLG was founded to provide solutions to the challenges presented by information access and management of digital resources. It served researchers by providing access to research materials held in libraries, archives and museums. It designs and delivers innovative information discovery services, organized collaborative programmes, and takes an active role in creating and promoting relevant standards and practices.

However, RLG merged with OCLC in 2006after three decades of its serving libraries. After its merger, its catalogue merged with OCLC WORLD Cat and its databases merged with OCLC First Search service. RLG merged with OCLC to be known as RLG Programs as part of OCLC Programs and Research Division. The latter was renamed as OCLC research in 2009 and the former as RLG Partnership. RLG Partnership was renamed as OCLC Research Library Partnership in 2011.

OCLC Research Library Partnerships provides following services to find out solutions to the problems faced by research libraries and archives:

- ***Shared Network Resources* :** The research library collections in print are available for sharing amongst the members.
- ***Sharing Special Collections* :** It is a document delivery service in which rare and unique materials are delivered to users. It also helps to economize the resources.
- ***COBOAT* :** It is a metadata publishing tool developed by RLP to transfer information between databases and different formats.
- ***SHARES Programme* :** It is a inter-library loan programme that strives to introduce innovative

methods for sharing of collections.

- ***Demystifying Born Digital*** : This programme focuses on enhancing the effective management of born-digital documents.

Besides, sharing and aggregating social metadata programme is also there wherein efforts are made in identifying user contribution to enhance descriptive metadata created by libraries.

1.4.3. JISC (Joint Information System Committee)

JISC, the Joint Information Systems Committee is a United Kingdom not-for-profit company whose role is to support post-16 and higher education, and research, by providing relevant and useful advice, digital resources and network and technology services, while researching and developing new technologies and ways of working. Joint Information System Committee (JISC) leads the Further and Higher Education community in the use of ICT for learning, teaching, research and administration. It is advisory in nature and is funded by all further and higher education councils. It has following sub-committees to facilitate the work:

- JISC Organizational Support Committee
- JISC Content Services Committee
- JISC Integrated Information Environment Committee
- JISC Learning and Teaching Committee
- JISC Network Committee
- JISC Support of Research Committee

JISC works with the following aims to fulfill the needs of the education and research communities:

- To develop solutions that help enable the UK education and research communities to keep their activities world class through the innovative use of information and communications technology.

- To provide advice to institutions to enable them to make economic, efficient and legally compliant use of information and communications, respecting the individual's and corporate rights and responsibilities.
- To help the sector provide positive, personalized user learning experiences and to aid student progression.
- To develop mutually advantageous partnerships with organizations in the UK and abroad, and
- To advise, inform and help to implement the strategies of government, funding councils and research councils.

As far as the services are concerned, JISC offers following services.

(i) Online Resources : It provides electronic collections to the education and research community in UK at subsidized rates. It acquires resources for members in consortium mode for ensuring economy and quality. The aims of its online resources' division are to:

- Provide leadership for national negotiations designed to lower the cost of access to electronic information resources;
- Facilitate debate and, where appropriate, action to help to implement possible long-term solutions to the rising costs of scholarly communication;
- Develop and advance strategy for cost-effective content acquisition and the delivery of electronic information resources which takes account of the dynamic nature of the information market place and the changing needs of the community;
- Assist the community in achieving and demonstrating the value for money;
- Commission research to assist the community in the effective exploitation of electronic information resources to support research and teaching;
- Work in collaboration with JISC to support the

enhancement of innovative resource discovery and library collection management services; and

- Communicate to all stakeholders to foster a mutual understanding of the issues around electronic information resources.

Thus, it ensures the best possible licensing terms and conditions and preservation arrangements for the library community.

(ii) Union Catalogue : Copac is the Union Catalogue of bibliographic records of more than 70 libraries which provides research materials in major libraries of UK and Ireland that include the national libraries, university libraries and research libraries. Copac also provides details of the collections of British Library and it is frequently updated on the basis of user feedback.

(iii) SUNCAT : SUNCAT is the union catalogue of serials held in libraries all over UK. It provides information on print and electronic journals, newsletters, magazines, newspapers and annual reports from 91 libraries in UK. It is developed and maintained by University of Edinburgh and designated as an EDINA service which is a JISC designated national data centre at the University of Edinburgh.

(iv) JISC Journal Archives: Its journal archives is very important in view of the fast changing information world which provides access selectively to over 4 million journal articles. Besides, Zetoc that is one of the world's most comprehensive research databases, is providing access to over 28,000 journals, 45 million article citations and conference papers through the British Library's electronic table of contents providing free access to higher education (HE) and further education (FE).

(v) Jorum : Jorum, is a free online repository of learning and teaching materials which is intended to integrate it with repositories being developed by other institutions and in different subjects. It is designed in a modified version of DSpace.

In addition, JISC offers different types of activities to enhance the competencies of library and information science professionals. It has specially worked for development in areas like digital literacy and e-learning. Its programmes have been organized regularly for professionals to update these skills which are essential today.

1.4.4. JANET (Joint Academic Network)

JANET that is a high-speed network for the UK research and education community provided by JISC, is a not-for-profit company set up to provide computing support for education in the year 1984. It was previously a private, UK government-funded organization, which provided the Janet computer network and related collaborative services to UK research and education.

JANET is dedicated to the needs of the UK education and research community. It connects education and research organizations in UK to each other, as well as to the rest of the world through the Internet. In addition, JANET includes a separate network that is available to the community for experimental activities in network development. JANET connects all universities in UK, FE Colleges, Research Councils, Specialist Colleges and Adult and Community Learning providers. It also provides connections between the Regional Broadband Consortia. Currently, it is serving 18 million users and is the busiest National Research and Education Network in Europe by volume of data carried.

JANET also allows video-conferencing and video streaming capabilities to be used to deliver lectures to remote groups of students. Its backbone allows the linking of large data storage and high-performance computing facilities at a national and international level for researchers and other users.

United Kingdom Education and Research Networking Association (UKERNA) manages the operation and development of JANET on behalf of JISC (Joint Information Systems Committee) for the UK Further and Higher Education Funding Councils. JISC also works in partnership with the Research Councils. UKERNA is funded by the UK government, with the primary aim of providing and developing a network infrastructure that meets the needs of the education and research communities.

JANET offers a wide range of network, support and information services to help the educational institutions to maximize their benefits from JANET. Major services offered by the JANET include the following:

(i) JANET Customer Service (JCS) : JANET Customer Service is the primary point of contact for enquiries concerning JANET. The JCS is in contact with technical experts and service managers both within UKERNA and throughout the education community, and is, therefore, able to provide relevant assistance at any level. JCS responds to a large volume of customer queries and facilitates provision of new and upgraded connections to JANET. It also assists in the registration of domain names and applications for IP addresses.

(ii) Mail Services : Mail services are available, including an electronic mailing list service, a Mailer Shield service, a SPAM-relay Tester System and the Mail Abuse Prevention System. Web Mail Service is also offered to a limited number of organizations, which do not have the resources to support an e-mail service themselves.

(iii) Networking Support Services : Networking Support Services include a co-location service for hosting equipment within the JANET backbone, a Network Time Service offering organizations a stable time reference and a Managed Router Service for those needing expertise in managing their network router.

(iv) Usenet News Services : Subscribing organizations with their own news servers can accept a news feed sent from central JANET servers. However, organizations without their own news server can let their users read news directly from a JANET server.

(v) Video-conferencing Services : Video-conferencing over IP networks and ISDN (Integrated Services Digital Network) is provided. A Booking Service lets registered users book a videoconference online. Its Video Technology Advisory Service evaluates products, develops documentation and offers an on-site consultancy service.

(vi) Web Services : A Web Filtering Service is available to provide protection against access to inappropriate content on the Internet and to allow the maintenance of lists of blocked or permitted URLs. Other services may include: Web Hosting and Web Mail which are available to small organizations only, such as specialist colleges or adult and community learning centres.

Other services also include Advisory Services, Domain Name Services, Information Dissemination services etc.

Besides, its training section was set up initially to provide for the needs of technical staff at sites new to JANET. It has been extended to include education and training for staff charged with the management of networking and networking services at JANET sites with Primary Connections. However, UKERNA ensures that the JANET community is kept up-to-date with networking developments by organizing workshops and conferences to cover either general networking issues or more specific topics. Its annual events cover a number of networking issues ranging from strategy to technical support. UKERNA also organizes events in conjunction with other organizations.

Super JANET is also there which is the core of JANET

network and is the backbone of the JANET. It ensures fast, and effective communication among the members of JANET and the network to meet the changing needs of the community. Super JANET is being implemented in phases. It was proposed in1989 with the aim to develop a high-performance wide area network based on optical fibers. Super JANET II started in 1995 to increase the spread of Super JANET and create MANs (Metropolitan Area Network). Super JANET III was aimed at consolidating the pioneering work of Super JANET I and II in 2001. Super JANET 4 was launched to increase the network capacity and strengthen the user base of JANET with further inclusion of education community and the use of Super JANET 4 backbone to inter connect school networks.

1.4.5. CALIS (China Academic Library and Information System)

China Academic Library and Information System (CALIS) that was launched in 1998, is a nation-wide resource-sharing system among Chinese academic libraries. Its mission is to serve directly those universities, which are funded by the central government, by providing document and information services to the users through the China Education and Research Network. CALIS also serves users in other universities and colleges so long as they have network connections to the China Education & Research Network (CERNET). CALIS is just like a nation-wide academic library consortium in China, which is half supported by the government and half by the libraries themselves.

(i) Aims and Objectives : CALIS aims to build a national information infrastructure along with CERNET. However, the priority of CALIS is to reveal what already exists in academic libraries in China and to increase its utilization. CALIS is committed: to build an information service network that contains hardware and software; and to introduce and produce various databases.

(ii) Governance and Organization : A top-level committee consisting of officers from related departments of the Ministry of Education and two university presidents from Beida and Tsinghua governs CALIS, which is supported by an expert team that acts as consultants. CALIS Administrative Centre located at Beijing University that coordinates and executes various activities of the network under the leadership of the committee.

CALIS is grouped into four national information centres, i.e., Science, Social Science and Humanities Information Centre; Engineering and Technology Information Centre; Medical Information Centre and Agricultural Information Centre. These centres provides information support to users. Besides, there are seven regional information centres which are divided as East China South Regional Center, East China North Regional Center, South China Regional Center, Central China Regional Center, Southwest China Regional Center, Northwest China Regional Center, and Northeast China Regional Centre – they provide secondary support to the information users.

(iii) Current Status of CALIS : CALIS has established a three-level resource and service infrastructure. It has also undertaken six major activities drafted in its plan in various cities and regions, which include: Coordinative Acquisition, Online Cataloguing, OPAC, ILL, Document Delivery and Internet Navigating.

A number of bibliographic databases and full-text databases are also being subscribed/ acquired either as central-funded acquisition or consortium acquisition, covering almost all the disciplines and subjects. Some major bibliographic databases and full-text resources include: Science Citation Index (SCI); Social Science Citation Index (SSCI); Engineering Information (EI); Biological Abstracts (B A); Chemical Abstracts (CA); Cambridge Scientific Abstracts (CSA); ABI/Global; ProQuest Academic Research Library; Science Online;

Elsevier ScienceDirect Onsite Academic Press; IEEE/IEE Electronic Library (IEL); Genome Database and China InfoBank, etc.

In addition, a series of databases are produced in-house which include: Union Catalogues of Books and Journals where 150 members have contributed 1.4 million titles and more than 3 million holdings; Current Contents of Chinese Journals where 28 members have contributed more than 2 million abstracts of 5500 Chinese journals; Chinese Dissertation and Proceedings Abstract Databases where 85 members have contributed more than 70,000 abstracts; Chinese Databases with Unique Features where 23 members have contributed 25 databases which contain more than 450,000 records.

Besides, an application platform operated on network is also there which is Unicode, Z39.50, ISO10160, and 10161 compliant. Its platform includes: Online cataloguing server and client, through which librarians can download and upload MARC records and holdings; data-making tools and database servers for TOC (table of contents) and other self-made databases; web-based search engines for accessing self-produced databases; and software for ILL and desktop document delivery services.

1.5. DEVELOPMENT OF LIBRARY NETWORKS IN INDIA

It was the mid 1980's when the telecommunication boom came to India and networking was given thrust by the Government of India. The Department of Telecommunication is responsible for maintaining national telecommunication infrastructure which is the backbone for network architecture of country. However, the major breakthrough was establishment of NICNET, established by National Informatics Centre (NIC) in 1977 that was started in the late 1987's. It was one of the largest VSAT Networks of its kind in the world, which was launched basically for getting and providing information from/to district levels to facilitate planning process. It linked for regional nodes at Delhi, Pune, Bhubaneswar and Hyderabad and established 32 nodes at state and union territory levels and 439 nodes at district headquarters.

INDONET at national level is India's first data communication and computer network that was started in March 1986 by CMC Ltd. as a solution to the growing need for providing timely, well processed data to various institutions. In the first phase, they have mainly network in Mumbai, Calcutta and Chennai. Later, Delhi and Hyderabad were also linked as additional stations (Gurikar, 2014). INDONET presently has an international gateway which provides access to the world wide pocket switched networks like USA's Global Networks Systems (GNS) and Internet.

Later, Education and Research Network (ERNET) (http://www.eis.ernet.in/) was launched by the Department of Education (DOE), Government of India in late 1986 with the financial assistance from United Nation Development Programme (UNDP) to provide academic and research institutions with electronic mail facilities. It is currently used by DSIR Labs, research centres and academic institutions.

Scientific and Industrial Research Network (SIRNET) was also established by INSDOC in late 1989 to interconnect all the CSIR laboratories and other R&D institutions in India. The success of the above networks and the initiatives taken by NISSAT, UGC, Planning Commission and other departments of Government of India have led to the establishment and development of library networks in India.

CALIBNET that was established by NISSAT in 1986 in Calcutta was the first library network visualized. It has become the centre for CD-ROM databases which are acquired from outside sources. DELNET was established in 1988 in Delhi by India International Centre with the initial financial support of NISSAT. It was the first operational library network in India. INFLIBNET that was established by UGC in 1988 and started its operations in 1991, is a network of university and college libraries. MALIBNET is the result of the need for interconnecting libraries and information centres in Chennai, which was visualized by INSDOC in 1991. MALIBNET was registered as a society in Chennai in Feb. 1993. Some other library networks in India are PUNENET (1992) in Pune, ADINET (1993) in Ahmedabad, BONET (1994) in Mumbai, MYLIBNET (1994) in Mysore (Chennai), and BALNET (1995) in Bangalore.

However, the development of INFLIBNET (Information and Library Network) in 1988 facilitated a nation-wide effort to improve information access and transfer, initiated by University Grants Commission (UGC). Besides, there were several networks developed for resource sharing among organizations. Table 1.1 gives a chronological overview on some important networks in India.

Table 1.1. Chronology of Development of Networks in India

Year of Establishment	*Name of the Network*	*Supported by*
1977	NICNET	NIC
1986	CALIBNET, Kolkata	NISSAT
1988	INFLIBNET	UGC
1992	DELNET, Delhi	NISSAT
1992	PUNNET	NISSAT
1993	ADINET, Ahmedabad	NISSAT
1993	MALIBNET, Chennai	INSDOC
1994	BONET	NISSAT
1994	MYLIBNET, Mysore	NISSAT
1995	BALNET, Bangalore	NISSAT

But due to growth and availability of Information Technology (IT) now Internet is being heavily used as communication channel. It has given a chance for these restricted networks to become global networks. Now, almost all the networks use Internet for dissemination of their service.

1.6. MAJOR LIBRARY AND INFORMATION NETWORKS OF INDIA

There have been several initiatives in setting library and information networks in India but not many of them are active. Some of the most active networks are: CALIBNET, INFLIBNET and DELNET etc. Some important of them are being discussed briefly below (Based on Murthy, 1996; Mustafa, 2002; Dhiman and Rani, 2007; Bhatt and Chand, 2014; Patil, 2014):

1.6.1. INFLIBNET (Information and Library Network)

INFLIBNET that was established in the year 1988 but started its working from 1991from its headquarter located at Gujarat University Campus, Ahmedabad. Initially, it was started as a project under Inter-University Centre for Astronomy and Astrophysics (IUCAA) to be converted later into a full-fledged programme of UGC. It has played an important role in automation and modernization of university library system in India. It provided universities and research institutions the bandwidth for accessing e-journals. It has also become a major player in enhancing scholarly communication in India. It has been shifted in its own building in Infocity, Gandhinangar (Gujarat) in January 2013 and working from there well.

(i) Objectives : INFLIBNET programmes are directed towards modernization of libraries and information centres and establishment of a mechanism for information transfer and access, to support scholarship, learning and academic pursuits. INFLIBNET was established with the following objectives (https://www.inflibnet.ac.in):

- To promote and establish communication facilities to improve capability in information transfer and access, that provide support to scholarship, learning, research and academic pursuit through cooperation and involvement of agencies concerned.
- To establish a computer communication network for linking libraries and information centres in universities, deemed to be universities, colleges, UGC information centres, institutions of national importance and R & D institutions, etc. avoiding duplication of efforts:
  - to promote and implement computerization of operations and services in the libraries and information centres of the country, following a uniform standard;
  - to evolve standards and uniform guidelines in techniques, methods, procedures, computer hardware and software, services and promote their adoption in actual practice by all libraries, in order to facilitate pooling, sharing and exchange of information towards optimal use of resources and facilities;
  - to evolve a national network interconnecting various libraries and information centres in the country and to improve capability in information handling and service;
  - to provide reliable access to document collection of libraries by creating on-line union catalogue of serials, theses/ dissertations, books, monographs and non-book materials in various libraries in India;
  - to provide access to bibliographic information sources with citations, abstracts, etc. through indigenously created databases of the Sectoral Information Centres of NISSAT, UGC Information Centres, City Networks and such

others and by establishing gateways for on-line accessing of national and international databases held by national and international information networks and centres respectively;

— to develop new methods and techniques for archival of valuable information available as manuscripts and information documents in different Indian languages, in the form of digital images using high density storage media;

— to optimize information resource utilization through shared cataloguing, inter-library loan service, catalogue production, collection development and thus avoiding duplication in acquisition to the extent possible;

— to enable the users dispersed all over the country, irrespective of location and distance, to have access to information regarding serials, theses/ dissertations, books, monographic and non-book materials by locating the sources wherefrom available and to obtain it through the facilities of INFLIBNET and union catalogue of documents;

— to create databases of projects, institutions, specialists, etc. for providing on-line information service;

— to encourage co-operation among libraries, documentation centres and information centres in the country, so that the resources can be pooled for the benefit of helping the weaker resource centres by stronger ones; and

— to train and develop human resources in the field of computerized library operations and networking to establish, manage and sustain INFLIBNET.

- To facilitate academic communication amongst scientists, engineers, social scientists, academics, faculties, researchers and students through electronic mail, file transfer, computer/audio/video conferencing, etc.;

- To undertake system design and studies in the field of communications, computer networking, information handling and data management;
- To establish appropriate control and monitoring system for the communication network and organize maintenance;
- To collaborate with institutions, libraries, information centres and other organizations in India and abroad in the field relevant to the objectives of the Centre;
- To promote R&D and develop necessary facilities and create technical positions for realizing the objectives of the Centre;
- To generate revenue by providing consultancies and information services; and
- To do all other such things as may be necessary, incidental or conducive to the attainment of all or any of the above objectives.

(ii) Services : Its various services may be listed as given below :

(a) *Document Delivery* : INLIBNET provides inter-library loan and document delivery services from its comprehensive collection of subscribed journals under JCCC @ UGC- INFONET. It has designated 22 libraries to fulfill ILL request from the users, affiliated to various universities covered under UGC. ILL libraries together subscribe 10,000 plus journals which are not available through consortia. Universities can request for articles from the journal holdings of those libraries wherever they find useful articles in JCCC search.

(b) *OJAS* : Open Journal Access System (OJAS) is an open source journal management and publishing software developed and freely distributed by the Public Knowledge Project at the University of British Columbia. INFLIBNET has installed and configured the software at its server and provides the facility of uploading the e-versions of journals of universities and even individuals for open access.

(c) *Library Automation* : INFLIBNET has developed a library automation package called SOUL, the Software for University Libraries. It has all the necessary modules which a library need. Besides SOUL, INFLIBNET has developed several small utilities for day-to-day libraries operations. It also develops solution on demand by university libraries, like retro-conversion, preparation of catalogue cards, duplicate checking of library records and so on.

(d) *Human Resource Development* : INFLIBNET runs several short-term courses for professionals in order to train them with new automated tools and techniques. It has conducted many programs for working university library professionals which contain training module in computer application for library and information centres.

(iii) Databases : INFLIBNET has developed following bibliographic databases pertaining to the collection of participating libraries to enable sharing of resources:

- Serials Holdings
- Current Serials
- Secondary Serials Catalogue
- Theses
- Books

Besides, the following databases are also developed to help the users, in particular the researchers.

(a) *Shodhganga* : INFLIBNET has been assigned the responsibility of hosting, maintaining and making available Ph.D. research work submitted in Indian universities to all in open access mode by University

Grants Commission, New Delhi. Thus, INFLIBNET has helped to form Shodhganga, a digital repository of theses and dissertations submitted in Indian Universities. It has been built using the open source software DSpace that is OAI- PMH complaint. It collects, stores, indexes, disseminates and preserves the rich knowledge reservoir of Indian universities.

Shodhganga provides a platform for researchers to share their research findings reported in their Ph.D. theses with the entire scholarly community in open access. Around 250,000 theses by 422 universities have been uploaded on the repository till December 2019 (https://shodhganga.inflibnet.ac.in/).

(b) *Shodhgangotri* : Shodhgangotri (https://shodhgangotri.inflibnet.ac.in) is a database of research-in-progress in universities in different disciplines. Researchers and their supervisors can send synopsis approved by appropriate bodies to be uploaded on the site. It helps researchers to know that areas actively being researched and the status of research. Thus, it helps to avoid unnecessary duplication of research. Once a thesis is approved the synopsis in Shodhgangotri would be linked to the thesis uploaded on the Shodhganga. There are available 6450 synopses on this site till December 2019.

(iv) Infoport : InfoPort (https://infoport.inflibnet.ac.in) is a subject gateway for Indian electronic resources that is designed and developed to serve as a comprehensive gateway to all Indian scholarly contents. It collects the Indian scholarly contents scattered over the Internet through an integrated interface that supports searching and browsing online resources of Indian origin available in open access. InfoPort is classified according to DDC, indexed subject wise and arranged alphabetically subjects.

Besides, INFLIBNET has also developed non-bibliographic databases on research projects and experts in different fields by the name "Vidwan" to help to improve communication and collaboration in research.

(v) NLIST : National Libraries Information Services Infrastructure for Scholarly Content (N-LIST) (https://nlist.inflibnet.ac.in) is a project of Ministry of Human Resource Development under National Mission on Education through ICT to provide access to e-resources to students, researchers and faculty from colleges and other institutions. Authorized users from colleges can access e-resources and download articles required by them directly from the publisher's website once they are duly authenticated as authorized users through servers deployed at the INFLIBNET Centre.

The registration of new colleges and renewal of existing colleges those are covered under section 12B of UGC Act is made with annual membership fee of Rs 5,900.00 including GST. However, non-aided colleges (except Agriculture, Engineering, Management, Medical, Pharmacy, Dentistry and Nursing)may also join NLIST on payment of annual membership fee of Rs. 35,400.00 including GST.

A total number of 8761 registrations have been done with the N-LIST programme till December 2019 that includes 3162 Government/Government-aided colleges covered under the section 12 B/2F of UGC Act as well as 208 non-aided colleges and 2021 Science Colleges.6000+ e-journals and 97,000 + e-books are provided under this programme.

(vi) Projects : INFLIBNEThas also undertaken various projects. Some of them include the following:

(a) *e-PG pathshala* : e-PG pathshala (https://epgp.inflibnet.ac.in/) is a project of the MHRD, under its National Mission on Education through ICT (NME-ICT), for development of e-contents at postgraduate level. It covers 77 subjects in different subjects across all disciplines of social sciences, arts, fine arts and humanities, natural and mathematical sciences, linguistics and languages. It caters over 22000+ modules comprising of text and video in these subjects.

(b) ***E-Shodhsindhu*** **:** E-Shodhsindhu was created after the recommendation of an Expert Committee of MHRD by merging three consortia initiatives, namely UGC-INFONET Digital Library Consortium, NLIST and INDEST-AICTE Consortium.

E-ShodhSindhu continues to provide current as well as archival access to more than 16,000 core and peer-reviewed journals and a number of bibliographic, citation and factual databases in different disciplines from a large number of publishers and aggregators to its member institutions including centrally-funded technical institutions, universities and colleges that are covered under 12(B) and 2(f) Sections of the UGC Act.

Besides, INFLIBNET also conducts annual events called Convention on Automation of Libraries in Education and Research Institutions (CALIBER) on different places in India, where the discussion is made on various topics which are recent and related to library automation. Earlier CALIBER was arranged on annual basis but now it is organized on alternate years bi-annually. In between a series of regional conventions, PLANNER (Promotion of Library Automation and Networking in North-Eastern Region) for north–east specific libraries have been started since 2003 on biannual basis.

INFLIBNETis also supporting creation for infrastructure by providing financial support beside running several courses as well as conducting workshops for training of library professionals.

1.6.2. DELNET (Developing Library Network)

DELNET (http://www.delnet.nic.in/) stands for Developing Library Network (formerly Delhi Library Network), is the first operational library network in India which was started as a project of the India International Centre in January 1988 with the initial, financial and technical assistance by National Information System for Science and Technology (NISSAT), Department of Scientific and Industrial Research, Govt. of India as Delhi Library Network. Later, it was renamed as Developing Library Network in the year . It was registered as a society in June 1992 under the Societies Registration Act of 1860 and is currently being promoted by the National Informatics Centre (NIC), Planning Commission, Government of India and India International Centre, New Delhi.

(i) Objectives : Its various objectives (a) Objectives include the following:

- To promote sharing of resources among the libraries by developing a network of libraries, by collecting, storing and disseminating information and by offering computerized services to the users.
- To offer guidance to the member libraries on cataloguing database services, circulation, acquisition, serials control, online services, selection of hardware and software, etc.
- To coordinate efforts for suitable collection development and for reducing unnecessary duplication wherever possible.
- To establish a referral centre, to monitor and/or facilitate catalogue search and maintain a central online union catalogue of books, serials, and non-book materials of all the participating libraries.
- To facilitate and promote delivery of documents manually and mechanically.
- To develop specialist bibliographic database of books, serials and non-book materials.
- To develop a database of projects, specialists and institutions.

- To possess and maintain electronic and mechanical equipments for the fast communication of information and delivery of electronic mail.
- To coordinate with other regional, national and international networks for exchange of information and documents, and
- To undertake, facilitate and provide for the publication of newsletters/journals devoted to networking and sharing of resources.

(ii) Membership : DELNET had 6834 (including 22 from outside India) libraries as its members, including both institutional and associate-institutional members.

(iii) Services : Various services of DELNET may be summarized as below:

(a) *Union Catalogue of Books* : DELNET maintains an online union catalogue of books available in its member-libraries. This union catalogue is continuously updated and is growing in size. The information can be retrieved by author, title, subject, conference, series, etc. It has 2,83,50,450 bibliographic records. The request for inter-library loan can be placed through its online system.

(b) *Union List of Current Periodicals* : DELNET has created a union lists of current periodicals in science and technology, social sciences and humanities. This database is available online to DELNET users. It now lists 38,184 periodicals and is regularly updated and new titles are added annually. It is a major resource for Document Delivery Service.

(c) *Union Catalogue of Periodicals* : DELNET maintains a union catalogue of periodicals, which contains full holdings of data of the libraries. At present, the database contains 20,235 records.

(d) *Database of Periodical Articles* : This database has the details of articles which can be searched under the title, author, compiler, name of the periodical and subject. The database is being extensively utilized by the researchers and scholars. At present the database contains 9,84,809 records.

(e) *CD-ROM Database* : It is a bibliographic database of CD-ROMs available with the member-libraries is being compiled. It has 61,750 records.

(f) *Union List of Video Recordings* : This is a database of video cassettes available in DELNET member-libraries and has about 6,000 listings.

(g) *Union List of Sound Recordings* : This union list consists of audio cassette records available in member-libraries. This database has 1,025 records.

(h) *Database of Theses and Dissertations* : This is a database of Theses and Dissertations submitted to Indian Universities which covers various subjects. The database has 1,30,753 records.

(i) *Union List of Newspapers* : This database has 70 records and contains information about the newspapers including title, name of the editor, published from, e-mail address and also the Web address of the INTERNET edition if available on the WWW.

(j) *Database of E-books* : This database has nearly 1613 records.

Besides, the DELNET was earlier providing CDS/ISIS software for storage and retrieval purpose, developed by UNESCO through NISSAT, but presently it is distributing its own software DELSIS. It has also created software: DELDOS and DEL-WINDOWS for creating MARC records. It also has a standardization committee which meets time to time. DELNET uses CCF for inter-library exchange of bibliographic data, accept AACR-II for cataloguing and LCSH is recommended for thesaurus.

DELNET also organizes national workshops, seminars and meets on library networking from time to time. DELNET has been organizing National Annual convention on Library and Information Networking (NACLIN) regularly and by 2019, 22 NACLIN have been organized. It also regularly conducts training programme on DELNET services, software, e-mail, subject heading of library of congress, AACR-II, Internet, etc. Recently, it has been advocated the open source software and teaching their use by conducting training programmes in KOHA and D-Space.

DELNET also publishes its newsletter called 'DELNET Newsletter' to communicate the activity of DELNET to professionals.

1.6.3. CALIBNET (Calcutta Library Network)

CALIBNET was formed as a metropolitan network in 1993 by linking 38 libraries in Calcutta with financial support from NISSAT. Its prime objective was to institute systematic inter-library co-operation and document delivery among the networked libraries for effective resource sharing. The participating libraries had computerized their in-house functions such as cataloguing, serials control, acquisition and fund accounting, circulation and user services and have been inter-connected through X.25 protocol. Its Network Services Centre provides global information services for all the users of the participating libraries which include current awareness, union catalogues, database, access to national and international networks.

The project is managed by the CALIBNET Society established under the West Bengal Government's Societies Registration Act 1961 and its centre is stationed at Jadavpur University Campus, Kolkata. CALIBNET provides libraries and their members an efficient solution for their information needs.

(i) Objectives : CALIBNET is established to pursue the problems of eastern region of country, mainly West Bengal. The primary objective of the organization is creating and facilitating access to available library and information resources in West Bengal. Oher objectives are as given below:

- Facilitating remote online access to the holding data of Calcutta libraries and other specialized databases; and
- Providing electronic access to globally available information, imbibing its information centre approach.

(ii) Services : Its various services are detailed out below:

(a) *Software Development* : Two software have been developed for supporting library activities by intense in-house research and development

- *Sanjukta* : It is developed for storage and retrieval which is used in Centralized Database of CALIBNET for providing online access from remote locations. The software provides options and flexibility for record generation, organizing and searching information.
- *Parapar* : Parapar is developed to support interchange of bibliographic data between different bibliographic standards like, USMARC, UNIMARC and CCF. It also converts other format data to ISO-2709 format which can be imported into the centralized Database of CALIBNET.

(b) *Current Content Service* : Its Confile Service is a current content service which covers almost 20,000 journals of different disciplines. It economizes library service on journal subscription and reduces the drain on precious foreign exchange resources.

(c) *Document Delivery Service* : Its Caliborder is a document delivery service which delivers full-text of any article and even patents on demand.

(d) *Selective Dissemination of Information* : Its ConAlert service is designed to give current and tailored bibliographic information. A user profile is created based on the keywords. Notification about the arrival or availability of the document is sent to the users. On demand document is also delivered at user's desk.

(e) *Institutional Resources Development Services*: CALIBNET supports institutes to build their library. It also assists and provides consultancy in library automation and creation of databases and electronic resources. Besides, it runs a wide range of training programs and customized courses based on institutional needs.

(iii) Databases : CALIBNET maintains a centralized database of holding of Kolkata libraries. It also maintains the databases of Asiatic Society Journals, and current serials acquired by Kolkata Libraries. Through website, CALIBNET also provides links to:

- Overseas Library Resources on India;
- Worldwide Library Catalogues; and
- National Libraries of the World.

CALIBNET is an active library network in West Bengal which can be contacted through its website http://www.calibnet.org.

1.6.4. ADINET (Ahmedabad Library Network)

ADINET was established for developing cooperative mode of working amongst the libraries and information centres in and around Ahmedabad in 1994 with the help of NISSAT. It was stationed in INFIBNET Centre, Ahmedabad. ADINET promotes sharing of resources and disseminates information among member libraries by networking them.

(i) Objectives : ADINET was established with following objectives:

- To bring about cooperative mode of working amongst libraries and information centres in and around Ahmedabad;
- To integrate the economic, scientific and technical

information systems into an effective network in and around Ahmedabad;

- To facilitate and promote sharing of resources amongst the libraries and information centres in and around Ahmedabad by developing and maintaining a central on-line Union Catalogue containing bibliographic information on books, serials and non-book materials of all the participating libraries;
- To coordinate with other regional, national and international networks, libraries, information and documentation centres for exchange of information and documents;
- To offer technical guidance to member libraries on selecting, storing, sharing and disseminating information;
- To coordinate efforts for suitable collection development and reduce unnecessary duplication whenever possible;
- To develop databases of projects, specialists and institutions in and around Ahmedabad;
- To create awareness amongst all users' groups and to educate them in the utilization of information;
- To develop resources and to propagate information in ways appropriate to the needs of users in and around Ahmedabad; and
- To help library and information centre users and also individuals who practice different professions in getting specialized information of their interest.

(ii) Services : Its various services Servicesinclude the following:

(a) *Document Delivery and Inter-Library Loan* : ADINET acts as referral centre for finding any periodical, book, report, theses and non-book material like audio-video materials, etc. It facilitates inter-library loaning among the libraries of Ahmedabad region. Besides, it procures and provides photocopies of articles from journals received by the libraries in the region.

(b) *Current Content for Library and Information Science (CUCOLIS)* : ADINET prepares consolidation of content pages of library and information science journals and provides the list to member libraries. On demand full-texts of selected articles is also provided under document delivery service. It is a database of over 5500 current periodicals received by over 140 libraries in and around Ahmedabad.16 volumes of CUCOLIShave been published by 2019.

Besides, ADINET performs several professional activities round the year. It runs course for fresh graduates of library science in Internet surfing and CDS/ISIS. It maintains a database of available jobs in and around and helps the professionals in finding suitable jobs. It also gives consultancy to several institutes for their requirement of suitable staffs and also conducts lectures of eminent scholars and professionals from time to time. ADINET also provides several services on demand like, cataloguing, classification of library documents, labeling and shelving of books, stock verification of library documents, staff training, and planning for library development, etc.

ADINET has also prepared a Directory of Libraries in Gujarat having 2,077 entries. ADINET can be contacted through its website on http://www.alibnet.org. However presently, its office is at: Sadvichar Parivar, Opposite: Ramdevnagar Bus Stand, Satellite Road, Ahmedabad (Gujarat).

1.6.5. MYLIBNET (Mysore Library Network)

Mysore Library Network (MYLIBNET) was formed in 1995 with the support of NISSAT at Central Food Technology Research Institute (CFTRI), Mysore. Of about 116 colleges/institutions affiliated to the University of Mysore; 34 college libraries are located within Mysore and these were networked in the first phase.

(i) Objectives : The objectives of the network are as follows:

- To share resources available with all the libraries;
- To provide a faster communication to all the libraries through electronic mail facility;
- To develop software tools for better library management;
- To create awareness in the field of latest information technology by conducting seminars/workshops/ training programmes;
- To setup a information base in collaboration with industries; and
- To flash arrival of new books/journals, announcement of events like seminar/ workshop/ training programmes.

(ii) Services : Its various services may be summarized as below :

(a) *E-Journals* : MYLIBNET provides links to several free online e-journals in the field of medicine, physics, mathematics and chemistry.

(b) *Union Catalogue of Journals* : It is a project that was initiated in 1990 by Academy of Information Science to conduct a survey in order to achieve the objective of 'Resource Sharing' for optimum utilization of available resources and to avoid as far as possible duplication and bringing out a hard copy of the "Union Catalogue of S&T Serials in Mysore City Libraries". The project is completed and its hard copy was published in 1991.

(c) *Experts Database* : Its database contains the list of library professionals and their details. One can search for details of an Expert either by selecting the Name of the Expert or by selecting the Name of the Institute. But the database is not very exhaustive and is still being developed.

1.6.6. MALIBNET (Madras Library Network)

MALIBNET was established in 1993 with the support of Indian National Scientific Documentation Centre (Now NISCAIR), Delhi. Now, it is a registered society of Tamil Nadu Government. It provides information to the users in and around Chennai. About 83 libraries in Madras are members contributing actively to the creation of various databases in MALIBNET. It has around 37 educational and research institutions as its members.

(i) Objectives : The main objectives of MALIBNET are:

- To foster growth in the field of information science and technology;
- To undertake scientific research in the field of library and documentation;
- To evolve a network of libraries and information centres in India;
- To establish appropriate links to national and international libraries and networks; and
- To facilitate resource sharing and information dissemination through networks.

(ii) Services : MALIBNET provides following services:

- Access to list of current serials subscribed in 50 libraries
- Full journal holdings of these libraries
- Access to specialized database giving article index with abstracts
- Door delivery system for document copies
- Access to International databases through INSDOC
- Contents, Abstracts and Photocopies from about 1200 important journals under CAPS service
  - Contents information of journals supplied as per user's choice
  - Each subscription covering 20 journals

  - — Contents data supplied in hard copy form, through E-mail or in diskette with retrieval software
  - — 12 dispatches under one subscription
- Standing order based/Demand based Abstract service from journals
- Full text of journal articles from member libraries supplied within 48 hours

Besides, MALIBNET also undertake the project to create specialized databases at user's request and also the library automation along with the training courses and consultancy project in networking and computerization. It also provides the facility of Internet search for which it charges the users for the time spent on searching. It is preparing Directories of Current Journals available in Madras City in different areas like Engineering Sciences, Basic Sciences, Medical Sciences and Social Sciences. MALIBNET can be contacted through its website with URL as http://www.malibnetonline.com.

1.6.7. BONET (Bombay Library Network)

Bombay Library Network (BONET) that was established in 1994 as a sponsored project of NISSAT is located in the National Centre for Software Technology (NCST, now CDAC) with a number of computers and software for shared use to the members. It has 25 members in the city of Mumbai.

BONET offers training related to library computerization and networking, and speed up computerization of Bombay libraries. BONET membership provides for access to its centralized catalogues and for e-mail among BONET members. BONET also benefits significantly from the experience gained, and facilities created, by the Education and Research Network(ERNET) project of the Department of Electronics, Government of India, assisted by the United Nations Development

Programme. Its main focus is on the inter-library activities, rather than on computerizing individual libraries, which no doubt computerizes their own operations and are likely to share their experiences with each other. BONET has an object of promoting cooperation among libraries in Mumabi.

BONET offers the following services:

- It provides consultation on standards and also organized training for selected staff of participating libraries, on-line catalogue of periodicals for the region, on-line catalogue of books for the region, on-line catalogue of preprints/reprints, inter-library lending of books and periodicals. It also fulfills inter-library request for photocopying, computer network support for book ordering, information retrieval services, on-line document delivery of items such as technical reports made available by participating libraries in machine readable form, and on-line access to foreign databases to those users who are willing to pay the costs incurred.
- It also has an e-mail interface for inter-library queries, e-mail facilities to order reprints from abroad, when necessary and dissemination of information, on new books etc.

Besides, BONET has also developed a database for 25,000 items in a bibliographic database on computers and software technology, union catalogue of journals and other periodicals in libraries in the region, tables of contents of 250 Indian periodicals created by the national centre for information, and a number of CD-ROM Databases which are mounted on a Novell Server for use of its members.

1.6.8. PUNENET (Pune Library Network)

PUNENET is a joint programme of the University of Pune, National Chemical Laboratory (NCL) and Centre for Development of Advanced Computing (C-DAC) funded by

NISSAT. It was established in 1992 that is accessed by 30 libraries and 15 professionals of Pune. It facilitates not only PUNENET data, but also the e-mail and internet services. PUNENET offers following databases to its members:

- Catalogues of holding of all member libraries
- Union catalogue of current periodicals in Pune libraries and information centres
- Union catalogue of books available in British libraries in India
- Publishers and Book Sellers Database
- Database on International Grants and Fellowships in Health Sciences
- Hard databanks in Biotechnology

The access to NICNET and databases available on NICNET, for example, the MEDLARS, US Patent Database, AIDS Database, access to internet and various databases available on internet.

Besides, many other metropolitan areas networks in India were sponsored by the erstwhile NISSAT in 1980s but these are not active today.

1.7. ISSUES RELATED TO LIBRARY AND INFORMATION NETWORKS

The main objective of library and information network is for resource sharing among libraries as well as easy access to information. But it requires heavy implementation of Information Technology (IT) which facilitates the access to information but unfortunately there are many issues needed to be addressed.

The libraries require high-speed connectivity to Internet which in turn require specific hardware and software for creation of system. Installation of a system is not the only issue which should be addressed. Libraries should make conscious effort for training the staffs who are involved in delivery of service and the users who are to be served. One of the major outcomes of such networks is accessibility of Online Public Access Catalogue (OPAC), which in turn requires adhering to particular standard.

Besides, the library network must follow a unique bibliographic standard but selection of a particular standard is a subjective issue which needs to be addressed in very beginning. However, India is big country with many different languages and, culture and growth of literature is there in all the language. In such a multilingual environment rendering service in once own language and script is very big challenge.

1.8. MAJOR SHIFT FROM ACQUISITION TO ACCESS

The impact of information and communication technologies has made rapid transformation of libraries and information centres. The advent of Internet and its subsequent proliferation has made dynamic changes in the communication and use pattern in libraries. The electronic publishing has made it possible to process and distribute the documents digitally. The transition to electronic publishing has provided the commercial publishers an excellent opportunity to produce the journals electronically where libraries are able to purchase large number of journals bundled in single package.

Thus, the Governments have developed consortia with the objective of collective responsibility to access those journals in order to combat the escalating cost of the journal. The reputed publishers started publishing e-books and they have also developed databases both full-text and bibliographic, indexes, abstracts, directories, encyclopedias, dictionaries and other reference works, etc., in electronic form. Contextually, the concept of open access publishing now has prevailed over the usual access publishing system in which the authors demand their work be made easily and freely available on the web for all users. The publishers and institutes producing the statistical resources also find it very suitable to convert the print document into their electronic counterparts due to emerging demand of the researchers.

Further, the problems like lack of continuous updating of information, expensive to distribution, aiming at one particular target, print depends on subscriptions, therefore reaching far less customers made the publishers shift from print medium to e-publishing. E-publishing instead takes the format of works published online, on a compact disk, e-mailed, or provided in a file format compatible with handheld electronic readers. E-publishing is an alternate form of publication especially attractive to new publishers.

E Books and e- journals, e-publications are the publication of any kind of information on any form of electronic media. They provide many advantages as compared to its print counterpart like portability, easy and any time access, search ability and space saving. Besides, customized content can be created and multimedia can be included which provide wider reach than print publications.

1.9. CONVERGING TECHNOLOGIES

There is seen a move from a physical world based on atoms to a digital world based on bites. Today, new techniques of information packaging and delivery ensure its availability at the point of demand instantly which can be achieved by exploiting the technologies provided by telecommunication, computer networking and broadcasting media (Doctor, 2003).

Further, the developments in information communication and technology that have pushed knowledge in the forefront of development of activities, are gradually transforming societies in knowledge-based societies, beside globalizing the world economy. It has also added voice and picture to information content, making it a better learning resource and thus, generated more interest in information use.

1.10. DAWN OF CONSORTIA MOVEMENT

The human race is on the threshold of a new emerging civilization that is known as the information civilization. It is an extension of and successor to the agricultural and industrial civilizations that had determined our social structure until now. Uplaonkar and Badiger (2017) states that "microelectronics technology applied in the form of computers is the essential ingredient in the making of an information society. Most of these technological innovations are born in research universities-their role is almost similar to that of a steel factory in an industrial society. Information is such a highly valued commodity that individuals who produce this are super elites of an information society". This superior class status is accessible through merit and education and attaining of knowledge through the sources and the retrieval agencies. Hence, the information seekers emerged with the advancement of communication technology.

Likewise, the object of sharing has changed over a period of years, so also the techniques. Now, resource sharing has come to mean sharing computing resources, unlike sharing of bibliographic materials like books, journals or journals articles on inter-library loan basis or preparing union lists of serials, etc. Many Indian university and college libraries are not in a position to subscribe to all the required journals and databases mainly due to lack of management support and financial constraints. Therefore, the libraries are forming consortia in order to facilitate knowledge sharing at a much cheaper rate. Hence, the development of consortia is the outcome of the desire for resource sharing that has evolved through library networks.

SUMMARY

This chapter started with the concept of library cooperation and their types which has led to the formation of library networks. Major library networks at the international and national level are discussed. Further, their role is described in brief with their contribution in the development of library services and automation activities etc. The chapter is ended with the evolution of library consortia in the scene.

BIBLIOGRAPHICAL REFERENCES

APT Partnership (1995). The Apt Reviews: A Review of Library and Information Cooperation in the UK and the Republic of Ireland. Library and Information Co-operation Council, Sheffield.

Bhatt, R.K. and Chand, M. (2014). Fundamentals of Social Sciences and Library Consortia. K.K. Publications, New Delhi.

Brodie, Maxine (1996). Connected Intelligence: the Power of Library Collaboration. Available at: http:www.csu.edu.au/special/raiss99/papers/mbrodie.html.

Dhiman, A.K. and Rani, Yashoda (2007). Resource Sharing and Library and Information Networks. Ess Ess Publications, New Delhi.

Doctor, G. (2003). Convergence of Computers, Communication - IR@INFLIBNET. CALIBER-2003 Paper. Available at: https://ir.inflibnet.ac.in/ir/bitstream/1944/213/2/03cali_44.pdf.

Evans G. E. (2002). Management Issues of Co-Operative Ventures and Consortia in the USA. Part one. Library Management, 23 (4/5): 213 – 226.

Gurikar, Rushmanasab (2014). Effective Use of Internet for Knowledge Retrieval in College Libraries. International Journal of Digital Library Services, 4 (3): 133-147.

Jaswal, B. A. (2005). Impact of Digital Technology on Library Resource Sharing: Revisiting LABELNET in the Digital Age. Pakistan Journal of Library & Information Science, 7: 87-104.

Jebaraj, V. Franklin David and Devadoss, Franklin Robert (2005). Library and Information Networks in India. Library Philosophy and Practice (e-journal). 29. Available at: https://digitalcommons.unl.edu/libphilprac/29.

Johnson, R. Sophia, Sheeba Zion, S. and Boselin Prabhu, S.R. (2019). ICT and Its Application in Library Services. Evincepub Publishing, Chattisgarh.

Kohl, D. (2003). Consortial Licensing vs. Tradition: Breaking up is Hard to do. Learned Publishing, 16 (1): 47-53.

Martey, A. K. (2002). Management Issues in Library Networking: Focus on a Pilot Library Networking Project in Ghana. Library Management, 23 (4-5): 239-251.

Merriam Webster s Collegiate Dictionary. Available at: www.merriamwebster.com/cgi-bin/book.pl?c11.html.

Mustafa, K.K. (2002). Network (DELNET): Objectives and Services. Available at: file:///C:/Users/amank/Downloads/Developing_Library_Network_DELNET__Objectives_and_Services._.pdf.

Murthy, S.S. (1996). Library Networks in India: An Overview. DESIDOC Bulletin of Information Technology, 16 (2): 3-9.

NCILS (1975). The National Commission on Libraries and Information Science. National Programme Document, USA.

Patil, Y.M. (2014). Consortium Approach to Resource Sharing in an E-Environment. Scientific Publishers, Jodhpur.

Payne, L.(1998).The Washington Research Library Consortium: A Real Organization for a Virtual Library. Information Technology in Libraries. 17(1): 13-17.

Potter, W. G. (1997). Recent Trends in Statewide Academic Library Consortia. Library Trends, 45(3): 416-434.

Rezaul Islam, Mirza Mohd. (2012). Present Status of Library Cooperation, Networking, and Resource Sharing in Bangladesh: Web-Based Library Cooperation for Access to World-wide Information. Library Philosophy and Practice (e-journal). 784. Available at: https://digitalcommons.unl. edu/libphilprac/784.

Sevukan, R. and Sharma, J. (2017). Unit-10 Library and Information Networks and Consortia: National and International. IGNOU, New Delhi. Available at: http://egyankosh.ac.in/handle/123456789/35262.

Uplaonkar, S.S. and Badiger, K.C. (2017). Library Consortia: An Overview. International Journal of Library and Information Studies, 7 (2): 132-139.

Wikipedia (2019). Library Networks in India. Available at: https://en.wikipedia.org/wiki/Library_Networks_in_India.

2

Library Consortium : An Overview

It is seen that the publishing industry is mainly represented by commercial, societal and academic publishers which are experimenting with newly emerging technologies and marketing strategies for several years. The latest one being making journals available in e - format along with print version. If the present trend continues, one day it may be ended up with only e-versions of journals and books. If this could be the trend, many questions will be raised. The foremost could be whether electronic versions are affordable by an average institution and if so, what could be the conditions for access? What will be the role of libraries in accessing/preserving technical information?

Moreover, print editions are converted into e-editions and bundle is made available for subscription at additional costs. This trend is directly affecting decreasing library budget which has forced library professionals to look for new ways and means to subscribe/access maximum number of journals/books on reasonable and affordable costs. This could be achieved only through negotiations with publishers/vendors or intermediaries keeping in view end users' requirements.

No institution could afford to be self-sufficient; thus, coming together of likeminded institutes is a dire necessity. Hence, the consortium concept has come into vogue, which is an institutional alliance bringing likeminded member institutions with common aims, policies and collective agenda. Indeed, it is for meeting across a table between willing buyers/sellers directly or through intermediaries/aggregators with "win-win situations" to all parties.

However, the experience has shown that the concept of consortium works well between organizations, which are similar in size, funding, subject areas, and those which are headed by enlightened library professional/ administrators. For consortium formation, one needs willingness, courage, time and determination. Patil (2004) and Carbone (2007) add that new possibilities may not come as easily as the earlier efforts. Nevertheless, good efforts are the well worth the payoffs: increased access to users, broadened access and recognition libraries receive for their spirit of cooperation. Thus, the library consortia have appeared and promoted for sharing of resources, cooperation in collection development policies. The consortia also have facilitated for set up of online union catalogues, inter-library loans, networks and applied to share the access to online resources.

2.1. HISTORY OF LIBRARY CONSORTIA

The history of library consortia can be studied under following headings.

2.1.1. Consortia: the Evolution of Cooperation

The evolution of library consortium is profoundly embedded in the history of library cooperative endeavors. Kraus (1975) in his seminal work entitled "Prologue to

Library Cooperation" precisely documents the historical treatise of library cooperation wherein he mentions the fact that library cooperative activities were being practiced in thirteenth century also. Wormann (1968) also reports examples of an exchange agreement amongst the Lund University, Abo Akademi University and University of Greifswald in 1740, that signifies concept of cooperation as a basic tenet of librarianship which was exercised through informal agreements, where tactic understandings appeared between individual libraries with an assumption that the growth of problems within library could be resolved by well-coordinated and cooperative efforts.

However, the real turning point in the cooperation among libraries was seen during 1800s when the concept of cooperation that is defined by Edmonds(1986) as, "reciprocally beneficial sharing of resources, developed or pre-existed by two or more bodies" was shifted towards relatively richer and broader concept of resource sharing which defines sharing of library resources and services by a number of libraries (Jackson, Kent and Lancour (1972). Morgan (1998) also mentions that "resource sharing is one of the fundamental principles for supporting library services, but the object of the sharing has changed over the years". Wylie and Yeager (1999) characterizes movement of resource sharing from the sharing of "things" to the sharing of "people, expertise, services", etc. Kopp (1998) follows the historical growth and development of "library collaboration" in the U.S.A. in the three documents namely, "Grouping of Places for Library Purposes by G L Campbell in 1879", "Reports of the Cooperation Committee of the American Library Association (ALA), published in the American Library Association Bulletin in the 1980s" as well as "A Library Journal by Melvil Dewey on Library Cooperation in 1886". He notes that resource sharing was the main purpose for libraries to collaborate and coordinate with each other. According to Bostick (2001) the early form of large-scale library resource sharing was cooperative cataloguing programme which was started by Library of Congress in early 1900s for sharing the cataloguing information amongst participating libraries.

Over the years, to fulfill the need of highly integrated and technologically advanced users, informal and early form of library cooperation and resource sharing was evolved into new form of cooperatives i.e. "collaboration", "partnership", "networking", and at present "consortia".

2.1.2. From Library Cooperation to Library Consortia

Library and information science literature shows how the early 1900s was the period when cooperative endeavors required the support of formal consortia. In this period, most of the libraries started transforming their cooperative activities from a "organizational self-sufficiency model" to "collaborative survival model" (Allen and Hirshon, 1998). Triangle Research Libraries Network that was established in 1933 by North Carolina and Duke University, is considered as the first major academic library consortium (Bostick, 2001). Wade (1999) in his study on "The Very Model of a Modern Library Consortium" examines various factors and circumstances under which the voluntary alliance of non-affiliated consortia should start thinking for a legal structure. While providing evidences of migration from the usage of word "cooperation" to "consortium", it is observed as to how the term "consortium" begun to flourish during the 1950s and the 1960s, the period when majority of the academic library consortia were come into existence (Kopp, 1998).

However, the exact date for the introduction of the term "library consortium" is not clear but the concept of a consortium as being an association or partnership has long been a concern of librarianship. The published literature indicates that the concept is not new, and it refers to co-operation, co-ordination and collaboration between, and amongst, libraries for the purpose of sharing information resources. However, a library did not use it widely until about the 1980s. The main drive for co-operation arose when there was increase in the output of publications or the information explosion, the rise in the cost of publications coupled with stringent budget allocations, and growth in student enrolment. Further, increasing demand for service from users together with the need to improve inter-lending services and the library collection are additional factors.

During 1980s, the concept of cooperation, i.e., how libraries can achieve their objectives better by working together, shifted toward the concept of resource sharing which is considered as a richer term that encompasses also the strategic aspect to link users with the required information or material. Sewell (1981) adds "the new term appears ... to assume a range of physical, intellectual and conceptual resources on the one hand and a body of people on the other, and covers the activities involved in organizing the one into a set of optimum relationships to meet the needs of the other".

Moreover, during 1980s, libraries concentrated their energies on implementing local integrated library systems and pioneering the use of technology, such as CD-ROMs installed in local networks, thus giving lower priority to consortia activities (Kopp, 1998). But the decade 1990s has opened up new vistas in terms of the proliferation of network - based electronic resources including indexing and abstracting databases, full-text electronic journals and e-books. etc. Thus, there was a paradigm shift from resource sharing to consortia approach as far as cooperative efforts were concerned. The decade could be not only the appearance of library consortia all over the world but also has seen many of these consortia organized themselves into an increasingly influential federation of library cooperatives.

Later, the Internet and world wide web (WWW) have facilitated for the emergence of e-environment, which provided access to a rapidly growing array of full-text electronic content and hyperlinks to cited references, etc. all in a well distributed network environment. This has further given impetus in development of 'virtual library', or 'electronic digital library' which could create a new environment well suited for what one may consider as a 'resurgence' of library consortia. With these developments, libraries were at cross roads. Library professionals were coping with developments but were also faced with ever increasing costs of print resources- serials leading to 'serials crisis'. The so-called 'serials crisis' was due to enormous increase in the growth of scientific information which took place in beginning of 1960s. This resulted in either down-sizing or right-sizing libraries. Policy makers were rather looking for more collaboration and cooperation in the ever-increasing cost and information itself.

The library consortia were appended during 1990s which was indeed an important phenomenon in the library activities and services. Immediate developments in forming consortia were visible particularly in USA and UK. The impact was felt in many countries and one or other form of consortia started appearing in Europe, Spain, Finland, Italy and Asia. The consortia concept has become a global phenomenon and many consortia emerged during these years across many countries.

However, the establishment of the International Coalition of Library Consortia (ICOLC) in 1996 was considered as a milestone in the evolution of consortium. Turner (2014) has mentioned that during the period 2000 to 2009, membership in ICOLC increased by 56 percent. Later, many consortia were created, primarily to leverage purchasing power for electronic resources and other library services, such as: "NILRC (1973)", "RLDC (1996)", "CCLC (1998)", "VALE (1998)", "the Carolina Consortium (2004)" and "Wyoming Community College Library Consortium (2006)" etc.

Westmoreland and Shirley (2004), and Evans (2002)

have carried out research on the historical development mention on the growth, objectives, and current status of several of the major academic consortia, such as "Tex Share (Texas)", "VIVA (Virginia)", "PALCI (Pennsylvania)", "GALILEO (Georgia)", and "Ohio LINK (Ohio)". Over time, the evolution of newer consortia like: "CARL in Colorado", "IDAL in Illinois", "SAILOR in Maryland", "MIRACL in Missouri", "CONZUL in New Zealand", "CAUL in Australia", "CRL in North America", "NCLive in North Carolina", "PORTALS in Portland", "WRLC in Washington", "CALICO, GAELIC, FRELICO, SEALS, CATNIP and EASELin South Africa", "CIC in South Asia" , "CURL in UK", "CALIM in Manchester", "Concord in Britain", "Metroweb in New York", "CALIS in China", came into existence in the international scenario. Thornton (2000) has investigated the impact of electronic resources on consortia base subscription to resources, foresaw an increase in cooperative collection development and so consortia will turn out to be significantly more essential because of electronic resources.

Reinhardt and Boekhorts (2001) show how in Germany, the consortium which originally was linked mainly to a legal context, was derived from an Anglo-American background and now assumes a broader meaning than it had, meaning more 'partnership, 'association' and referring to joint actions of libraries. There are other initiatives of library consortia at an international level such as ThaiLIS (Thailand), CALIS (China), CBUC (Catalonia), GAELIC (South Africa) and RUSSNet (Russia) (Ghosh, 2002).

Ashoor (2000) suggests a few guidelines for the Arabian Gulf regions and concludes that libraries in the region should enter into partnership to establish a consortium. Fordyce (2004) has discussed different consortium-related issues. He adds that the committee of New Zealand University Librarians Acquisitions Consortium was developed to gain maximum value from expenditure on print monograph resources, to achieve operating efficiencies and to improve levels of service.

Mclean (1999) writes that the consortia movement in Australian was driven by resource sharing. Wade (1999) says there is a stage and circumstances under which an informal consortium needs to think about changing from an alliance of non-affiliated institutions to a formal, legally incorporated body in Australia. However, in Europe, with the exception of a few countries with strong inter-library cooperation traditions, mostly of the northern area, cooperative activities among libraries began to take shape during the 1970s which were mainly based on the automation of cataloguing processes. But the phenomenon of the rise of academic library consortia is relatively new in Europe. A study by Tammaro (2009) on the literature on resource sharing in Europe pays particular attention to its development in Europe starting from 1998 in Spain, Catalonia, France, Greece, the United Kingdom, Finland, Germany, Poland, the Netherlands and Switzerland.

It also involves most of the Italian academic libraries, and assumes different attitudes depending on the different contexts. Likewise, in the other European countries, during these years the first interesting cooperative initiatives were linked to the automation of public library catalogues, through a national automation programme, the Servizio Bibliotecario Nazionale. Most of the academic libraries followed this programme after the promulgation of Act 168/89, with which the Ministero dell' Universitae della Ricerca Scientifica was created and the financial and administrative autonomy of the university was established (Galluzzi, 2001).This new context created the premises for the organization of the academic library systems from which at the end of the 1990s some of the academic library consortia alliances found their basis; for example, the consortia groups Center for International Private Enterprise and Comitato Inter-universitario Basi Dati ed Editoria in Rete.

2.2. CONSORTIA EFFORTS IN USA

USA is the home place of many library consortia or networks (Wade, 1999). Triangle Research Libraries Network (TRLN), a well-known consortium was formed in 1933 by the combined efforts of the University of North Carolina and the Duke University, are the earliest known library consortia, which are still in existence today.

However, USA has a long history of library cooperation where the library consortia were seeming to be existed for over a century and gone through several phases of developments. Initially, during 1900s, the Library of Congress began cooperative cataloguing and began distributing catalogue cards to all participants in the project on a nation-wide basis. It resulted in developing a formal library consortium during 1960s when library automation was introduced. With TRLN consortia on the scene, further developments took place, for example, the Big Twelve Plus and the Committee on Institutional Cooperation (CIC) have come out with this model. Illinois Libraries Computer System Organization (ILCSO) is one of the consortia belonging to earlier groups for resource sharing.

But the consortia in the USA came in different formats ranging from simple buying clubs to full-fledged networks. Consortia types differ from a single city (Kansas State City Library Consortium) to single state (OhioNet), to multi-state (SOLINET - the Southeastern Library network). Also, libraries were forced to participate in more than one consortium.

2.3. CONSORTIA EFFORTS IN UK

In UK, there are two models for resource sharing, e-content, viz. library purchasing consortia and access schemes. It is seen that many library consortia were formed at national, regional and local levels that provide access but the thrust was for cooperation with the focus for best practice. Society of College, National and

University libraries (SOCNUL), which has participants including most of the colleges, universities and national libraries in England and Ireland offer for many schemes for access. National Consortia consists of Consortium of University Research Libraries (CURL) and UK Libraries Plus. Access to libraries for Learning (ALL), Access to Libraries in Swansea (ATLIS) and Access to Libraries in North amptonshire (ALIS) are some examples of regional consortia.

Joint Information Systems Committee (JISC), the most important committee of UK that funds higher education has evolved a programme - Distributed National Electronic Resource (DNER) with several activities. Significant contribution of DNER is the National Site Licensing Initiative (NESLI) -a loose consortium for the purchase of electronic copies of academic journals. It has set up to secure better value in journal subscriptions for UK's academic libraries and buildup electronic resources.

2.4. CONSORTIA EFFORTS IN CHINA

China has also taken a leading role for its consortia activities, where the library consortia have emerged during 1980s. Large scale regional consortia among Chinese academic libraries were achieved in the 1990s, while cross - regional consortia and national consortia began to gain popularity after 2000.

China Academic Library and Information System (CALIS - 1998) and China Academic Humanities and Social Sciences Library (CASHL - 2003) are two most influential and successful nationwide academic library consortia projects in China (Xu, 2010).

2.5. CONSORTIA EFFORTS IN INDIA

The concept of consortia formation in India is of recent origin that has been discussed about since 1990s. Though, some efforts were made notably for: 'Forum for Resource Sharing in Astronomy (FORSA)'s Indian

Astrophysics" Consortium earlier to 1990s, but in real sense, the formation of library consortia may be claimed to be started with the formation of 'Consortium for Material Science and Aerospace Collection' of the NAL in 1998 for a few databases, though it could not sustain for various reasons. This was followed by TIFR Consortium formation in 2000 and the formation of IIM Library Consortium in the same year, i.e. 2000. TIFR has used the consortia model offered by Springer for multisite licensing and cross sharing of content among all branch libraries affiliated to TIFR. Perhaps, this is the first known successful consortia in the country. Thereafter, few leading libraries and publishers/vendors joined together and formed few open and non-informal consortia projects.

This was followed by CSIR E-Journals Consortium (now National Knowledge Resource Consortium of DST and CSIR Libraries); DAE Consortium for its affiliated institutions with single publisher- Elsevier. INDEST took its birth in 2003 which is the first well planned, multi sector, consortium with both funding and management commitment. Likewise, many consortia emerged in India, viz. HELINET, UGC-INFONET, SNDT for LISA; CeRA of ICAR; DRDO; ISI Libraries Consortium; ERMED Consortium of NML; MCIT Consortium; and DBT Consortium etc.

2.6. CONSORTIUM: CONCEPTS, DEFINITIONS AND OBJECTIVES

The concept, its definitions, and major objectives of the library consortium can be studied as under.

2.6.1. Concepts of Library Consortia

The concept of consortia is based on a group of libraries coming together with common aims, objectives and policies. The basic aim of consortia is to achieve set goals which otherwise members of the group cannot achieve at an individual level.

Bhatt (2011) mentions that over last few decades, the concept of consortia has emerged as a potential area directly concerning to librarians, publishers and end users of information. Consortia is a term that is derived from Latin word for 'fellowship' - the meaning being coming together of separate groups with a common purpose. It involves relatively informal, cooperatives, founded to realize economies scale in purchasing to highly organized, centrally staffed/funded organizations, intended to share resources and to engage in all manners of collaboration within a group of member libraries.

Consortia are resource sharing organizations formed by libraries, invariably termed as cooperatives, networks, collective alliances or partnerships. The library consortia are association of libraries established by formal agreements where cooperative purchase of e-resources is one of the key activities. Collaborative acquisition of electronic resources can result in lower price and savings in terms of actual cost, time and staff efforts. Moreover, access to resources is considered more important than collection building itself if the access is perpetual in nature. A consortium with the collective strength of resources of various institutions available to it is in a better position to address and resolve the problems of managing, organizing and archiving the electronic resources.

Further, the recent technologies have changed users' perceptions, expectations, their patience, and willingness to accept services that are available on demand. The available resources on web-based services are apt answers to the expectations of researchers. The availability of full-text resources and bibliographic databases to scholars improve their research productivity in terms of research papers given the fact that there exists a correlation between scientific literature availability to researchers in a research organization and scientific productivity of researchers and number of research papers produced.

Thus, the consortium, as an effective tool and platform for number of libraries not only facilitates sharing the print and electronic resources, it also acts as spring board to trigger other activities that require collaborative efforts, such as union catalogues of books, joint automation projects and exchange/sharing expertise and research outputs etc. (Arora, 2005).

2.6.2. Definitions of Library Consortia

Consortia is the plural form of consortium but is often used in place of the singular form. The term is derived from the Latin word for "fellowship"; the meaning emphasizes the coming together of separate groups for a purpose. Homogenously, it is used as "alliance," "coalition," "collaboration," "cooperation," "partnership" etc. Consortia are complicated organization but "an association" in the sense that is not commonly understood; i.e., a consortium is not a library association, although some associations of libraries engage themselves in consortia activity (Scepanski, 1998). However, these consortia embrace a group of libraries with a common interest, objectives and policies and one of the group members acts as a coordinator to liaise with publishers and deal with negotiations, licensing and legal matters etc. Thus, consortia are strategic alliance of institutes that have common goals to achieve.

The following are some of definitions of the consortium as given in different sources.

Online Dictionary of Library and Information Science (ODLIS) defines library consortia as "an association of independent libraries and/or library systems established by formal agreement, usually for the purpose of resource sharing. Membership may be restricted to a specific geographical region, type of library (public, academic, special), or subject specialization" (Reitz, 2012).

While, according to *American Heritage Dictionary,* a consortium is said to be "a cooperative arrangement among groups or institutions" or "an association or society" which has its root in Latin word, *consortia* that first was adopted in the 17th century.

According to the *Oxford English Dictionary,* library consortium is "a community of two or more information agencies which have formally agreed to coordinate, cooperate or consolidate certain function" to achieve mutual objectives.

While, according to *Merriam Webster Dictionary* a consortium is "an agreement, combination, or group (as of companies) formed to undertake an enterprise beyond the resources of any one member", but it "usually involves horizontal collaboration among direct competitors" (Aldrich, Bolton, Baker and Sasaki, 1998).

Hirshon (1998) defines the consortium as, "a generic term to indicate any group of libraries that are working together towards a common goal, whether to expand cooperation on traditional library services (such as collection development or electronic information services)". It is now used perhaps too broadly and encompasses everything from formal legal entities to information groups that come together solely to achieve better pricing for purchasing electronic information.

Kopp (1998) writes that "use of the term for relationship or association did not come about until the 1820s, and it was not until a hundred years later that it began to appear in relation to manufacturing and banking enterprises.". However, the concept of consortium as being an association of partnership has long been a tenet of librarianship. It refers to cooperation, collaboration and coordination between, and amongst libraries for the purpose of sharing information services (Nfila and Darko-Ampen, 2000).

Thus, library consortia are the "community (a cooperative) of two or more information agencies which have formally agreed to coordinate, cooperate or consolidate certain function" to achieve mutual objectives. It is an association of a group of libraries to achieve mutually the joint benefits. It provides a way for its members to conduct business in a comparative manner.

Library consortia are, thus, can be the networks for buying and accessing e-information in a cooperative arrangement among a group of libraries in providing instant access to greater resources for the users of the individual libraries, where coordinator for identification of libraries for each publisher, negotiation, legal matters etc. is selected from one of the member libraries. The degree of centralization of consortium is the primary factor affecting not only how member institutions interact with one another, but also maintain relationship with external party (publisher/vendor). More decentralized the consortium, the greater the degree of autonomy each member retains. But the library consortia may vary from being decentralized to highly centralize in nature.

2.6.3. Characteristics of Library Consortia

Okerson (2004) has identified the following characteristics of library consortia:

- Always institutions/libraries participate, not individuals;
- Can be formal or informal, big or small;
- Many choices for name and structure, depending on mission, organization, and message;
- Some are becoming very large and complex but some have broad programmes; and others do principally licensing of electronic resources;
- Can be restricted to specific library types (special libraries, academic libraries, etc.) or government agencies;
- Can be open to all local, or regional, or country wide group libraries; some include all libraries in their region including elementary school and public;

- Underlying structure can be "informal" or "formal," some or lots of centralization, many activities or highly focused;
- Most informal: no central office, leadership may rotate, volunteers are key; this can work for a startup, or for a narrowly focused set of consortial goals and/or limited financial resources;
- Most formal: legally incorporated or an organized office in a government or NGO, permanent staff, an ambitious set of ambitions and goals and many members, and
- Can change over time.

There is seen a growing number of large/small, informal/formal consortia worldwide but their functions vary considerably; for example, the shared cataloguing, MARC records, reciprocal borrowing, collection sharing, integrated library systems, virtual union catalogues, servers and virtual reference collections. However, the consortia can be loosely clustered into the various types: technical processing, user services, special subject, product areas, inter-library loans or reference networks and multi-type: reference, book, journal, databases, e-services.

2.6.4. Purpose of Library Consortia

Though, a library consortium is formed to achieve shared purpose, yet the resource sharing is the main purpose. However, electronic resources licensing is other major goal, aiming to reduce the costs per unit through formation of purchasing consortia.

Library cooperation is, therefore, a major purpose but the means toward greater access to resources is beyond the ability of any single library (Shachaf, 2003). Some other purposes of library consortia are:

- to control and reduce information costs;
- to improve resource sharing;

- to share licensing issues with each other;
- to subscribe to electronic resources for members at highly discounted rates;
- to impart training to the users, librarians, research scholars, and members of the faculty;
- to provide platform interaction amongst the member libraries;
- to evaluate the usage of the resource subscriptions; and
- to identify newly required resources for subscription.

But the ability of consortia to achieve these purposes entirely depends upon the cooperation and commitment from each one of the member libraries, from the publishers as well as the availability of funds. However, the consortia are usually economically motivated, and in this modern world most of them are formed with the objective of increasing bargaining power for accessing expensive electronic databases.

2.6.5. Objectives of Library Consortia

The consortium serves the libraries/publishers/ users with the following set of objectives (Patil, 2014).

- Consortia have been formed mainly for cooperative acquisitions and sharing of e-journals. Libraries buy licenses for number of print/electronic resources from different publishers and use different modes for information delivery;
- Shared subscription to electronic resources through consortia of libraries is a means to access electronic resources across institutions at a negotiated cost, and download required materials remotely;
- Consortia based subscription meets diminishing costs, increased users' demands and contains ever increasing costs of journals;
- Consortia are formed of all types, at all levels with

the aim of taking advantage of global network to promote better, faster and more cost-effective ways providing access to e-resources and meets ever increasing demands of users; and

- Consortia formed at national level possibly seek national site licensing for products of common interests to many participants across several institutions in the country.

But the objectives could be widened to make them efficient instruments of sharing of all types of library resources, viz. journals, e-books, reference materials, full-text databases etc.

2.6.6. ELements of Library Consortia

Every library differs from one another according to its collection, information needs of users, working method, sources of finance, processing of information, etc. but various elements can be adopted by a consortium for functioning standing on a common platform. These are:

Agreement for establishment of a Consortium: A concrete agreement is needed to establish for the participating libraries in consortia to achieve a common target. Only then, every library will be able to work in such a manner that they are mutually exclusive, but they follow the common mission of a consortium as a whole. So, a managing committee should be formed for making agreement etc. for a consortium.

Administration of Library Consortium: A statutory body is very essential to be formed to run the total functions of a consortium smoothly by taking Chief Librarian / Chief Information Manager from every library/ Information Centre. One of them will act as a Chief Coordinator on rotation basis. Each library has to inform about its collection, databases, user service, training of human resource for handling new equipment, etc. to the Chief Coordinator through hierarchical management level.

Financial Control: As libraries form a consortium because of financial problems for providing better service to the users, the crucial activities of the members of management committee is to take action on the following financial points :

- Whether a consortium fund be created to subscribe the core journals in different subjects in multiple copies at a discount rate;
- How to manage the fund of a consortium and how much money is to be collected from each library as a contribution;
- Whether the participating libraries to whom the responsibility to negotiate with some publishes are vested by the managing committee will send remittance to the publishers for multiple copies from its own fund and adjust it subsequently among the participating libraries.

Joint Work : All the participating libraries under library consortia are expected to work jointly just like a joint venture in business sector to make the consortia a total success. Each library will subscribe the core journals and prepare the union list of titles to be covered under resource sharing programme. However, the member libraries may also send full content page service of all issues of the title to another library.

Evaluation: All the activities of a consortium, i.e. individual as well as co-operative, must be evaluated on the basis of the pre-determined objectives after a certain period. If there is any lacuna in between the work performed and to be performed should be adjusted by taking corrective measures in activities in future. If there is a need for any change in the path of action, it should be changed immediately to achieve the objectives of a consortium.

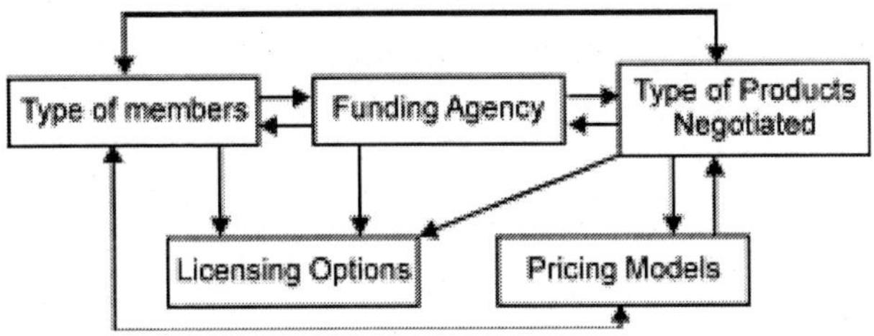

Fig. 2.1. Elements of Library Consortium

However, Birdie (2005) has listed five essential elements as shown in Fig. 2.1 that constitute a consortium arrangement. These requirements are to be well defined before starting any consortium arrangement. But these five elements may vary according to the objectives for which the consortia came into existence.

2.7. CONSIDERATION OF POINTS BEFORE CONSORTIA FORMATION

Various factors that can be taken into account for the effective functioning of successful consortium are (Bedi and Sharma, 2008):

- Selecting a coordinating agency to deal on the behalf of entire group of participants and execute and monitor the work;
- Clear administrative/official/organizational policy and need of liberal economic policies and liberal organizational attitudes;
- Sources of funding to meet the subscription costs;
- Identifying and negotiating the potential publishers/ vendors or aggregators to provide access under consortia purchase;
- Legal issues involved in contracts and usage of material within the consortia;
- Resource identification on the basis of usage and usability;

- Long-run planning of the technology infrastructure;
- Access to back runs of periodicals clearly spelled out in the license contracts;
- Copyright and licensing;
- Issues related to backup and archiving of database;
- Economically favourable price issue; and
- Designing and launching of long-term sustenance and robust models of library consortium.

Besides, permanent staff should be there for innovative development of services and processes. But the lack of permanent staff can be a major obstacle when developing content provision and all the related services in society. Volunteer work may give good results in the short term, but it is very difficult to offer permanent services based on that kind of solution.

2.8. FACTORS RESPONSIBLE FOR FORMATION OF LIBRARY CONSORTIA

Various factors that necessitated the formation of library consortia. Based on Allen and Hirson (1998), Hirson (1995), Piotrowicz (2002) and Pandian and Karisiddappa (2004), these can be studied under following four sub-headings.

2.8.1. Changes in Technology

Information and telecommunication technologies have great impact on the way a library processes information, where libraries have to look for new methods of serving heterogeneous needs of varied users. These factors have transformed libraries to move from being access oriented to content oriented. In fact, it is assumed that the concept of a digital library was not demand driven but very much a product/service-driven approach. Libraries have gone from print indexes to librarian-mediated online searching, from CD-ROM user-friendly systems to highly powered Web-based systems that provide index entries, abstracts and full text and image of articles. With emerging development in the implementation of the Z39.50/OAI-PMH standard for systems interfaces, libraries today are increasingly able to search across multiple databases simultaneously and to receive merged retrieval sets.

2.8.2. Changes in the Scholarly Research and Publishing

It is seen that Web has changed the mode of access of information where much information available is free of charge but still it is given secondary importance because scholarly information is mostly available in databases and in scientific publications, though it is slow. Probably, a lack of understanding in pricing the information in the electronic environmentis the major reason for publishers being slow in providing their publications electronically. This economic crisis is occurring at the time when technology is dramatically changing the ways in which scholars share their research results. Scholars in some disciplines are disseminating information quickly on the Web rather than waiting for the protracted publishing processes that make publication irrelevant by the time of availability. Traditional print publishers are feeling new pressure to make information available more quickly and in more formats. So, they opt for the electronic publishing, which is offering great potential to become a faster, more fully featured, widely accessible medium of scholarly communication.

2.8.3. Economic Competition

Libraries have been under increasing pressure both from the educational sector and the requirements of the licensing field which have forced various academic institutions into competition, especially regarding cost-effectiveness and cost reduction. These phenomena have increased competition among funded institutions and, consequently, caused the collapse and disintegration of library funding, significantly and reducing of their budgets with a simultaneous increase in the number of users. Further, the economic pressure has caused individual libraries to maximize the use of their financial resources, and the creation of library consortia undoubtedly seems to be at least a partial remedy.

2.8.4. Quality Improvement

The libraries have directed their attention to electronic information resources in order to maintain high professional standards of customer service and expand the range of proposed services; however, electronic resources are costly, but they could be used more optimally. Academic libraries also have started implementing structural and organizational changes and took initiatives toward developing self-education and improvement of professional qualifications of their own personnel in keeping with the idea of supporting research and educational processes. These libraries saw a chance for a dynamic development through partnership agreements, formation of consortia and creation of an organized network of institutions with common access to valuable information resources. Consortia are the required forum for libraries' activities related to sharing information about library procedures and cost reduction within the field of customer service.

Nfila and Darko-Ampem (2002) add that as per the Report of System Development Corporation (SDC) USA, the main reason for the formation of the consortia was perhaps the thinking that the consortia approach offers an attractive solution to many outstanding problems of the participating libraries. However, the main driving force for collaboration among libraries, especially academic libraries, has been the increase in numbers of publications and the rise in the cost of publications as well as the decline in library budgets. Further, the increase in user enrollment in higher education and increasing demands for library services and collections were other factors given, from the 1980s, onwards, for collaborative efforts for formation of library consortia.

2.9. CONSORTIA GOALS

Consortium is a unique organization, with a set of goals, funds and members. It must try for integration with its environment, in order to collaborate with publishers, vendors and libraries. Though library consortia are formed to achieve shared goals but the main goals of cooperation vary. One of the most common goals is resource sharing through union catalogues and inter-library loan agreements. Electronic resources licensing is another goal aiming to reduce costs per unit through formation of purchasing consortia (Shachaf, 2003).

Further, the consortium can have its own organizational structure for governance and can act as an agent on behalf of members with set goals and benefits. Malviya and Kumar (2007) have listed some of important goals as enumerated below:

- Increase the access base of all relevant resources for all participants;
- Judicious utilization of funds and pay up-front products and not for Research & Development;
- Ensure continuity of subscription keeping in view users' needs;
- To make available the quantitative and qualitative electronic resources;
- Enhance the visibility of library resources;
- Improve and enhance existing library services;
- Cost sharing for technical and training support; and
- Increasing user base-access from users' computer.

2.10. CONSORTIA MISSION/VISION

The consortia of libraries are made to create and

sustain a rich, supportive and diverse knowledge environment that furthers research, teaching, learning and resources through the sharing of collections, expertise and programmes. However, the basic consortium mission is to facilitate access by researchers to the global information network and remove access barriers to e-products at an affordable cost with least time and efforts (Kirlidog and Bayir, 2007). Other include:

- Maintaining liaison with the contents providers and assessing proposals;
- Negotiating the deals and acquiring database usage clauses with model license;
- Analyzing usage statistics;
- Creating awareness about availability of resources at the users' computer;
- Conducting use-based training programmes to both library staff and users of resources; and
- Conducting evaluation and monitoring usage of resources.

In the process of change, the consortia assist libraries in programme implementation and also how each of its members is coping with various issues. In an ideal situation, the following parameters could be of importance, viz. (Katsirikou, 2003).

- To explore all related issues objectively;
- To understand and articulate trends as they are emerging; and
- To create and follow standardized methodologies that the individual libraries can employ and customize at their own institutions.

Further, the library consortia may:

- Promote the organization for collaborative activities;
- Expand the higher education opportunities for the learning community by reducing inter-institutional barriers;

- Stretch the scarce resources of the region through the effective use of educational and research technology, of each institute's resident expertise and of improved strategic and operational and management activities; and
- Facilitate the development of joint efforts to meet the needs of the local and regional learning communities.

2.11. BASIC FUNCTIONS OF THE CONSORTIUM

There are three basic functions of consortia formation as enumerated by Potter (1997) are given below:

- Share physical resources among participants by means of union catalogues, local systems linked together, inter-library loan protocols established, courier services provided, etc. for document delivery;
- Provide connections to the Internet and world wide web (WWW), including the provision of e-mail facility and workstations; and
- Provide access to electronic resources either by mounting them on a local server or providing access to resources on publishers or vendors platforms or third party.

2.12. WHY CONSORTIUM: THE NEED

It is observed that during last 15-20 years there have been marked developments in libraries, which have moved from organizational self-sufficiency to a collaborative survival model as seen with growth of library consortia. Recent developments in ICTs are now enabling a level of cooperation that is much broader and deeper than ever before (Allen and Hirshon, 1998). With proliferation of e-products, there have been marked increases in prices of e-resources and due to ever growing demands of users, libraries are unable to sustain collection development. Thus, the libraries have turned from ownership to access, from a "just in case" attitude to a "just in time" in order to overcome this problem (Xenidou-Dervou, 2001). There is also a paradigm shift from physical ownership to lease or licensing of information resources. Potter (1997) has observed that libraries are forming institutional alliances to meet various challenges arising from developments in information technology and impacts of Internet and World Wide Web.

2.12.1. Challenges of Consortium

There was an urgent need to form consortia due to serials crisis and ICTs applications on global stage in order to consolidate proliferating electronic resources and provide access on a larger scale. Hiremath (2001) adds that it was also necessary to know various challenges, constraints and whether these are the part of growing or permanent aspect to consortial arrangement.

2.12.2. Changing Role of the Librarian

The role of the librarian has changed from keeper of library documents to that of navigator of information with the advent of Internet and world wide web (WWW). Also, the role of library is changing from purchasing content to facilitating access to content. Library professionals come closer willingly for actively sharing information and buying selectively, involving in selection, negotiations and licensing keeping in view present scenario of proliferations of electronic resources.

2.12.3. Uncertainty in Costs

There is annual increase in prices to the tune of 7 to 15 percent at institute level. There is made a cut in subscription on annual basis keeping this in view and fixed library budget. Being in consortia as a participant, negotiations can lead to reduced pricing and bulk purchases. This cannot be done at an individual level.

2.12.4. Uncertainty in Pricing

Due to proliferation of electronic resources, pricing is evolving continuously confusing both for consortia and publishers. On one hand, publishers are looking to protect declining print sales and enhance electronic sales whereas on the other hand libraries are looking to delink print from online version. In such a scenario, publishers are offering different models based on capability of buyer - at an individual, institutional and the consortium.

2.12.5. Lack of Trust

There is always a feeling of uncertainty and distrust in any cooperative ventures while dealing with any undertakings and it is more so in any consortia negotiations. There is a feeling of low trust in many of consortial undertakings in the beginning. There is also a likelihood of strong hesitation to trust unknown negotiators from the other side. Each member of the negotiation committee felt a compelling need to participate in both negotiations with the vendor as well as a personal study of proposals received. It is intriguing factor over length of time as a participant in negotiation for comparatively a bigger consortium for purchasing a license as well as reluctance of vendors to deal with the avoidably complicated transactions come to mind most easily. The feeling of distrust could diminish with a couple of meetings and eventually, a mutual trust and confidence will be built up over a period of time. Hence, as suggested by Allen and Hirshon (1998) "the pivotal issues get addressed early, and the informal or divisive issues get deferred until some success has been achieved".

2.12.6. Consortia Obligations

It is also seen that the library in a case where multidisciplinary research is being carried out in an institution may not be able to provide requisite information even by joining or being a participant in a consortium.

One may explore to join other consortia or 'buying clubs' from where it could meet its user requirements. One consortium member may be participating in more than one consortium for a variety of reasons like some may be strategic or political in nature. The political reasons may not be underestimated as they are frequently tied up to funding, especially government supported institutions. There may be smaller or bigger institutions in the group of consortia which must reflect the common needs of entire spectrum of consortium, by developing links amongst them and other smaller consortia.

However, this could be succeeded with consortia obligations (Alexander, 1999) as mentioned below:

- Develop a strategic plan which is to be achieved and how to do it;
- Familiarize with strategic plans of other consortia to which another consortia participant is a member;
- Use meetings and other conferences to develop good 'diplomatic relations' with consortial colleagues; and
- Avoid working at cross purposes or potentially competitive situations by looking for opportunities to cooperate with other consortia.

2.13. FORMING LIBRARY CONSORTIUM

It is clear that the consortia are evolved as group initiatives keeping in view effective management practices including legal structure, sound policies and best practices which are critical for success of any consortium. The important parameters to be looked into forming consortium are: development, governance, and management (Hawthorn, Frey and Roy, 1999; Satyanarayana, Krishnan and Arora, 2004). However, as pointed out by Helmer (1999), when we are trying to form a consortium, the following questions are raised to find means to an end.

- Why library consortia are experiencing renaissance at this time?
- Is there an ideal model for library consortia, or, lacking an ideal, can one at least identify some indicators of success or 'best practices'?
- How do consortia with overlapping membership and similar missions most effectively and efficiently coexist?
- How can member libraries minimize the 'dark side' of consortia comprising of time, cost, bureaucracy, loss of local control, political entanglement, while maximizing the benefits of collective action.

Helmer, himself answered that, 'there is no single best model for a library consortium'. Nevertheless, the consortia formation has become important as a result of changes in scholarly publishing, increase in cost of e-products, cost escalation, declining library purchase power and needs for libraries to make use of their funds judiciously (Ward, 1999 and Friends, 1999). One business link between publishers and libraries is in expanding use of site licenses and allow both to negotiate differences across the table (Tenopir and King, 2001). The market pressure for 'one-stop-shopping' at handful sites is leading to proliferation of 'aggregators/intermediaries' which sell packages of journals and whose aim is to become the 'first port call' access through a single, powerful and user-friendly interface (Butler, 1999).

Keeping the above in view, it was felt necessary to establish a consortium in order to fulfill information needs by means of library cooperation and sharing the resources (Nikisch,2002). Now, it is needless to say that the development of the consortium is an outgrowth for the desire for resource sharing. If one participates in formation of the consortium and have ongoing participation, then interests are likely to be considered and protected in decision-making process (Morgan, 1998). As such, the goals of libraries do not coincide with the goals of business, and since there is enough strength in membership it is important to form a consortium for effective negotiation for products available in marketplace. Consortium as a group allows speaking with authority across the table for negotiation with publishers/vendors.

There exist various factors which need to be considered while forming a consortium are such as the: stakeholders in the group, resources identification/ selection keeping in view overall requirements of the participants; long term planning of technology infrastructure, current and back files access features, copyright and licensing issues; archival issues - whether access is from publisher/vendor's platform or otherwise; negotiations for affordable costs and economic viability. Anyhow, the consortia should be viable and sustain on a long-term basis (Patil, 2004).

Besides, the project of forming consortium also involves forming a committee with set bylaws/policy matters, make recommendations, and discuss the feasibility of structured collaboration. The policy could also include timely meetings to be held in order to make recommendations for purchase of required resources. Further, the coordinator of the consortium with available staff is also expected to keep project operational, collect data from participants, prepare a report and convene a meeting with funding proposals and monitor thereof the consortium activities on regular basis.

2.13.1. Guidelines for Design/Management of Consortia

The consortium is developed on multi-organizational network which affects its activities. Some guidelines are proposed for consideration by planners and policy makers while designing and forming a consortium (Glazer, 1982).

- The first issue could be addressed is complete autonomy to the consortium;

- Actively cooperate in areas of strength;
- Public versus private support and their implications;
- Governance should be at the level most concerned with the delivery of cooperative services; and
- The ideal consortium will have four requisites, viz. academic complementarity; join long range planning; a willingness to take risk, and preferred central budget.

The above criteria will benefit individuals within institutions themselves, which are essential for success of any consortium. Besides, the feasibility study has to be made before forming a consortium keeping in view existing and working models including methodologies to be adapted, models, action plans and responsibility assigned to smaller working groups. Satyanarayana, Krishnan and Arora (2004) have listed the following factors which are to be taken into consideration while planning and developing a consortium:

- Scope and areas of resource sharing — which need not be too ambitious in the beginning and coverage could be widened in a phased manner;
- Mission — set a clear mission, which could serve as a driving force;
- Goals - should be specific, workable, achievable and measurable;
- Participants — whether homogeneous or heterogeneous;
- Funding — needs to define funding channels clearly for long term sustenance of the consortium;
- Model — there are no set models. Can develop one ideal model in context to observing other working, models and as per needs;
- Identify Required Services — which should be geared up after realization of consortium;

- Action Plan to be Drawn — should reflect progress with consortium idea and to achieve set goals;
- Bylaws/Policy — define bylaws/policies which gives legal framework for the consortium;
- Draft Memorandum of Understanding (MOU) — in order to commit responsibility with participants is a starting point for the consortium which could conclude later in a formal bylaws/policy of the consortium.

Last but not least the consortium has to be given appropriate name in order to fulfill legal obligations.

2.13.2. Approach to Consortium

The consortium needs willing, supportive and dedicated professionals in the beginning in order to place it in sound footing keeping in view some set factors based on institutional objectives, policies and programmes. Some basic steps could be enumerated as follows (Patil, 2014):

- Send feasible study report to the members for their comment and consensus to make a comprehensive plan document;
- Execute an MOU briefing set policies/plans of the consortium with all participants;
- Draft Bylaws/policies for the consortium which are dynamic in nature;
- Identify, designate a consortium team with place of working;
- Constitute different working committees to implement, supervise various programs, and the policies of consortium;
- Identify the channels of funding with the budgetary provision for purchase of resources keeping in view actual users' requirements;
- Develop a Website, portals and Listserv for the consortium;

- Complete various resource selection, get proposals from publishers based on RFPs and initiate action for licensing negotiation;
- Initiate training programs for effective usage of resources, both for library staff and users and distribution/display of materials at strategic locations; and
- Develop a review mechanism for continuous monitoring and evaluation.

2.13.3. Consortia Documentation

Further, the consolidation of consortia documentation is required for the purpose of good administration. It may include the following:

- Memorandum of Understanding (MOU);
- Bylaws/policies;
- Resource sharing and licensing agreements;
- Strategic plans;
- Request for proposals (RFP);
- Access infrastructure;
- Consortium responsibilities; and
- Provision of funding and identification of funding agencies.

2.13.4. Constraints in Consortia Formation

It is revealed looking into past experiences of consortium formation and functioning of participating libraries and their institutions, and funding that there are number of reasons which are obstacles in realizing consortium. These may include the following (Arora, 2001 and Scott, 2004):

(i) Lack of Understanding : There is no awareness of consortium concept and lack of understanding in subscription of electronic resources. Further, the librarians are not very keen to go with mindset in formation of the consortium;

(ii) Funding Constraints : Electronic versions are preferred over print editions for many reasons. One has to pay a little more for electronic versions, as prices of which are linked to print versions. Librarians are in dilemma with extra payment as it is a recurring commitment and adds additional burden to existing fund constraints.

(iii) Consortia as Legal Entity : The consortium needs to be a legal entity since it would be involved in collection of subscription amount from each participant and in turn to make payment to publishers. Also, the consortium coordinator needs to sign licensing agreements and dealing with banking transactions for foreign remittances on behalf of all participating libraries. A consortium needs to have legal entity with permission and authority to deal with its activities in order to fulfill these obligations.

(iv) Problems with Transfer of Funds : The funds required for consortium governance needs to be pooled together from all participants for consortium-based subscription as well as to meet overhead charges. Besides, administrative problems exist in transfer of funds from participants to the consortium.

(v) Geographical Distances : The participants could be spread across the country or a region where coordination among them could be difficult due to geographical distances in spite of available technology and networking. These problems need to be addressed for formation of consortia and for implementation of consortia-based subscription.

(vi) Availability of Infrastructure : All participant libraries are expected to have availability of hardware and software and networking technology, accessibility of Internet and web - based online journals subscription and access with adequate bandwidth, which sometimes, may not be there in many libraries.

(vii) Potential Pitfalls : There are number of obstacles even before start of consortium, such as, the lack of understanding and consensus regarding consortium's vision and goals; differing levels of commitment and collaboration from members; real or perceived inequities in the costs and benefits of membership and different views or needs of different types among member libraries.

(viii) Human Factors : Ultimately, the development and successful consortium is all about the active and willing participants' commitment and involvement. It is necessary to have shared vision, active cooperation and firm commitments to consortia activities in order to meet every one's needs and expectations. One might even consider hiring a consultant or managing agent to help in realizing consortium ensuring that all stakeholders are involved and their views are heard and discussed.

SUMMARY

This chapter provides an overview on the library consortia. Some important initiatives taken at world level, especially in USA, UK and China and at national level are discussed. Later, aims and objectives, purpose and benefits of forming library consortia are also discussed well. Further, the needs for forming library consortia, factors responsible and challenges of library consortia are explained.

BIBLIOGRAPHICAL REFERENCES

Aldrich, H.E., Bolton, K.M., Baker, T. and Sasaki, T. (1998). Information Exchange and Governance in U.S. and Japanese R & D Consortia: Institutional and Organizational Influences. IEEE Transaction on Engineering Management, 45(3): 263–275.

Allen, B. M. and Hirshon, A. (1998). Hanging together to avoid Hanging Separately: Opportunities for Academic Libraries and Consortia. Information Technology and Libraries, 17(1): 36-44.

Alexander, A. W. (1999). Multi-Consortial Obligations: Too Much of a Good Thing. Library Consortium Management: An International Journal, 2 (7): 135-144.

Arora, J. (2001). INDEST – A Proposal for Strategic Cooperation for Consortia Based Access to Electronic Resources. International Information and Library Review, 33 (2-3): 149-165.

Arora, J. (2005). Managing Electronic Resources through Consortia" An Overview. In H.K. Kaul and G. Sin (Eds.): NACLIN Proceedings -2005. DELNET, New Delhi. Pp. 145-170.

Ashoor, M. Saleh (2000). Planning the Electronic Library: Suggested Guideline for the Arabian Gulf Region, The Electronic Library, 18 (1): 29-39.

Bedi, S. and Sharma, K. (2008). Library Consortia: A Step forward the Information Society. Available at: dlist.sir.arizona.edu/2289/01/Shalu_Bedi_and_Kiran_sharma_LIBRARY_CONSORTIA. Pdf.

Bhatt, R. (2011). Libraries in India: Collection to Connectivity. Ane Books Pvt. Ltd., New Delhi.

Birdie, Christina. (2005). Library Consortia and Open Access Initiatives: Collaboration at Different Level. SLib 2005 Papers. PETRONAS, in Collaboration with Librarians Association of Malaysia, Kuala Lumpur. 241-261.

Bostick, Sharon L. (2001). Managing Technology. The Journal of Academic Librarianship, 27(2): 128-130.

Butler, D. (1999). The Writing is on the Web for License Journals in Print. Nature, 397: 105-107.

Edmonds, D. J. (1986). Current Library Co-Operation and Co-Ordination: An Investigation. Majesty's Stationery Office, London.

Evans G. E. (2002). Management Issues of Co-Operative Ventures and Consortia in the USA. Part I. Library Management, 23 (4-5): 213 - 226. Part II. Library Management, 23 (6-7): 275–286.

Fordyce, Marilyn. (2004). New Zealand University Library Acquisitions Consortium for the Supply of Print Monograph Resources, University of Otago Library: Annual Report. Available at: www.library.otago.ac.nz/pdf/annualreport_2004.pdf.

Friends, F.J. (1999). New Wine in New Bottle: Purchasing by Library

Consortia in the United Kingdom. Information Technology and Libraries, 18 (3): 145-148.

Galluzzi, A. (2001). Coperate: Un Concetto in Evoluzinone. Bibliotime, 4 (3): 1-10.

Ghosh, M. (2002). Indian Academic Library Consortia (IALC) : A Proposal for Electronic Resource Sharing. In Proceedings of the Crimea - 2002- International Conference: Russian National Public, Library for Science and Technology, Sudak, 2: 594-600.

Glazer, J.S. (1982). Designing and Managing an Inter – University Consortium in Period of Decline. The Journal of Higher Education, 53 (2): 177-194.

Hawthorn, M., Frey, D. and Roy, V. (1999). Getting to the Summit: How Do You Get There from Here? A Climber's Guide to Consortium Formation. The Serials Librarain, 36 (3-4): 415-420.

Helmer, J.F. ((1999). Epidemiology of the Consortia Spore. Information Technology and Libraries, 18 (3): 119-120.

Hiremath, U. (2001). Electronic Consortia - Resource Sharing in teh Digital Age. Collection Building, 20 (2): 80-87.

Hirshon, Arnold. (1995). Library Strategic Alliances and the Digital Library in the 1990s: The OhioLINK Experience. The Journal of Academic Librarianship, 21(5): 383-386.

Jackson, W., Kent, A. and Lancour, H. (1972). Encyclopedia of Library and Information Science. Marcel Dekker, New York.

Katsirikou, A. (2003). Consortia and Knowledge Management: the Functional Contexts and An Organizational Model. Library management. 24 (6-7): 337-347.

Kopp, James J. (1998). Library Consortia and Information Technology: the Past, the Present, the Promise. Information Technology and Libraries, 17(1): 7-12.

Kirlidog, M. and Bayir, D. (2007). The Effects of Electronic Access to Scientific Literature in the Consortium of Turkish University Libraries. The Electronic Library, 25 (1): 102-113.

Kraus, Joe W. (1975). Prologue to Library Cooperation. Library Trends, 24(2).

Malviya, R. N. and Kumar, A. (2007). Networking and Consortia Management Techniques. DESIDOC Bulletin of Information Technology, 27(3): 21-30.

Mclean, Neil (1999). The Evolution of Information Resource Sharing Infrastructure: An Australian Perspectives. Library High Tech, 17(3): 256-264.

Morgan, Eric Lease. (1998). Resource Sharing and Consortia, or, becoming a 600- Pound Gorilla. Computers in Libraries, 18(4): 40-41.

Nikisch, J.A. (2002). What Kind of Consortium Do We Have and What Kind Do We Have? Library Cooperation and Consortia. Article – EBIB No.7/2002. Available at: http://ebibl.oss wroc.pl/2002/36/nikisch.

Nfila, R.B. and Darko-Amphen. (2002). The Development in Academic Library Consortia from the 1960's through to 2000: A Review of Literature. Library Management, 23(4): 203- 212.

Patil, Y. M. (2004). Resource Sharing through Consortia: An Experience with FORSA Libraries. In Devika P. Madalli (Ed.): Proceedings of the Symposium on Consortium Approach to Resource Sharing: Issues and Polices. DRTC, Bangalore.

Patil, Y.M. (2014). Consortium Approach to Resources Sharing in an E-Environment. Scientific Publishers (India), Jodhpur.

Pandian, M.P. and Karisiddappa, C.R. (2004). Emerging Role of Z39.50 for Library Consortia in India. CALIBER-2004 Paper. Inflibnet, Ahemdabad. Pp. 327-337.

Piotrowicz, G. (2002). The University Libraries Consortia: Yesterday, Today and Tomorrow. EBIB: Electronic Information Bulletin for Librarians, No. 7. Available at: http://ebib.oss.wroc.pl/english/grant/piotrowicz.php.

Potter, W.G. (1997). Recent Trends in Statewide Academic Library Consortia. Library Trends, 45(3): 416-434.

Reinhardt, W. and Boekhorts, P.T. (2001). Library Consortia in Germany. Liber Quarterly, the Journal of European Research Libraries, 11 (1): 67-79.

Reitz, J.M. (Ed.). (2012). Databases. Available at:// www.abcclio.com/ODLIS/odlis_d.aspx#database.

Satyanarayana, N.V., Krishnan, S. and Arora, J. (2004). Library Consortia and Resource Sharing Initiatives in India: A White Paper. Rajiv Gandhi University of Health Sciences, Bangalore.

Scepanski, J.M. (1998). Collaborating on New Missions- Library Consortia and the Future of Academic Libraries. In Conference on New Missions of Academic Libraries in 21st

Century, Beijing, Peking. Available at: from, www.ait.org.tw/ events/docs/ 20070501-Jordan.pdf.

Scott, L. (2004). Fact Sheet: Establishing A Consortium of Health Libraries. Canadian Health Library Association, Toronto (Canada).

Sewell, P. (1981). Resource Sharing: Co-Operation and Co-Ordination in Library and Information Services. Deutsch, London.

Shachaf, P. (2003). Nationwide Library Consortia Lifecycle. Libri, 53: 94-102.

Tammaro, A.M. (2009). Resource Sharing: Academic Library Consortia in Digital Age, A Literature Review. Available at: http://dspace-unipr.cineca.it/bitstream/1889/1153/1/zorzi.pdf.

Tenopir, C. and King, D.W. (2001). Lessons from the Future of Journals. Nature, 413: 672-674.

Thornton, Glenda A. (2000). Impact of Electronic Resources on Collection Development, the Roles of Librarians, and Library Consortia. Library Trends, 48(4): 842-856.

Turner, Christine N. (2014). E-Resource Acquisitions in Academic Library Consortia. Library Resources & Technical Services, 58(1): 33-48.

Wade, Rona. (1999). The Very Model of a Modern Library Consortium. Library Consortium Management: An international Journal, 1(1-2): 5-18.

Ward, P.L. (1999). Editorial. Consortia Library and Information Management Online, 4 (4): 1-2.

Westmoreland, T. and Shirley, B. (2004). The State of Consortia: Promises to Keep. Texas Library Journal, 80(2): 52-58.

Wormann, Curt D. (1968). Aspects of International Library Co-operation: Historical and Contemporary. The Library Quarterly, 338-351.

Wylie, Neil R. and Yeager, Tamara L. (1999). Library Cooperation. New Directions for Higher Education, 106: 27-35.

Xenidou-Dervou, C.(2001). Consortial Journal Licensing. Interlending and Document Supply, 29(3): 120-125.

Xu, D. (2010). CALIS, CASHL and Library Consortium Trend in China. Library Managment, 31 (8-9): 690-701.

3

Consortia: Types and Models

Library consortia around the world are organized with different aims, objectives and policies. They range from informal to formally organized operations either sponsored by a single member institution or owned by all member institutions through a separate incorporated entity or supported by government agencies/private organizations. However, experiences have shown that the concept of consortia works well between organizations that are similar in size, funding and those that are headed by enlightened library administrators. Further, a library consortium may be academic, public or special library consortium depending upon the nature of the libraries for which they are formed. Thus, research libraries being special libraries seem to be in better situation with reference to the facilities and funds available but establishing a consortium between homogeneous group of members is slightly easier than bringing the heterogeneous group of members together (Birdie, 2002). Besides, the library consortia may be national, state wide or regional types depending upon the geographical area they covered.

In addition to funding, the different groups have different models for contract negotiation and resource acquisition. Some consortia coordinators prefer to deal directly with the publisher from the start - and work outward to determine the interest among members and reach to mutually agreeable offers for negotiation. Many others prefer to work from the "bottom up" asking publishers to generate interest among their members first, then having those members officially request a proposal from the consortium. Another approach is "top- bottom" where government agency instructs its organizations to be in the consortium for negotiation keeping in view their interests on e-resources. When it comes to acquisition, the most popular arrangements are "opt in" in which the member institutions join the agreement as their budget and content needs dictate, or a one-price-fits-all agreement in which the consortium provides access to all of its members for a single, discounted price.

3.1. CONSORTIA TYPES

It is seen that during the last few decades, various consortia have been developed and many of them exist today, each being characterized by a number of cultural, socio-political, and financial needs. However, type is a grouping based on shared characteristics; and library consortia may be grouped on their geographical characteristics.

Thus, there may be basically three approaches to cooperation, namely national, statewide and regional and on the basis of them many models have been developed and utilized successfully. Some are relatively simple, others far more complex, but all of them have considerable potential in a variety of environments.

3.1.1. Nationwide Consortia

A nationwide consortium means there exist only nationwide consortium in a country; for example, Australia – CAUL, is there which is a consortium of Council of Australian University Librarians for Electronic Information Resources that involves 39 academic libraries; and in China –China Academic Library and Information System (CALIS) which involves 70 academic libraries (Shachaf, 2003). Nationwide may further be two types: national centralized and national decentralized consortia.

A national centralized consortium is based on the authoritative role of the national library with long term projects of electronic resources management and licensing. Libraries can join the programme through any agreement with central office and take part in decisions through a structured system of governance, in which each member is represented. This model is also defined as 'Nordic approach'.

While, national decentralized consortium is mostly developed in a University context, which may not be formalized in a legal structure. University library administrators may play vital role in this structure which generally has main reference point, a board nominated by the membership of the consortium. The main activity of this type of consortium is to negotiate licenses for e-resources which are acquired by different institutions without central funding. This type of the model is in operation in Italy and France.

3.1.2. Statewide Consortia

Statewide consortium may be restricted to a state and it has a central funding which augments what each member can purchase from their own fund. It is possible to obtain contracts and make available resources that each campus could not afford alone. Member libraries have more of an incentive to collaborate than with any of the other models with a central source of dedicated funds.

3.1.3. Regional Consortia

It is a form of cooperation structured in a regional or inter-regional context, with legal basis and administrative autonomy, which aims also to develop shared library services and technologies. This model is in existence in Spain. ISPOR-Asia consortium (International society for Pharmaco economics and Outcomes Research) can also be cited as an example to this type of consortium (Sunil and Ojha, 2017).

However, the main difference between the US and the European consortia is represented by the objectives of the consortia: in US they tend to have a multiple-function role and to encompass a wide range of library services, while in Europe, it is generally limited to the management of electronic resources (Tammaro, 2004; Malviya and Anil Kumar, 2006; Rowse, 2003).

Further, the consortia may be of academic, public or special library types depending upon the nature or libraries to which they are serve.

3.2. MODELS OF LIBRARY CONSORTIA

It is inferred that thousands of library consortia around the world are organized in many different ways which range from informal gatherings of library directors for the purpose of sharing information and promoting a united front to more formally organized operations, either sponsored by a single member institution or owned by all member institutions through a separate incorporate entity (Wade, 1999).

Thus, models are needed to run any organization satisfactorily that provide a base to set up the library consortium. If there is uniformity in its set-up, it will be easy to cooperate among organizations. Hirshon (1999) has suggested three potential partners for libraries wishing to participate in a consortium:

- Information providers (publishers),

- Service providers (vendors, aggregators) and
- Others (archives, museums, art galleries, educational groups, etc.).

Though, the needs and requirements of the members determine the type of model and the activities of a consortium but the activities usually include reciprocal borrowing, inter-library loan arrangements, negotiating database licenses, human resources development and union catalogue linking. These activities do not require a formal legal structure and the members operate independently. However, in the provision of joint services, the consortium provides services to end users on behalf of its members which are to be utilized by all members or alternately the members can participate in different services over time.

Consortia models are not well defined but generally they depend upon the types of libraries participating, parent organizations they belong to, subject areas they cover, purpose of coming together and so on. Consortia could be a club of highly decentralized or highly centralized organization. Further, the characteristics of consortia model are also influenced by other players like publishers and vendors. It is seen that highly decentralized models suffer due to non-availability of common agenda, no external funds, central sponsor and central staff but on the other hand, highly centralized models overcome these lacunae and also get maximum discounts. Participant's oriented models may be a group of organizations of a particular geographical location, a discipline or the ones from same parent organization while purpose-oriented models may serve to give access to e-journals and other contents, and avoid duplicate acquisitions or train library personnel. Further, the members of a consortium may belong to different parent organizations, following different administrative rules; and the subject areas covered, geographical location and user categories are other variations. Besides, the publishers, aggregators, vendors, subscription agents and document delivery centers may have their own policies.

Thus, the types of library consortia may be described based on the following factors:

- Participants
- Parent organizations
- Subject coverage
- Purpose
- Clients
- Affiliation etc.

3.2.1. Based on Participants

The participant-oriented models may be a group of organizations of a particular geographical location, a discipline, or the one from the same parent organization. Here, each consortium is categorized by the type of libraries participating in the consortium. Large consortia and small consortia are based on the number of participating members, whether it is either too large or too small.

(i) Informal or Loosely Federated Consortia : This is an informal gathering of libraries for the purpose of sharing information and promoting a united front. There is a loosely defined partnership based on the interests and needs of each institution. There is no central office and the leadership rotates. This type of consortium is formed, by a contract that delineates the rights and obligations of each member. The members retain their separate legal status, and the consortium control over each participant that is generally limited to activities involving joint endeavours. Informal consortia have no designated staff and it is completely a voluntary effort to run the projects. However, if some members wish to advance the cause of cooperation more than others, they must carry the burden which are quick and flexible.

The consortium has a uniform Web platform through which members share union catalogue, digital databases, and inter-library loan services. This model supports cooperative acquisitions and cataloguing, training and certification of library staff in processing materials based on established standards, and coordinates the development of the digital project and virtual reference service (Zou and Dong, 2007). But resource sharing in this consortium model tends to become decentralized as libraries want to gain freedom in forming partnerships with peer institutions. Indian Institute of Managements' venture in India can be cited as an example for this type of consortium.

(ii) Formal Consortia : The formal consortium has formally organized operations either sponsored by a single member institution or owned by all member institutions through a separate incorporate entity. The mission and goals are clearly specified and it is accountable to members and fund providers. Such consortia have a legally incorporated or organized office. When, the consortia project moves beyond the collaborative efforts to the joint provision of services, the need for coordination and some level of joint responsibility becomes apparent. With the joint provision of services comes the need for operational resources, for clear and frequent communication with the member libraries and for the coordination of activities of the members with the service provider which require the appointment of staff that is independent of any member library. They own assets, such as the hardware, software licences, a union database or even a building, in common or need to take on contractual obligations in their own right. A consortium at this point usually initiates the process of becoming a legal entity. International Federation of Library Associations and International Coalition of Library Consortia are the examples of this type of consortia.

(iii) Homogeneous Model : In this model, like-minded professionals come together for cooperation, coordination and collaboration in resource sharing and initiate need-based consortia formation. However, the participating libraries should be of the same type and the size. Consortium for e-Resources in Agriculture (CeRA) in India is the best example of this type of consortium.

3.2.2. Based on Parent Organizations

These are publisher-initiated consortia models, where the publisher offers a deeply discounted consortium price to the participating libraries on a national level. But the pre-condition is that there should not be any drop in their print subscriptions. Emerald Full-Text Library published by the Emerald Publishing Group is an example of this type of consortium.

3.2.3. Based on Subject Coverage

This type of consortium is formed by the organizations which are working in a particular discipline. The Forum for Resource Sharing in Astronomy and Astrophysics (FORSA) is an example of this type of library consortia model, which is a subject-oriented model in astronomy and astrophysics.

3.2.4. Based on the Purpose of Coming Together

The purpose-oriented models may serve to give access to e-journals and other contents for avoiding duplicate acquisition or to train the library personnel. These are also loosely organized bodies whose members, unite for the purpose of obtaining discounts only and provide the service locally in their own way. Indian Institute of Management (IIM) Library Consortium is a best example of this type of consortium.

3.2.5. Based on Source of Funding

Consortia have different types of funding- some operate without funding with annual membership fees and others receive some form of funding. Membership fees are generally charted on a sliding scale according to the size of members, number of transactions, number of clients, size of collections etc. Various models based on the funding are described in the following sections.

(i) Centrally Funded Model and Self-Sustained : The existence of the consortium solely depends on the central funding agency in this model. The strength of this model is that the financial responsibility of running the consortium is shouldered by the parent body. One central library provides its resources and services to the sub-libraries of the system. Information resources are acquired and processed centrally or cooperatively, and inter-library loan services are provided to other libraries in a one-way direction. Although there is a certain degree of sharing, this model does not focus on equal sharing among the members of a system because the contribution is overwhelmingly unbalanced between the central library and branch libraries (Zou and Dong, 2007). Council of Scientific and Industrial Research (Now NKRC), Indian Council of Medical Research Consortia etc. are the best examples of this model.

(ii) Shared-budget Model : The participating libraries in this model take the lead and form the consortium while, the operational aspects of the consortium, especially the management of funds etc. are individually handled. However, entering into a memorandum of understanding for a better and strong footing is always recommended for this type of model. IIM and FORSA are examples of this model.

3.2.6. Based on Governance and Organizational Structure

These consortia are categorized by the governance structures which may be highly informal, semiformal or formal, or on the basis of organizational structure which may or may not have a central office with dedicated staff. Various models based on governance and organizational structures are described in the following sections.

(i) Highly Decentralized : These consortia are like loosely affiliated buying clubs which generally has one negotiating body but allows purchasing decisions to be made at the level of individual institutions. Highly decentralized models suffer from non-availability of a common agenda, external funds, central sponsor and central staff. IIM Consortium is an example of this type of consortium.

(ii) Highly Centralized : These consortia are alternatively tightly affiliated and highly organized virtual groups which have permanent staff. Each types of consortia have an organized body with centralized management, a legal charter and provides a wide range of services to its members. Highly centralized models overcome the lacunae of the highly decentralized model and also get maximum discounts. CSIR E-Journal Consortium (now NKRC) in India can be cited as an example of this type of consortium.

3.2.7. Based on Clients

Client-oriented models are based on the age of clients like children and senior citizens, their interests like sports and music or their educational background like technical and professional. FORSA in India is a best example which is dealing with interests of astrophysicists and astronomers.

3.2.8. Further, the Consortia can be categorized by the type of libraries or organizations that participate in each consortium. These can be divided up into one of four main models.

(i) Single Sector : Consists of libraries which are all of the same type, for example, the academic libraries, public libraries, etc. There is no overlap with other library sectors.

(ii) Single Sector with State or National Library Involvement : Consists of a single sector of library but also has the State or National Library as a member or partner.

(iii) Multi Sector : Consists of members from all types of libraries but may include non-library partners.

(iv) Mega Consortium : Consists of joined consortia which came together with other consortia and /or other groups.

3.3. MODELS BY EXPERTS

Some of the experts have given different library consortia models. Sinclair (1973) has described four models of cooperative activity among libraries. These are:

3.3.1. Bi-Nodal Partnership Model

It is simply a pair of libraries that have agreed to exchange information and materials. Libraries in Singapore, Taiwan and Hong Kong are the examples which have adopted such model.

3.3.2. Multi-Nodal Partnership Model

This is very common model where a number of libraries contribute and cooperate. This can be said as the extension of the bi-nodal model.

3.3.3. Service Partnership Model

One library and all participating libraries contribute to the output in this model. Information Resource Sharing Service Network linking over 100 academic libraries in Beijing is the best example of this type of consortium.

3.3.4. Outsourcing Partnership Model

An external organization which is typically a bibliographic utility or aggregator, is engaged in this model by the participating libraries to provide a common service. Online Computer Library Centre is an example.

3.4. LICENSING MODELS

The electronic journals are made available through the web at varying price models, in most of the cases linked to printed counterparts. It means that the e-journals may be offered free with subscriptions (e.g. publications of APS and ASCE) or priced at a fixed percentage over the print subscriptions (e.g. journals of Elsevier Science, Springer Verlag and IEEE) or may also be offered exclusive in electronic media. Here, the publishers, generally view a site as a single, geographically contiguous office building complex, or campus location-plus dial-in access via the licenses secure network which is not a mailing address and may include more than one library. Such type of consortia provides a union strength to negotiate with electronic publishers for the best possible price and rights. Based on Bhatt and Chand (2014), each of them is briefly described below:

3.4.1. "Title-by-Title Subscription Model"

This practice followed in most of the libraries to subscribe print journals but the only concession library may get in this model is the special rates if one subscribes few (Physical Reviews package from American Physical Society/AIP) or all publications (ASPP from IEEE) from the publisher, regarded as set price schemes.

3.4.2. "Print Plus" Model

The pricing of the electronic journal product is expressed as an "add on" to the price of the print product, or the price quoted is linked to a "no-print cancellation" clause in the contract.

3.4.3. "Electronic Plus" Model

Here, the electronic journal contentsare supplied for a base price and the price for print copies added to that base price. ICOLC argues for keeping the purchase of the print copies as optional, and the base price for the electronic content is no more than 80 percent of the price for the electronic-plus-print and the combined electronic and print price is no more than current print-only prices.

3.4.4. "All-You-Can-Eat" Model

Some publishers offer their total contents for the price that a library might have paid for a limited number of print journal subscriptions.

3.4.5. "Pay-by-the-Drink" Model

It is a provision to purchase blocks of journal articles, or may pay only for the delivery of the articles that are actually used.

3.5. PRICING MODELS

It is observed that there exist marked variations in pricing models and many models currently available in the market, viz. from print plus free online, print plus online with an up-charge, standard online only pricing with varying amounts of back files to tiered online pricing, custom online quotes per institution, as publishers sought the best way to package and price their content. As such, pricing model keeps changing depending on prevailing business conditions (Sloan, 2000; Bosch, Henderson and Klusendorf,2011).

However, the pricing models vary between print and e-journals due to various parameters involved in the process of supply chain, i.e., creation, publishing, distribution, servicing and archiving but the business model transformed into a well-established subscription model may not be cost-effective and may not fit in all situations. Further, the current situation demands perpetual access and archiving rights and as a result new models are evolving to meet changing requirements. Content providers project their model which depends on investment level, publishing/hosting and access rights, etc. Pricing models are closely related as they are mutually influencing factors over each other (Satyanarayana, Krishnan and Arora, 2004). Various pricing models are discussed below:

3.5.1. Publisher Hosted Model

Pricing is done exclusively by the publishers or content owners keeping in view the market strength and strategies. However, they may not have expertise in respect of availability of technology and many related issues. In such a situation, they either license technology or contract a third party for hosting their e- content. The hosting company manages publisher's content, including archiving, provides the search engine, and user interface for browsing, searching, down loading, printing, etc.

In majority of cases, publisher-hosted access model is used by many consortia but this model has inherent limitations and not feasible in a long-term basis. These limitations are (Patil, 2014):

- Users have to visit multiple publishers' sites to find an article. Thus, this model cannot support search beyond publishers' own journals.
- Publishers may part with to provide contents for local archival hosting at consortia or participants site and may not the technology itself. Even if mirror site is provided at consortia/libraries sites, it is not feasible for libraries to maintain locally an array of distributed contents on different software and technology platforms.

Besides, the uncertainty of publishing world which requires that library has a common archive and hosting site independent of publishers' sites. But local digital archiving is beyond the means of individual libraries as availability infrastructure and technology may not be adequate to meet such purposes.

3.5.2. Aggregator Model

Aggregators are one of the important content providers for libraries. It is seen that the libraries have been working with the publishers and aggregators for many years, but the issues related to aggregators are not well documented.

However, consortia sales of bundled collection and aggregation raise a variety of issues relating to pricing, market coverage, primary subscription retention, and revenue allocation (Crow, 2010). This is a matter of fact, aggregation of journals provides a major value for e-journals, and facilitates a common access platform of multiple publishers. It is a proven distribution channel for all those who publish e-journals/ products for-potential, library markets (Cox, 2000). As such, smaller publishers may not handle all activities by themselves keeping in view the cost factors and resort to aggregators in order to manage their sites and other issues. Aggregators may cumulate contents of various small publishers and make it searchable from a single interface. They also invest considerably in the technology for hosting the contents, maintain the archives and offer tailor made services. There are two types of aggregators, differentiated by their pricing and access models. These are(Cox, 2000):

3.5.3. Publishers Group as Aggregators

Some publishers representing a common market segment join together to host their journals by creating a joint brand and create their own platform but this model is particularly prevalent among professional society publishers. Notable examples are: IEL of IEEE and IEE; and American Physical Society representing publishers like American Institute of Physics, Acoustical Society of America, etc.

3.5.4. Publishers Selling Packages

Many larger serials publishers have resorted in

selling 'packages' of journals direct to individuals or library consortia. The notable examples are: Academic Press's IDEAL, Elsevier's SciVerse, Science Direct, Springer's Springer Link, and Wiley Online. This is of particular interest to consortia that have a heterogeneous membership of libraries. Moreover, the publishers have benefitted considerably by incremental increases in revenue in return.

3.6. PRICING MODELS AND ACCESS RIGHTS

The publishers with the passage of time are still experimenting with various options of pricing models, which are dynamic entity and are still evolving. The pricing models so far developed are nothing but permutation and combination of two basic models, viz. print based and e-only with several limiting terms of rights. There are several pricing models that are applicable to consortia and other bundle providers which are briefed below (Woodward, 2002; Crow, 2010):

Table 3.1. Pricing Models and Access Rights

Format Option	*Description and Pricing*
Print only or Online only:	Format available independently, either at the same price or at different prices, typically with online only at a lower price.
Print and Online:	Both formats bundled for one price. Sometimes, the bundle is priced at the former print-only price; sometimes at a slightly higher price.
Print-plus-Online:	Online available for a surcharge on the top of the print-only price.
Online-plus-Print:	Print available for a surcharge on top of the online-only price.
Institutional Size:	Price is based on FTEs (Full Time Equivalents).
Transactional Pricing:	Unpopular in academic libraries but of interest to some commercial and corporate organizations.

3.6.1. E-Only Models

This model is independent of print plan. Here, the publishers offer set of e-journals with their fixed prices, which is open for consortia negotiation; and they develop a subject specific package with deeply discounted price keeping in view current print spending to ensure any loss of revenue due to future print cancellations.

It is seen that many publishers are moving to e-only model and grants consortia wide archiving and perpetual access for the subscribed period of content. Back file access fee is either included in the offer price or a one-time additional payment or on yearly basis. Thus, the total amount payable in early model, according to percentage applied to the base price, could be lower than the cost of the same serials on paper (90 percent) or the same (100 percent) in this model.

3.6.2. Full-Time Equivalent (FTE) Model

It is also called population-based model where pricing is based on the total number of user population per site; full-time equivalents - FTEs, which are defined as full-time enrollments in research or employees in corporate, government and professionals. However, the price may vary according to type of institutions with 3 or 2 years' academic institutions (bachelors/ masters degrees) or other levels with different number of users ranging from 1-100; 101-200, etc.

3.6.3. Concurrent Users Model

This model treats all members of the consortia as a single site and allows access rights by number of simultaneous users for a journal across the consortium. However, in this model, pricing is done by publishers according to number of users in the consortium. This model is prevalent among database providers. Examples are: IELXplore and SciFinder.

3.7. ALTERNATIVE MODELS

In addition to the above-mentioned models, there are some alternative models which are also in practice like, Tiered Models, Pay-per-Viewing models. F urther, prior year plus a premium, variations on the title subscription price, population-based models, and usage-based pricing models are also there. Some important of them are briefly discussed below:

3.7.1. Tiered Pricing Model

It is seen that all institutions in normal course pay the same subscription rate. However, society publishers have the option of charging differential pricing for the reason that libraries receive intensive use than individual subscriptions. Thus, there may be two approaches to journals pricing- Cost Plus and Value-based.

(i) Cost Plus Pricing bases a journal's price on society's costs of producing it, plus a margin sufficient to sustain the journal's operation. Societies often apply this approach to print journals.

(ii) Value - based Pricing tries to determine the price that institutions would be willing and able to pay. Establishing a price for an online edition in this way allow a society to tap the value created by the online version and increase the revenue available to sustain the service going forward. Such value - based pricing for online journal services often leads to a form of tiered pricing schedules.

(iii) Tiered Pricing allows a publisher to earn revenues while keeping journal prices moderate and equitable. Online journals are offered via banded pricing schemes based on the type of institution, on the number of full-time equivalent (FTE) at an institution, the number of sites included in the license, and the number of concurrent users able to access the service or some combination of these measures(Crow, 2010).

Tiered pricing sets prices for content upon

parameters such as the amount of back file included with the subscription, institutional FTE, the number of students enrolled in specific disciplines, and/or Carnegie Classification as in American Physical Society Pricing Plan. With electronic access, a single price means that a small college with handful of users could be paying the same subscription as a large research university with potentially large number of users (Bosch, Henderson, and Klusendorf, 2011; Stern, 2003). But differential pricing in tiered pricing model is based on projected local use, ability to determine a 'fair' institutional price based on an estimate of use, as determined using criteria such as population size, institutional research level, and the use statistics, etc.

3.7.2. Pay-per-Viewing Pricing

Pay-per-view model (PpV) allows publishers to reach out to the reader directly bypassing the library and their dependence on academic and research libraries as the source of all their revenues. However, PpV distribution requires that the journal has e-commerce functionality, either through its online publishing system or via an online fulfillment service. The institution which has downloaded maximum numbers should be in position to subscribe the journal than PpV.

It can negotiate a fee and licensing term with the publishers. The articles acquired under this model can be archived for perpetual access that is not openly addressed by either party - publishers and libraries. However, the consortia may negotiate and get permission from the publisher to locally archive and share articles acquired under this model. Thus, pay per view business model though not widely accepted as the most sustainable business model, will eventually, with the improvement in the strategy, prove to be the choice of future publisher's business practice.

3.8. BENEFITS OF CONSORTIA PARTICIPATION

Various benefits in participating in consortia are summarized as below (Kumar and Gaur, 2015):

3.8.1. Foster Resource Sharing

The members of consortia can share a variety of resources. Helmer (1999) emphasized that "for libraries, consortia provides shared expertise, access to new electronic and print resources, professional development, new sources of funds, and safety in numbers...." The resource that can be shared by consortia includes catalogues, collections and the content creation. Equally, the electronic resources and archiving of resources can be done along with sharing staff expertise and risk for success and professional glamour.

3.8.2. Enhance Library Services to the Users

A consortium enables the member libraries and their users to enter into the rapid changing world where things have been changed with the jet speed.

3.8.3. Improves Quality of Library Services

The quality of library services and reduction in the cost of operation are part of the process. Hence, libraries turned to consortia formation as a way to share and to foster the information about best practices, and to reduce the unit cost of providing core services. Thus, consortia consolidate the library services in a good deal.

3.8.4. Increase Financial Benefit

One of the most common reasons that libraries join consortia is to gain some financial benefit. Thus, all library consortia have one goal in common: pooling their collective financial resources to leverage greater economic control over their marketplace.

3.8.5. Encourage for Discussion, Collective Thinking and Leadership

Intangible benefits, such as the encouragement of discussion and collective thinking is a valuable part of being a member of a consortium. It is pointed out that the value of increased communication between libraries cannot be overlooked. Leadership is also an important part of library management. Consortium services manage more than the cost and a consortium can do this by providing leadership for its members that generates cooperative action for the advancement of educational environment, institution's fiscal situation and the quality of services for the client of library.

3.8.6. Demonstrate Reduced Cost

Consortia act as an agent on behalf of the member libraries to seek a reduced group purchase price for information resources that is lower than that which any one institution could achieve alone. Therefore, it considers new ways to consolidate global resources amongst the participating libraries in order to maximize their resources within limited budget.

3.8.7. Facilitates the 'Change Management'

One of the most complex issues facing libraries today is change management. The decisions face is becoming more complex, the risks are greater, and the resources are both human and fiscal. A library consortium seems to be valuable in managing the change, but the process of change management normally proceeds through a series of steps. However, each of these steps risks and optimizing the opportunities.

3.8.8. Provides Training and Workshop

The libraries must have an understanding of emerging issues to manage change. Here, the consortium can play an invaluable role by providing training and organizing new programmes or promotional activities on library improvement plan, schools of library computerization, etc. and to upgrade the existing staff.

3.8.9. Enables Better Access

Consortia promote better, faster and more cost-effective ways of providing access to electronic information resources to the information seekers. Increasing amount of access to electronic resources is possible, across the institutions, at a lower cost or at an optimum cost possible for the subscription through consortia agreements.

3.8.10. Facilitates Better Management

Consortia can manage electronic information resources in a better way and save the library from the complications of print-resource management. It enhances buying power through the consolidation of collection and services.

3.8.11. Sustains and Pressure

It successfully meets the pressure of diminishing budget, increased user's demand, and rising cost of library resources.

3.8.12. Protects from Duplication

A consortium also protects the duplicate manpower - expert, guide, online serial-control manager, system analyst, network manager, problem counsellor, architectural consultant, etc. by providing collective technical expertise in general or even detailed and specific levels of assistance, to member constituents. Thus, the duplication of cost on materials, time, and effort can be minimized and by that, savings and access can be maximized.

3.8.13. Accelerates Sustainable Growth of Libraries

The collection strength of consortia members facilitates the libraries to get the equal benefit of wider access to electronic resources at an affordable cost and at the best terms and conditions. It also demonstrates the benefits to offer not only in terms of discounted subscription rates but also value-added services like Document Delivery and Search Interfaced and finally it brings the uniform growth, standard, and compatibility among the member libraries in a better situation.

Besides, other benefits are manifolds where consortia facilitate ongoing communication, coordination, awareness, creates information super highway professional improvement, force to maintain standard cultural broadness, increased visibility and preferred partnership marketing and advertising opportunities.

3.9. WHAT MAKES A SUCCESSFUL CONSORTIUM

It is seen that a consortium can take many forms depending upon their membership, purposes, funding, governing structures and the commitment of the participants. Therefore, the consortium can realize varying degrees of collaborative success. But there are some prerequisites to effectiveness in a consortium and practices that lead to a 'successful consortia'.

Further, any cooperative activity, whether resource sharing or collection development, requires a high level of managerial skill and commitment if it is to succeed. So is the case with a consortium model; thus, a consortium success has to fulfill following criteria (Gorman and Cullen, 2000):

3.9.1. Committed Leadership

The senior management of a library, the governing body and the executive of the parent organization, must all be fully committed to cooperation. Close commitments by senior management are the need for a formal governing structure, which includes broader staff involvement and clear lines of command.

3.9.2. Formal Governing Structure

The governing structure can be a library system, a network, an area authority, a consortium or even a parent institution. Whatever the structure and degree of formality, the governing structure must have responsibility and authority to make and review policy, to review activities and to issue directives for management of the cooperative venture.

3.9.3. Staff Participation

The staff who are directly involved in day-to-day management of the cooperative activities must be represented in the decision-making process of the governing structure. However, less involvement in decision-making may result in less commitment to the programme.

3.9.4. Staff Training

Both the managers and the line staff need to have practical knowledge and skills in collection assessment, collection development and other aspects of collection management. This knowledge should be extended from the operational staff up to the senior management of all participating libraries by providing training so that everyone knows precisely the amount of work that is involved in each activity.

3.9.5. Sufficient Funds

Sufficient funds must be there with a detailed budget for the acquisition of materials for the cooperative scheme. The funds must also be for the additional management and associated costs of operating the joint activity.

3.9.6. Agreed Collection Description Guidelines

A mutually agreed collection development and assessment framework and methodology are important criteria of a successful programme. Thus, all participants must have agreed to use the conspectus, then information on collections can be readily exchanged making the evaluation and monitoring a much simpler process.

Besides above, the following issues are also be taken into consideration for an effective functioning of a successful consortium:

3.9.7. Culture of Shared Vision and Mission

Consortia members should have a high degree of respect for the value of increased collaboration/shared subscription because having a "consortium culture," one can emphasize over common interests, values, vision and needs. Shared vision and mission may, on occasion, results in members having to compromise individual institutional goals to help to advance the common good and to achieve the greater common goal.

3.9.8. Deep Interest to Obtain Real Benefit

A set of ground rules require each member to come to the table taking a consortial perspective rather than merely considering consortial interests. Thus, it is essential that an individual library must feel that they obtain real benefit from their membership in consortia, those benefits that cannot be realized as easily through their own efforts.

3.9.9. Constant Support and Commitment

There should be a constant support throughout all levels of the organization. Staff must receive support to make the partnership successful, and be encouraged to generate a result greater than what any individual institution could do on its own. It is also necessary to ensure that "organizational and financial commitments once made, stay made."

3.9.10. Authority to Take Action - Take Risk

A consortium, with institutional head (President/

Director/Vice Chancellor/Chief Librarian) directly in its governance, is able to make decisions and take actions at the highest level. So, someone should be there with authority to speak for the library and with the ability to act relatively quickly. Moreover, both consortia and library managers need to possess high grade of 'leadership quality' so that they must not be afraid to lead, to take risks, to commit resources, and to encourage actions.

3.9.11. Centralized Staffing

This is a general rule "more centralized the consortia, more likely to have dedicated staff". However, the availability of staff to initiate, organize, coordinate, and maintain programmes is instrumental to success. Though some consortia have been able to function without dedicated staff (but volunteers), increasingly the value of having paid employees whose job is basically to stay focused on joint efforts is being recognized but many large consortia do have full time staff (though never enough) and a large number rely on volunteers.

3.9.12. Centralized Funding

Centralized consortia may have a sponsoring agency to advocate for external funds which can provide assured purchasing power for the consortium. Some people suggest that the availability of pooled or centralized funding is a good idea to support the subscriptions having limited interests coming from the individual members who desire it. This is essentially important, when publishers/ aggregators do not offer a discount to consortia, in such a situation centralized consortium may serve as the integrator of the publisher.

3.9.13. Linkage

It is important to build linkages at all staff levels, especially involving the first like staff. However, effective staff communication that often depends on personal encounters - is an essential ingredient for the mutual efforts. So, careful attention must be given to establishing right combination of face to face versus virtual encounters.

Besides, a number of licensing issues are also involved with the publishers/ aggregator in order to get maximum flexibility in sharing (access) electronic resources as well as to enjoy best pricing practices in forming a consortium. Hence, healthy negotiation in relation to the number of simultaneous users, number of participants in the consortium, selection of resources, wider and consistent access, user friendly interface, pricing formulas, etc. can make the success of the consortia. Ultimately, adequate technology infrastructure in support of wide area information access and management in a consortium is the key to success.

If understood and attended to all these, it will greatly facilitate the formation of consortia and thereby lead to an enhanced access to e-resources. Besides, staff must receive support to make the partnership successful, and be encouraged to generate a result greater than, what any individual institution could do so on its own. Further, designing of the new and useful programmes keeping in mind the changing needs and information seeking habits of end users would also help to succeed. Lastly, but not least develop library staff and information professionals to remain effective and relevant in this fast-changing environment. Therefore, the consideration on above-mentioned points will have the great potential impact on successful consortia.

SUMMARY

This chapter dealt with the types and models of library consortia based on many factors and characteristics. Various factors are there, such as the: participants, parent organizations, subject coverage, geographical area, purpose of the cooperation, varieties of the clients and affiliations to the organizations on which the models are based and formed worldwide. The chapter ends with the characteristics of committed leadership, formal governing structure, staff participation, trained staff, sufficient funds and a mutually agreed collection development and assessment framework with the methodology for a successful consortium.

BIBLIOGRAPHICAL REFERENCES

Bhatt, R.K. and Chand, M. (2014). Fundamentals of Social Sciences and Library Consortia. K.K. Publications, New Delhi.

Birdie, G. (2002). New Acquisition with New Partners: Are We Ready Yet?. Available at: http://www.iatul.org/doclibrary/public/Conf_Proceedings/2002/birdie.pdf.

Bosch, S., Henderson, K. and Klusendorf, H. (2011). Under Pressure, Times are Changing: Periodicals Price Survey-2011. Library Journal, 36 (8): 30-34.

Crow, R. (2010). Subscription Options and Pricing. Available at: http://cnx.org/content/m34287/latest.

Cox, J. (2000). Developing Model Licenses for Electronic Resources: Cooperation in a Competitive World. Library Consortium Management, 2(1): 8-17.

Gorman, G. E. and Cullen, R. (2000). Models and Opportunities for Library Co-Operation in the Asian Region. Library Management, 21(7): 373-384.

Helmer, J.F. ((1999). Epidemiology of the Consortia Spore. Information Technology and Libraries, 18 (3): 119-120.

Hirshon, A. (1999). Libraries, Consortia, and Change Management. The Journal of Academic Librarianship, 25(2): 124-126.

Kumar, N. and Gaur, R. (2015). Library Consortium: A Collaborating Approach towards Promotion and Provision of E-Resources for Modern Academic Pursuits on Single Platform. International Journal of Digital Library Services, 5 (4): 134-141.

Malviya, R. N. and Kumar, A. (2007).Networking and Consortia Management Techniques. DESIDOC Bulletin of Information Technology, 27(3): 21-30.

Patil, Y.M. (2014). Consortium Approach to Resources Sharing in an E-Environment. Scientific Publishers (India), Jodhpur.

Rowse, M. (2003). The Consortium Site License: A Sustainable Model? Libri, 53(1): 1-10.

Satyanarayana, N.V., Krishnan, S. and Arora, J. (2004). Library Consortia and Resource Sharing Initiatives in India: A White Paper. Rajiv Gandhi University of Health Sciences, Bangalore.

Shachaf, P. (2003). Nationwide Library Consortia Lifecycle. Libri, 53: 94-102.

Sinclair, M.P. (1973). A Typology of Library Cooperatives. Speical Libraries, 64 (4): 181-186.

Sloan, B. (2000). Understanding Consortia Better-What Vendors can Learn? Library Journal, 15: 57-58.

Stern, D. (2003). Comparing Consortial and Differential Pricing Models. the Bottom Line: Managing Library Finances, 16(4):154-156.

Sunil, and Ojha, N.K. (2017). Library Consortia in India At a Glance. International Journal of Library and Information Studies, 7 (3): 246-254.

Tammaro, A.M. (2009). Resource Sharing: Academic Library Consortia in Digital Age, A Literature Review. Available at: http://dspace-unipr.cineca.it/bitstream/1889/1153/1/zorzi.pdf.

Wade, R. (1999). The Very Model of a Modern Library Consortium. Library Consortium Management: An International Journal, 1 (1-2): 5-18.

Woodward, H. (2002). Results and Analysis from a Study of the Impact of the Consortium Site License on Academic Libraries. In A. Pearce (Ed.): The Consortium Site License: Is It a Sustainable Model? Ingenta Institute, Oxford (London).

Zou, T.J. and Dong, E.X. (2007). In Search of a New Model: Library Resource Sharing in China- A Comparative Study. World Library and Information Congress: 73rd IFLA General Conference and Council Paper held during 9-23 August 2007 at Durban (South Africa)> Available at: https://archive.ifla.org/IV/ifla73/papers/096-Zou_Dong-en.pdf.

4

Library Consortia: Components and Benefits

Electronic publishing or e-publishing includes the digital publication of e - books, e-journals and other reference materials which finally facilitate the development of digital libraries. Electronic publishing provides wider dissemination and their distribution is being done via the Internet and web. Hence, a number of journals, while retaining their peer review process, established electronic versions or even moved entirely to electronic publication. Though, the term "electronic publishing" is primarily used today to refer to the current offerings of online and web-based publishers, but the term has a history of being used to describe the development of new forms of production, distribution, and user interaction with regard to computer-based production of text and other interactive media.

It is seen that the journals have played a pivotal role in the creation and transmission of knowledge as the primary channel of formal scholarly communication and remained unchanged in the form, function and service since last over three centuries. Since their first appearance in the middle of 17th century, journals served as the principal medium for one-to-many communication among the scientists and scholars. The publication of the first scholarly journal was made in French - Le Journal des Scavans, which was started in 1665, followed by the Philosophical Transactions of the Royal Society, London. The journals number reached to 750 by the turn of the 18lh century and the figure has reached over 150000 in the recent times (Banks, 2018). Out of 150000 journals, more than 60000 titles cover scholarly journals, 14000 titles are electronic versions, accessible through the Internet and over 8790 titles are freely accessible as per the Directory of Open Access Journals. Due to barriers of access and copyright, there emerged Open Access Movement, with three distinct parameters attached: Open Access Journals, Open Archives and Institutional Repositories to facilitate scholarly communication (Bjoernshauge, 1999). There are now 25400 journals in science, technology and medicine and their number is increasing by 3.5 percent and in 2009 they all together published over 1.5 million articles (Fraser and Dunstan, 2010).

Since the beginning of 1990s, libraries had access to Internet and since 1995s, World Wide Web (WWW) have become universally accessible - these two important epochs making events made tremendous impact of the combined computing and telecommunication technologies on scientific scholarly communication as it manifested in the scholarly journals. Over the last three centuries, the scholarly journals have proved to be an important medium for communication with the following attributes:

- Issued successively in separate parts;
- Identified by chronological or numerical designations; and

- With no predetermined terminate date.

Thus, the technologies have been playing pivotal role in shaping the publishing industry specifically, the making of paper in Europe during late 13th century, Gutenberg's printing press during 15th century, lithographic offset printing in the 20th century and digital scholarly publishing during 21st century - all together have served their role in the evolution of the publishing industry, which we are harnessing today (Hargrave,2013). These changes in information landscape have directly affected the trinity of publishers, libraries and the end users. In spite of journals direct benefits to science and scholars, the journal publishing system has been criticized, mainly due to escalating costs, problems with peer-review process and inordinate delays in publication. The impact of ICT and World Wide Web have completely changed publication landscape with creation of alternate form of the print journals. Later, the desktop publishing has emerged during 1980s as a viable alternate to traditional printing (Goudar and Poornima, 2004). Now, the e-publishing has made revolution in e-journals publication, submission, access, archival and delivery mechanism.

Further, the introduction of the Internet and the emergence of World Wide Web opened new vistas and opportunities for making scholarly communication available in a network-based environment. Engineering and scientific/technical databases were introduced to scholars during 1970s; for example, industrial standards, patents, product catalogues and bibliographic databases have been around since the creation of online services such as DIALOG, ORBIT and STN (Osoria, 2002).

Now, the information resources are available in formats such as digital full-text, sound, graphics, images, multimedia and hypertext as well as print documents. Further, the changing economy, technological development, and necessity to serve more users have shifted the cooperation activities from the informal among a few libraries in the same locality, to large formal systems beyond the physical boundaries. It is a fact that acquiring information is vital, but many times a lot of funds and time are wasted to acquire the same information simultaneously by multiple organizations and occasionally by various departments within the same organization. Library consortia are seeking not only to have an effect upon the national and international agendas concerning issues such as pricing policies and copyright laws but also to pressure the information providers to reduce the cost. Consequently, libraries have been sharing their resources to work more efficiently and effectively by maximizing available resources and exchanging information, expertise and experience. Ultimately, this has transformed into e-resource sharing or consortia in the networked environment.

For many libraries, especially the academic and special ones, the consortia have emerged as a principal tool for obtaining electronic content in subscription/ purchase form. Library consortia have major role in licensing as they negotiate for and offer the packages that are serial in nature. These packages are database subscriptions, e-journal packages, renewable e-book packages, library services for monitoring the electronic, content of packages and providing links to the full-text. So, participating institutions in a consortium have access not only to their own resources but to information sources in the other institutions as well at an affordable cost (Pandian, Jambhekar and Karisiddappa, 2002).

Thus, the consortium approach is a win-win situation for all its stakeholders: users, publishers and the libraries. Users are the ultimate end beneficiaries of such initiatives.

4.1. CURRENT SITUATION

If the trend continues converting print to the e-format, soon most of the scientific/ technical information will be available in e-format only. Now, the question arises whether publications in print form are affordable by average institutions and under what conditions? What will be the role of libraries and publishers in handling preservation of scientific/technical information? Some of the issues about current scenario are given below (Patil, 2014):

- It is fact that the mode of operation of traditional libraries is in deep crisis due to continuous price rise combined with the lack of adequate funding resulting in yearly cancellation of journals;
- It has become difficult to purchase all required information due to exponential growth of literature and also becoming more dependent on inter-lending to fulfill requirements of users;
- A constant pressure for new products, viz. hardware/ software, education/training of library staff is seen due to rapid technological developments; and
- Overwhelming application of new technologies - especially the World Wide Web - has contributed to rapid escalating expectations of users for their research requirements.

Precisely, the very technological developments seem to include the opportunity to solve the crisis. Thus, library consortia have emerged as a good solution of above problems.

4.2. NEEDS OF LIBRARY CONSORTIA

Though, the main reason for forming a library consortium is to improve information resources and services to the library users and to gain financial benefits but the standardized policy in collection development and bargaining power of a consortium can help in reducing the costs of documents (Haneefa, 2007).

However, the following are the reasons that compel libraries, users and publishers to look for library consortia (Tripathi and Lal, 2016):

4.2.1. For Libraries

- Growth of knowledge in different subjects poses challenges for libraries in acquisition and dissemination in accordance with growing information needs of clientele;
- Cope with diminishing library budgets;
- Changing demands caused by the developing technology;
- Gain consistency of information access in accordance with, technological development and also to guarantee equality of access amongst a group of libraries at all levels;
- Consortia deal proves to be more cost-effective for libraries; and
- Provide end user autonomy and reliance on remote mediated information services, especially in poorly resourced and/or remote geographic areas.

4.2.2. For Users

- Way of improving users' satisfaction with rapid availability of e-information;
- Users with a personal networked computer can have direct access from their desktop;
- E-information service through consortia is independent of geographical location;
- Users can retrieve additional information relevant to their topic;
- E-information takes less time for its publication and delivery than its print counterpart; and
- Consortia-based services overcome language barriers.

4.2.3. For Publishers

- Internet publishing poses challenges and competition to publishers;

- Publishers as content providers face erosion of print subscriptions;
- Willingness of information producers to negotiate with the multiple institutions rather than to insist on individual contracts with individual libraries;
- Publishers need additional costs for new production and technological requirements;
- Improved return on investment to owners; and
- Safeguard the vital interest of authors and societies.

Thus, user expectations rose with the enhancement of technological changes and libraries had to meet these user requirements "with advanced capabilities". But budgetary limitations forced libraries to provide the scholarly publications collectively. This gave rise to resource sharing and providing services through a common gateway (Varatharajan and Ravi, 2004) that is library consortia.

4.3. COMPONENTS OF LIBRARY CONSORTIA

The stakeholders are the persons, groups or organizations that have a direct or indirect stake in an organization because they can affect or be affected by the actions, objectives and the policies of the organization (Business Dictionary, 2010).

Wikipedia (2019) states that a stakeholder is a person or organization that has a legitimate interest in a project or entity, while, a corporate stakeholder is a party that can affect or be affected by the actions of the business as a whole.

Stakeholders are the essential components of the consortium without whose support the consortium is bound to cease. They are the entities that influence the organizational and functional set of the consortium. Stakeholders also influence programmes, products and services.

Various stakeholders in a library consortium are the publishers & subscription agents, library users & libraries and the institutions (Goudar and Poornima, 2004).

4.3.1. Publishers and Subscription Agents

Hunter (1999), the Vice President of Elsevier Science, points out that "publishers, consortia and aggregators have barely begun the process of learning how to work together" and stresses the common interest of working together and identifying best practices that guarantee "better deals" for both parties. It is interesting to notice how, after a big debate against open access initiatives in which large publishers like Elsevier contrasted the new trend, publishers themselves now also seem to be changing their attitude (Harnad and Hunter, 2004). So, the publishers have changed their policy and given the possibility to authors to deposit post prints on personal or institutional Web pages for articles published in their periodicals.

Cox (2000), Fogg (2001) and Prior (2001) have highlighted the importance of a new role for subscription agents. It is relevant to notice that the same booksellers and subscription agents have been subjected to a transformation within the, supply chain. They have been in danger of disappearing in slowly responding to the changes of the market, depending on the activities of consortia and of big publishers wishing to deal directly with libraries over online journals. It is noticed that the "the big five publishers (Blackwell, Dawson, EBSCO, Faxon, and Swets) have become the big two (EBSCO and Swets), all within eight years" (Cox, 2003) due to publishers starting to deal directly with clients.

4.3.2. Library Users

The profile of the user population is also changed because the demand for lifelong or continuing education and off-campus studies has increased (Cox, 2000), where the change in the use of information technology in learning and research in recent years has a direct impact on the users. Librarians and publishers have the opportunity to better know their users and the new habits. Further, usage statistics of the use of electronic content can help both the librarians and publishers to identify the needs of the other stakeholder, the users.

Sanville, the director of OhioLINK consortium is to say that "librarians should no longer presume to know exactly what patrons will need in the electronic world based solely on past patron behaviors in the controlled print environment...To move forward, [librarians] must assume that there is an evolution on information use at work and libraries and their consortia must be enablers rather than gatekeepers" (Sanville, 1999).

Sanville further, adds - the role of consortia is also to expand information use by creating and making available systems of information access and retrieval "friendly, fluid and flexible," with the aim to create "a sustainable economic model of information purchase that maximizes information use by the patron populations" served. However, the point of the use of information is particularly relevant as recent studies emphasize how students and staff members find it difficult to use high-quality electronic publications made available by libraries. An evaluation and monitoring framework in the United Kingdom carried out by the Joint Information Systems Committee (JISC), and reported by Wise (2003), has emphasized how high-quality information resources are relatively underused and stressing because the users begin their search by using free search engines without moving on to using other tools.

4.3.3. Libraries and Institutions

Libraries are themselves actually the consortia users (Sloan, 2000) as they recognize the advantages offered to libraries by participating in consortia and they also have the concerns about the contracts established by consortia (Rowse, 2003). In the case of purchasing electronic material, consortia have to contemplate clauses regarding archiving and fair use of information as far as document inter-library loan and delivery services are concerned. As far as copyright is concerned, archiving and fair use of information, together with cost and access, are the main concerns for libraries (Ashcroft, 2002). However, the institutions willing to guarantee free research have to support open archives initiatives (Oliver, 2000; Prosser, 2004) and offer digital spaces to preserve the institutional digital scientific production.

4.4. E-RESOURCES

E-resources consists of surrogates of print formats. Hence, they may be of as much types as the print formats exist. However, main of them are tabulated in table 4.1.

Table 4.1. Types of E-Resources

Sl. No	*Types of E- Resources*	*Description*
1	E Books	E Books are available in many formats competing for prime time, including Adobe PDF, Microsoft Reader, eReader, Mobipocket Reader, EPUB, Kindle and iPad.
2	E-Journals	E-Journals and electronic serials, are scholarly journals or intellectual magazines that can be accessed via electronic transmission.
3.	E-Newspapers	E-Newspapers are also known as online newspapers or web newspapers that exist on the World Wide Web or internet.
4	E-Magazines	E-Magazines are very important part of every library collection. They are like print format but published online on internet.
5	Indexing and Abstracting Databases	These are the reference sources which provide bibliographic information about the journals including abstracts of the articles.

6	Full-Text databases	These are the organized collection of information on a particular subject or multidisciplinary subject areas, whereas the information within e-databases can be searched and retrieved electronically. There are available a number of databases on the network which are either free or with charges.
7	Reference Databases	These are the Dictionaries, Almanacs and Encyclopedias etc. which are available on internet in electronic format.
8	Statistical Databases	These databases contain the numerical data useful for the mass community.
9	Image collection	E-images are the collection on various themes of the photographs available electronically.
10	Multimedia Products	These are the databases which may include the images, videos, audios and the text etc.
11	E-Theses	These are databases which contain the PhD theses and Master Dissertations published through e-format.
12	E-Clipping	E-clipping is retrospective search and comprehensive analysis of news items electronically.
13	E-Patents	E-patents are the exclusive right granted by the government to make use of an invention for a specific period of time.
14	E-Standards	These are the written definition, limit rule, approved and monitored for complains by authoritative agency.

Some important of e-publications are discussed here:

4.4.1. E-Journals

Journals are the periodicals, especially onc containing scholarly articles or disseminating current information on the research and development in a particular subject field. They are considered to be a major source of communication of nascent thought among sources of information. They are considered the note chord of any library's collection and have become indispensable for research in any field. In fact, without journals, it is difficult to ensure the growth of any research in any discipline.

The term 'scholarly' applies to both the nature of the content and the type of author. Scholarly journals contain a high proportion of articles of original scholarship contributed by authors, which upon publication with peer-review process, brings recognition to authors as well as institutions.

Journals were originally published by learned societies but now commercial publishers are also publishing a large number of scholarly journals since the middle of the 20th century. The growth of science and technology saw emergence of new areas of research in a number of fields, which resulted in to inter-disciplinary and multi-disciplinary approach for research that can facilitate proliferation of scientific literature. Besides the pressure exerted on researchers to produce more published work under the well-known *mantra* 'Publish or Perish', resulting in publication of even more articles (Campbell and Meadows, 2011).

Print journals which are referred to conventional print editions, are published and distributed as paper copies could not be able to accommodate the new research. Hence, e-journals/online journals which are referred to electronic editions started to make available online through computer networks. The journal editions available online through the Internet are called electronic journals (e-journals) (Chandra and Mahesh, 2003).

Thus, the web and online electronic publishing; however, has changed the way of accessing information for scholars and the researchers (McKnight, 1993). With the application of information and communication technology (ICT), particularly the Internet, there has been a shift from traditional print journals to online journals.

E-journals are available commercially since early

1990s, although publishing of journals electronically had been discussed in literature for several decades. However, due to lack of standards, cost-effective delivery and storage mechanism initially kept them in the realm of a futuristic 'wish list'. *"Adonis"*, one of the first e-journals, appeared on pilot form during late 1980s was launched as a commercial product in 1991. This provided page imaging of journals from major scientific publishers, which were distributed to subscribers on CD-ROMs. But with introduction of WWW, publishers could post their materials for users to access using standard web browsers. With these developments, the libraries and users were willing to give a chance to web-based e-journals and publishers began producing electronic versions of their print journals and thereby, libraries began subscribing them.

Presently, e-journals have become the largest and fastest growing areas of the digital collections for most of the libraries. For instance, e-journals, which numbered just a few hundred titles a few years ago, are now running in the many thousands. Further, the advancements in digital technologies and the recent proliferation of e-publishing across the world have brought a revolution in journal publication, subscription, access, and delivery mechanism. E-journals possess numerous additional features as the electronic equivalents of their print counterparts.

E-journals are the ideal solution for users because they permit full-text access via computer terminals irrespective of location. There is no more user frustration arising out of the unavailability of material on the shelf for whatever reason. Electronic publishing has reduced time lag from 3 to 6 months, as an electronic version can be made available and accessible within the minimum possible time (Chand, Murthy and Chandel, 2005).

(i) Definitions : There are other terms for an online journal—some call it a "paperless journal," some say "virtual journal," and some say "electronic journal." But the most common definition of an online journal defines it as "a journal that is provided by any electronic means, for example, the Internet or CD-ROM, although not necessarily exclusive by electronic means" (Ashcroft and Langdon, 1999).

Glossary of Library and Information Science states tha tit is "an online journal is a publication, often scholarly, that is made accessible in a computerized format and distributed over the Internet" (Ali, 2004).

Lancaster defines an e-journal as "a journal created for the electronic medium and available only in this medium." It is different from an electronic serial that may be defined very broadly as any journal, magazine, or newsletter that is available over the Internet (Lancaster, 1995).

Electronic Journals: A Selected Resource Guide explicitly defines electronic journals as "serial publications available in digital format. Some are distributed on CD-ROMs, some over the Internet. Of the Internet-available ones, some are delivered over the World Wide Web, some by e-mail. Some are ASCII texts; some are HTML WWW pages; some use proprietary formats such as Adobe's PDF (Portable Document Format). Some have paper equivalents; some are purely electronic. Some are published in electronic form; some are digitally reformatted print journals. Some are free; some are available by subscription only. Some are peer-reviewed scholarly journals; many are not quality-controlled" (Harrassowitz, n.d.)

Thus, for simplicity, an e-journal is the journal which is distributed to some or all of its primary subscribers in electronic form. In contrast, a paper journal (p-journal) is one that is distributed exclusively in paper form.

(ii) Types of E-Journals : E-journals can be produced in different formats, such as a CD-ROM, which was the first step toward electronic publishing. As such, during late 1988 to early 1990 various journals were published on CD-ROMs mostly because of its increased storage capacity. However, there are new forms of e-journals that have all of the print-version features and can therefore replace print. These journals are available through the vendor sites or directly from the sites, and most of them are in Acrobat format.

Thus, there are two distinct eras of e-journal development: (1) ASCII text-based pre-Web era, and (2) graphics-enabled post-Web era. In the pre- Web era, these ASCII text-based e-journals appeared in different forms, as newsletters, non-referred e-journals, referred e-journals, and tailored and structured journals (Peek and Pomerantz, 1998). With the arrival of the Web, e-journals in all disciplines have proliferated, finding widespread, enthusiastic acceptance by end users. Some electronic publications replicate existing print publications while others exist only in electronic form.

Kling and McKim (1997) have classified at least four kinds of e-journals in the post-Web era:

- Pure e-journals that are originally distributed only in digital form, for example, the *Electronic Journal of Communication, Journal of Digital Information, Information Research.*
- E-p journals that are primarily distributed electronically but may have very limited distribution in paper form also, for example, the *Journal of Artificial Intelligence Research, Electronic Transactions on Artificial Intelligence.*
- P-e journals that are primarily distributed in paper form but are also distributed electronically, for example, the *Nature, Science, Physical Review.*
- P-e journals that are initiated with parallel paper and electronic editions which may be widely distributed, for example, the *Organic Letters.*

(iii) Benefits of E-journals : E-journals are becoming increasingly in demand both as a means of rapid desktop access to current research materials and as a way to view past volumes. They offer a range of potential advantages to libraries and end users (Boyce, 1997; Neal, 1997; Moret, 1997):

- **Speed of Publication :** E-journals are published more quickly resulting in speedy information delivery. This means that the information is much more up to date than can be achieved with paper.
- **Availability of Hyperlink :** The availability of hyperlinks to related resources in the articles is compared to traditional citations. The intrinsic value of the links is nearly as great as the content itself.
- **Interactivity :** The articles can be read, commented on and amended much more quickly than can be done with print.
- **Accessing and Searching Facility :** Search ability and accessibility are the main features of a digital format. Further, the access is available at a 24 × 7 × 365 days. Besides, the availability and monitoring of usage statistics is easy.
- **Storage Space :** It saves physical storage space and provides a scope for developing a union catalogue among participating libraries. Further, the increase in the cost of keeping printed materials makes electronic forms more attractive from an economic point of view.
- **Inexpensive :** Getting deep discounts through joint-pricing negotiation results in lower unit cost of information.
- **Flexibility :** E-journals are able to evolve quickly as they are not tied to a format, printer, or distribution network.

(iv) Disadvantages of E-journals : However, along with various advantages, there are also disadvantages of e-journals which may include the following (Gessner, 1996):

- **Difficulty in Reading On Screens :** Often not included in indexing and abstracting services, reading a large amount of data on the screen is very difficult and causes health problems such as back pain or vision problems.
- **Archiving :** Both storing large files of data and maintaining access to them have additional costs in terms of staff, time and other resources.
- **Perishable Citation and Authenticity :** The change in website URLs or their frequent disappearance causes loss of data. Thus, the authenticity of sources and authority of e-journals are to some extent questionable.

Besides, the proliferation of e-journals and various pricing models for the information has further complicated the acquisitions issue both for the libraries and publishers.

4.4.2. E-Books

E-books are digital publications, that is to say, texts that use electronic files instead of paper as support. They may be called electronic books (e-books) or soft books or digital books. They are said to be originated back in 1971 when Michael Hart, the founder of Project Gutenberg decided that the greatest value created by computers would not be computing but the storage, retrieval, and searching of what was stored in our libraries. The first "e-book" was born as, "a copy of the Declaration of Independence." E-books appeared on the Web, easily shared and stored on a hard drive or storage disk, and quickly began to proliferate. However, early e-books were generally written in specialty areas, intended to be documents that only small groups might share and therefore, were few and far between (E-Book, 2011).

E-books are different partly because of the extent of

their individual content. Library users are either tied to a screen to read large volumes of text or obliged to print the text themselves. Initially they were intended to be read on dedicated hardware devices but now they can be downloaded to a computer, PC, Mac, laptop, PDA, or any other kind of computer, and is read on the screen and even they can have numbered pages, a table of contents, pictures and graphics, exactly like a printed book (Sasson, 2009).

(i) Definitions : Although the idea of e-books is not new, there is still much confusion about e-books, even at the level of the basic definition of what an e-book is (Tedd, 2005). At present, there is no commonly accepted universal definition of an e-book (Bennett, 2006) and the term has been used ambiguously in the literature. Although they have the potential to support learning activities and transform the scholarly environment has been acknowledged, but their uptake is slow (Cox, 2004). A report entitled "Promoting the uptake of e-books in Higher and Further Education" referring to these issues, highlight that "within the context of academic publishing, there is not an adequate definition for the term 'e-book,' and this is a source of confusion and therefore a barrier to uptake" (Gold Leaf, 2003).

However, the JISC defines electronic books as "an online version of printed books, accessed via the Internet" (Gold Leaf, 2003). Armstrong, Edwards and Lonsdale (2002) are of the opinion that "any piece of electronic text regardless of size or composition (a digital object), but excluding journal publications, made available electronically (or optically) for any device (handheld or desk-bound) that includes a screen" can be an e-book.

International Encyclopedia of Information and Library Science has updated the definition of e-book continuing to use the book-analogy approach as: "the result of integrating classical book structure, or rather the familiar concept of a book, with features that can be provided within an electronic environment is referred to as an electronic book (or e-book), which is intended as an interactive document that can be composed and read on a computer" (Landoni, 2003).

Further, the National Information Standards Organization (NISO, 2005) Data Dictionary for Libraries and Information defines e-books as "digital documents, licensed or not, where searchable text is prevalent, and which can be seen in analogy to a print book (monograph). The use of e-books is in many cases dependent on a dedicated device and/or a special reader or viewing software."

Though, these key definitions vary in their nature and extent but more specifically, the term e-book refers variously to "hardware, software, and content" of e-books (Wilson and Landoni, 2001). Even those sources that purport to present an overview of perspectives on e-books typically develop their own, slightly unique "working definition" of the term, shaping it to their own domain of interest and purpose of their research studies.

Thus, Vassiliou and Rowley (2008) have proposed a sustainable definition of e-book in a two-parts, as "(1) An e-book is a digital object with textual and/or other content, which arises as a result of integrating the familiar concept of a book with features that can be provided in an electronic environment; (2) E-books, typically have in-use features such as search and cross reference functions, hypertext links, bookmarks, annotations, highlights, multimedia objects and interactive tools".

(ii) Formats : E-books have many formats competing for prime time, including Adobe PDF, Microsoft Reader, eReader, Mobipocket Reader, Optical Packet Switching (OPS), OpenReader, and Kindle. Today, e-books are available in a range of formats and accessible using a diversity of devices such as PCs, PDAs, BlackBerrys, Pocket PCs, Tablets, Sony Readers, mobile phones, and iPods. Each format has its own features and specific reader software is needed to enable the e-book to be read or viewed on a device (Sasson, 2009). Even, e-books can have numbered pages, table of contents, pictures and graphics, exactly like a printed book. Thus, if desired, it is very easy to print an e-book after download.

As far as the types are concerned, many different types and kinds of electronic books are available. These may include: textbooks, reference materials such as dictionaries, scholarly monographs, directories, gray literature, including technical reports, working papers, standards, conference papers and proceedings, official publications, trade literature, privately published material, theses, and translations, and out-of-print and free e-books (Armstrong and Lonsdale, 2003).

(iii) Features : E-books have become known as one of the prominent electronic resources in this competitive information age. They are easy to use for browsing, keyword searching within a book and across a collection of books and customizable search interfaces, extracting, comparing, and assessing relevance and quality of information presented. E-books possess following features (Tripahti and Lal, 2016):

- Easier access for users and no need to go to the library;
- Increased flexibility and availability to more users over a wider area;
- Help to increase access to those unable to acquire a print copy;
- Improve circulation, but only if the user license reflects the demand;
- Important for distance learners, but authentication issues may mean it is more trouble than its worth;
- Have a higher turnover rate than print versions; therefore, there are more borrowers in a shorter time providing maximization of usage;

- Increased access to resources outside the institution, but users are dependent on their access to the technology and their IT skills;
- Require no handling and can be issued/returned instantly;
- Free up staff time from shelving;
- Ease pressure on physical space;
- Less need for stock editing;
- Issues of vandalism and hidden/missing books solved;
- Cannot be damaged like regular books;
- If the content goes out of date it can be easily updated; and
- Extend access to a wider range of material on individual subjects but only if the material is available in e-format.

Besides, they might be able to afford a wider range of reference materials and might be more cost-effective for short-life titles.

(ii) Benefits of E-books : Now, more and more people prefer e-books to traditional ones because they can save time and money. Sasson (2009) gives the following advantages of e-books:

- E-books are delivered almost instantaneously. They can be purchased, downloaded, and started to be read within minutes. There is no need to go to a bookstore to buy them, and no need to wait for them for days, weeks, and sometimes more to arrive in the mail;
- Practically, no space is needed to store them. There is no need of a library or a room for them. Hundreds and thousands of e-books can be stored in the computer;
- E-books are portable and hundreds of books can be carried in CD, laptop, notebook, or any e-book

reader, without worrying about their weight;

- E-books can be read any-where, on the bus, train, airplane, even while standing in line;
- E-books are more safely stored and carried from one place to another than ordinary books.
- E-books can show links for easy access to more information and related websites;
- E-books are searchable, where any information can be easily searched without turning page after page;
- E-books are interactive and may contain audio, video and animations which enhance the message that the author is trying to convey;
- E-books are delivered through the Internet, there are no packing and shipping expenses;
- E-books are also printable so that if one wishes to read an e-book in the traditional way, he can very inexpensively print it with a home printer or at any printing shop;
- Fonts in e-books can be resized, making it easier to read for people with disabilities. It is also possible to turn some of the e-books into audio books with additional software;
- E-books are very simple and easy to purchase and download an e-book. People living in big modernized cities, in a remote village, in a faraway country, or on a small island can equally access them. It takes them the same amount of time to purchase and download an e-book provided they have an Internet connection.

Besides, it is possible to purchase an e-book 24 hour a day, every day of the year, from the comfort of one's own house or office. Even, they can be purchased and downloaded even when one is on a vacation but has a laptop with Internet connection.

(iii) Disadvantages of E-books : With various e-books flooding the market, more and more people are aware of the disadvantages of e-books. The disadvantages of e-books given by Garry (2009) and Tian (2008) include:

- E-books require special devices or personal computers to read. Many e-books are typically produced to be compatible with certain software, which in turn may be not easily available;
- Since e-books are dependent on other equipment, certain hardware or software failure may affect it. Unless the hardware, Internet connection, or battery power that is required by an e-book reader is readily available, its electronic documents are useless;
- Some people do not like reading books on a computer screen because screen glare and eye strain are a serious concern for many potential users of e-books. Further, the display resolution of computer screens and electronic devices is considerably less than the print quality produced by a printing press;
- Reading from a computer lacks the familiarity and comfort of reading from a book. A paper book can be opened and flipped through while some electronic text is more difficult to navigate;
- E-books can be lost if someone's hard drive fails and he/she has not kept a backup; and also, e-book reading devices are surely more expensive than printed books.

Besides, there is a growing concern that the e-books at present may not be accessible to or compatible with future e-book software or devices. E-books also have an unreliable life span, where paper has a much longer life span than most digital forms of storage. Further, because of the rapid development of new computer systems it is difficult to judge whether the software or hardware will become outdated. As new hardware is developed, structures must be put into place to allow for the migration of existing materials to the new platforms so that they can still be accessed. E-books might also be hacked, copied, or distributed without the permission of the author or publisher.

4.4.3. E-Databases

E-databases which are also known as the online databases are the record of logically related information, recorded in computer files in a uniform form to facilitate easy and efficient retrieving of data by means of internet or communication networks. These systems are the results of many research and development activities that were carried out more than 60 years ago. However, before 1960s, the major function of information retrieval was to organize information but now, the emergence of online databases has introduced a new era for information searching and retrieval from traditional retrieval systems to network based information retrieval systems.

Online Information Retrieval Systems can be characterized as the Information Retrieval systems that allow remote access with searches conducted in real time. Users generally search information from four types of online IR systems: "online databases, online public access catalogues (OPACs), Web search engines and digital libraries". Online IR systems are also known as professional online systems, which are also abbreviated as online systems or online databases (Chu, 2009). Therefore, an online database is widely recognized as a typical online IR system.

Online databases include information that is organized and represented in a logical manner. Structurally, online database made up of records, further divided into a number of fields (author, title, etc.) for categorizing, searching and retrieving information. Initially, online databases were used to provide bibliographic information, later they started to comprise full-text information to provide actual information, since then they were called as full-text online databases. They provide access to those digitalized resources which are not generally available on the World Wide Web. These databases make use of computers and communication to offer various types of information for serving the academic and research community globally.

It is seen that the availability of these databases enables users to search information in a variety of forms and formats, such as HTML, PDF, RTF, etc. In online databases, contents are arranged in such a way that it can be easily searched and retrieved without the help of any intermediaries. Therefore, these are excellent tools for in-depth study, providing a range of consistent and scholarly literature from well-known online database producers or publishers.

(i) Definitions : E-databases are variously defined. Gray (1976) has defined online database as "a collection of bibliographic information stored in a computer or a central computer and retrospective search is made possible remotely from a distance computer through the use of software".

ODLIS defines these databases as, "a large, regularly updated file of digitized information (bibliographic records, abstracts, full- text documents, directory entries, images, statistics etc.) related to a specific subject or field, consisting of records of uniform format organized for ease and speed of search and retrieval and managed with the aid of database management system (DBMS) software. Content is created by the database producer (for example, the American Psychological Association), which usually publishes a print version (Psychological Abstracts) and leases the content to one or more database vendors (EBSCO, OCLC etc.) that provide electronic access to the data after it has been converted to machine readable form (PsycINFO), usually on CD-ROM or online via the Internet, using proprietary search software" (Reitz, 2012).

While, according to the University Santo Tomas (2008), "Online databases [e-databases] are [the] collections of computerized information or data such as articles, books, graphics and multimedia that can be searched to find information. Databases can be general or subject based in form of abstracts and or full-text".

(ii) Features : These databases possess following characteristic features.

- **Organized Collection :** Contents are arranged logically to facilitate easy access and retrieval. Further, the documents in such types of systems are organized in a suitable manner for carrying out easy and fast retrieval of information.
- **Credibility :** Recorded contents of information are reviewed by subject experts and publishers to maintain the credibility and authenticity of the resources. The contents of database are finely evaluated in terms of their accuracy and credibility.
- **Usability:** The well-defined organization of information contents and search capabilities of these databases allow users to search and retrieve results more efficiently and effectively.
- **Conversational Searches :** Searches in these databases are conducted as a two-way communication between the searcher and system, in which each get a chance to communicate with each other. Therefore, online databases are referred to as interactive or conversational.
- **Expert System :** E-databases are characterized as expert systems that provide information on specialized areas of knowledge; for example, a nuclear database gathers specific information on nuclear sciences from experts or specialized associations and provides particulars of the nuclear sciences.

- **Controlled Vocabulary :** Usually they have their own controlled vocabulary to support the searching. Controlled vocabulary is largely used for information presentation and retrieval, though the keyword searching is also supported by almost all the online systems.
- **Permanence :** Published documents, such as journals, reviews and books, etc. in these databases do not change frequently. Thus, these information documents remain in databases for a long time in the form of archives to again retrieve the information.
- **Up-to-Date :** These databases comprise of current information on its concerned areas. Online database providers or publishers regularly update their contents by adding new information to provide current and copyrighted scholarly materials.
- **Real-Time :** Real time in online database operations implies that the remote terminals respond quickly to the user's search processes. Remote terminals receive data, search the information, and return the results more frequently to be utilized by the users in ongoing activities.
- **Time-Sharing :** On-line time-sharing implies the sharing of machine processing time among a number of terminals. It means that the processing time of the computer is equally shared amongst independent activities. Many users can search the information simultaneously either from the same place or variant locations by time sharing.

(iii) Types : On the basis of information incorporated in e-databases, they are divided into two main categories: Reference and Sources databases. *Reference databases* direct seekers towards the source of information, while *source databases* include actual information itself (Chowdhury, 2010).

On the basis of content, scope and the information incorporated, online databases are grouped under the following categories:

- On the Basis of Information Incorporated
- On the Basis of Scope of Data
- On the Basis of Contents, and
- On the Basis of Providers

However, on the Basis of Information Incorporated, the most common forms of online databases may be grouped into following four types:

- Full-text Online Databases
- Reference Databases
- Numeric Databases
- Multimedia Databases

Each of them is briefly discussed below:

(a) Full-text Online Databases : A full-text database is a compilation of documents or other information in the form of database in which complete text of each referenced document is available for online viewing, printing or downloading. In addition to, text documents, images are often included as graphs, maps, photos and diagrams. Full-text online databases are comprising of full-text information of the publications that are basically either print or online in origin. It includes large files of text such as, all the paragraphs of a journal article or all the chapters from a book along with abstract or citations of the text files incorporated in them.

Bandyopadhyay (1999) mentions that full-text online databases are now being using as effective and important sources of periodical literature that are not usually available in local collection of libraries. Examples may be cited for the JSTOR, Emerald insight and Wiley Online Library etc.

(b) Reference Databases : The references databases

include terms descriptive of content on which retrieval is based, while some databases also provide abstract to give brief description of original documents. The retrieval of information in these databases is mostly based on the words appeared in abstract. The retrieved data helps the requester to identify where an original source can then be found. Reference databases provide bibliographic descriptions to published literature. They provide abstract, references or citations to documents.

These databases are divided into two main categories: Bibliographic Databases and Referral Databases. *Bibliographic database* is one of the most important forms of reference databases. These databases are widely used as reference tools and provide citations or references, abstracts and index to published literature. Online bibliographic databases provide quick information about publications, which may or may not be available in library's own collection. These are the excellent means to access information, rather than merely an item of information in the collection of any library. Bibliographic databases contain elements of bibliographic description that are used to describe books, journals, documents, and other publications or portions. These databases which are typically online bibliographic files, are the online equivalent of print abstracts and indexing services and mostly used for bibliographic verification of literature. Examples may include: LISA, Indian Citation Index, Scopus and Web of Science etc.

Referral databases direct the users towards the particulars of actual source of information i.e., name of a person or institution. It offers references to information, such as names, address, specialization of persons, institutions, information systems, and so forth. Ulrich's Periodicals Directory and Electronic Yellow Pages are the best example of reference databases.

(c) Numeric Databases : Numeric databases are the computer-readable collection of data that are primarily numeric in nature. These are also known as the fact sources and non-bibliographic databases. These are mostly used for supporting business or financial research. Numeric databases include organized numerical data along with brief textual description and provide the access in the form of statistics, demographic and financial reports, stock market quotations, chemical and physical properties and chemical nomenclature and graphic structures, etc. These are the files of primarily statistical information from which a user can extract specific forms of data. Examples may include the COMPUSTAT and ProQuest Statistical Insight.

(d) Multimedia Databases : Multimedia databases are the collection of related multimedia data objects of different types. A multimedia database contains various data types such as images, sound recordings, video recordings, signals, graphics together with text data etc. Multimedia databases host different types of media file, such as .txt for documents, .jpg used for images, .swf deals with videos, .mp3 use for generating audio files etc. These databases involve the activities related to acquisition, generation, storage, processing and transmission of multimedia data over the networks. These databases primarily provide access to art prints, animations, photos, audio clips, videos and others multimedia contents. Artstor and Academic Video Online are the good example of multimedia databases.

Thus, it is seen that e-databases or the online databases which have developed as benchmark systems of information retrieval, mainly designed to retrieve documents required by the users. They work on the principle of providing right information to the right user instantly and they are designed with the aim of providing scholarly information in one or more areas of education and research. Online databases deal with a variety of information in variant forms and formats, comprising of textual information, bibliographic information, numeric and multimedia information including text, audio, images and video. Thus, online databases may be treated as a bridge between the generators of information and the seekers of that information.

4.5. CONSORTIA APPROACH TO E-JOURNALS/E-PUBLICATIONS

Cooperative e-acquisition has become a compelling proposition in a library consortium environment due to increase in costs, proliferation of electronic resources and dwindling library budgets. User community also has been greatly influenced by newer technologies facilitating seamless access to information. Users are also demanding for providing electronic information services. As such, the current library scenario has reached a critical mass both in terms of e-products as well as increased number of users. Hence, the library professionals due to journals crisis, and cuts in library budgets are forced to come together in forming consortia for subscription of e-publications (Sreekumar and Sunitha, 2005).

E-products, especially the journals are becoming increasingly popular for the fact that delivery of information is at the desk-top facilitating ease of use and faster access to information. Consortia provide expanded use of information by potential users and enhance collective buying power of group of libraries. Consortia as such have the greater capability in negotiating for purchase of information. Libraries and consortia together have to purchase the information by adopting suitable purchase models that provide for expanded journals access (Sanville, 1999; White, 2001).

Further, due to proliferation of e-resources and existing constraints with print editions and developments in computers and communication networks, especially world wide web has facilitated the creation of an alternative electronic form of the conventional paper journals. The scholarly publications have brought about a revolution in journals subscription, access and delivery mechanism with better means of archiving for future use. Thus, scholarly journals may be subscribed through purchase or lease by consortia on behalf of group of libraries or consortia participants.

4.6. ADVANTAGES OF LIBRARY CONSORTIA

With subscribed resources accessible online in electronic format, the member libraries would have less pressure on space requirements for storing and managing print-based library resources. Moreover, all problems associated with print media such as their wear and tear, location, shelving, binding, organizing, etc. would not be an issue for electronic resources. Thus, for participating libraries, consortia offer several benefits:

- A comprehensive collection;
- A single interface and access point;
- Access to the otherwise unsubscribed materials;
- Avoidance of duplication of core collection;
- Scope for electronic archives;
- Availability and monitoring of usage statistics;
- Provides access to wider number of electronic resources at substantially lower cost with optimum utilization of funds;
- Reduced storage costs as e-journals demand less library space with no shelving costs; also, they cannot be stolen;
- Developing common resource databases;
- Effective document delivery systems and better library services like current awareness service (CAS) and selective dissemination of information (SDI); and
- Available 24 h a day, 7 days a week.

Besides, consortia bring economy, efficiency, and equality in information availability and use and also offer better terms of licenses for use, archival access, and preservation of subscribed electronic resources, which would not have been possible for any single institution. Further, the publishers are able to market their products/ journals/databases to a large number of libraries. However, small vendors may be at a loss due to capturing of market by large vendors.

4.7. DISADVANTAGES OF LIBRARY CONSORTIA

There are seen a number of benefits of forming library consortia but the problems also exist, such as the poor technological-infrastructure, economic and cultural barriers, and separation of effort etc. Thus, the disadvantages of library consortia may include the following:

- Funding problems
- Absence of a printed copy of journals
- Training of staffs required for handling electronic documents etc.
- Initially require high investments in licensees and information and communication technology; and
- Copyright problems.

Besides, unreliable telecommunication links and insufficient bandwidth may disturb the scene. Last but not least, the users may not accept e-products, especially e-journals on par with the printed journals.

SUMMARY

This chapter discusses about various components of the library consortia such as stakeholders– users, publishers and the library documents covering e-journals and e-books. The journals are the major source of communication of nascent thought among sources of information. They are considered the note chord of any library's collection and have become indispensable for research in any field, inspite of the presence of other form of e-publications such as the e-books and e-databases etc. In fact, without journals it is difficult to ensure the growth of any research in any discipline. However, to change from library-centered services to user-centered ones, e-books are needed. Now, more and more people prefer e-books and other e-publications to traditional ones, because they save time and money.

This chapter ends with the advantages, disadvantages, and criteria for the success of library consortia, and the collective strength of members which provides it the power to bargain with the publishers for better subscription rates and terms of licenses. Further, the members of the consortium must work together for better functioning of the consortium. Hence, the cost of subscription to electronic resources decreases as more and more institutions are joining the consortium.

BIBLIOGRAPHICAL REFERENCES

Ali, A. (Ed.). (2004). Glossary of Library and Information Science. Ess Ess Publications, New Delhi. P. 259.

Armstrong, C.J. and Lonsdale, R. (2003). The E-Book Mapping Exercise: Draft Report on Phase 1. JISC E-books Working Group, London. Available at: www.jisc.ac.uk// uploaded_documents/eBook_mapping_exercise_Final Report_0403.pdf.

Armstrong, C.J., Edwards, L. and Lonsdale, R. (2002). Virtually There? E-Books in UK Academic Libraries. Program: Electronic Library & Information Systems, 36 (4) : 216-27.

Ashcroft, L. (2002). Issues in Developing, Managing and Marketing Electronic Journals Collections. Collection Building, 21(4): 147-154.

Ashcroft, L. and Langdon, C. (1999). Electronic Journals and University Library Collections. Collection Building, 18(3): 105-113.

Bandyopadhyay, A. (1999). Accessing Sci-Tech Literature: Commercial Document Delivery Services and Online Full-Text Databases. Collection Building, 18(1): 10- 15.

Banks, D. (2018). Thoughts on Publishing the Research Article over the Centuries. Publications, 6 (1). DOI 10.3390/ publications6010010.

Bennet, L. (2006). E-Books- the Option: A Manual for Publishers. The Publishers Association, London.

Bjoernshauge, L. (1999). Consortia Licensing: Implications for Digital Collection Development. INSPEL, 33 (2): 116-121.

Boyce, P. (1997). Electronic Publishing in Astronomy. Available at: http://tiepac.portlandpress.co.uk/books/online/tiepac/sessionl/ch3.htm.

Business Dictionary (2010). What is a Stakeholder? Available at: www.businessdictionary.com›definition›stakeholder.

Campbell, R. and Meadows, A. (2011). Scholarly Journals Publishing: Where Do We Go from Here? Learned Publishing, 24 (3): 171-181.

Chand, P., Murthy. T.A.V, and Chandel, A. S. (2005). Usage of Electronic Journals Under UGC Infonet E-Journal Consortium in North Eastern University Libraries. Planner-2005 Paper. Assam University, Silchar (Assam). Pp. 417-425. Available at: http://ir.inflibnet.ac.in:8080/ir/bitstream/1944/1417/1/57.pdf.

Chandra, P. and Mahesh, G. (2003). CSIR Electronic Journals Consortium. In Y. Singh (Ed.): 21st Annual Conventional and Conference of Society for Information Science (SIS): Challenges in Management and E-Learning in the Age of Globalization. IIT, Roorkee. Pp. 181-188.

Chowdury, G. G. (2010). Introduction to Modern Information Retrieval. Facet Publishing, London.

Chu. H. (2009). Information Representation and Retrieval in the Digital Age. Ess Ess Publications, New Delhi.

Cox, J. (2000). Developing Model Licenses for Electronic Resources: Cooperation in a Competitive World. Library Consortium Management, 2(1): 8-17.

Cox, J. (2003). Vendors: Extinction or Reincarnation? Serials, 16(2): 141-144.

Cox, J. (2004). E-Books: Challenges and Opportunities. D-Lib Magazine, 10(10). Available at: www.dlib.org/dlib/october04/cox/10cox.html.

E-Book (2011). E-Book / Digital Book History - History of Information. Available at: http://www.historyofinformation.com/expanded.php?cat=90.

Fogg, H. (2001). A Review of Subscription Agency Services to Law Firm Libraries: Investigating Current and Future Service

Relationships. Serials, 14(1): 57-62.

Fraser, A.G. and Dunstan, F. D. (2010). On the Impossiblity of Being Expert. British Medical Journal, 341: 6815.

Garry. (2009). Disadvantages of E-books. Available at: http://www.publishyourownebooks.com/5-disadvantages-of-ebooks.

Gessner, A. (1996). The Electronic Journal: Is It becoming Academically Respectable? Connect. Available: at: http://www.nyu.edu/its/pubs/connect/archives/96spring/gessnerejournal.html.

Gold Leaf. (2003). Promoting the Uptake of E-Books in Higher and Further Education. JISC, London E-Books Working Group. Available at: www.jisc.ac.uk/uploaded_documents/PromotingeBooksReportB.pdf.

Goudar, I. R. N. and Poornima, N. (2004). Emerging Pricing Models for E-Journals Consortia and Indian initiatives. In Proceedings of the International Conference on Digital Libraries (ICDL 2004). ICDL, New Delhi. Pp. 333-341.

Gray, D.E. (1976). Veterinary Information: The Current Situation and Future Trends. The Veterinary Records, 98(14): 271-274.

Harrassowitz, (n.d.) Electronic Journals: A Selected Resources Guide. Available at: http://www.harrassowitz.de/top_resources/ejresguide/providers.html.

Haneefa, M. (2007). Application of Information and Communication Technologies in Special Libraries in Kerala (India). Library Review, 56(7): 603-620.

Hargrave, J. (2013). Disruptive Technological History: Paper Making to Digital Printing. Journal of Learned Publishing, 44 (3): 221-236.

Hamad, S. and Hunter, K. (2004). Elsevier gives Authors Green Light for Open Access Self-Archiving. Available at: https://mx2.arl.org/Lists/SPARC-OAForum/Message/759.html.

Kling, R. and McKim, G. (1997). A Typology for Electronic Journals: Characterizing Scholarly Journals by their Distribution Forms. Centre for Social Informatics, SLIS Indiana University, Bloomington.

Lancaster, F.W. (1995). The Evolution of Electronic Publishing. Library Trends, 43(4): 518-527.

Landoni, M. (2003). Electronic Books. In J. Feather and P. Sturges

(Eds.): International Encyclopedia of Information and Library Science. 2nd Ed. Routledge, London. Pp. 168-171.

McKnight, C. (1993). Electronic Journals: Past, Present, and Future? Aslib Proceedings, 45: 7-10.

Moret, B. M. E. (1997). Bridging the Gap between Theory and Practice. Journal ofElectronic Publishing, 3(1). Available at:http://www.press.umich.edu/jep/03-01/JEA.html.

Neal, J. G. (1997). The Use of Electronic Scholarly Journals: Models of Analysis Drawn from the Project Muse Experience at Johns Hopkins University. Available at: http://www.arl.org/scomm/scat/neal.html.

Oliver, M. (2000). SPARC: An Alternative Lifestyle for Academic Libraries. Collection Management, 25(2): 37-49.

Osoria, N.L. (2002). Consortia and the Big Deals: A New Way of Doing Business or the End of the Technical Library. IATUL Proceedings (New Series). Vol. 12. Kanas City USA. Available at: http://www.iatul.org/doclibrary/public/Conf_Proceedings/2002/Osorio.pdf.

Pandian, M. P., Jambhekar, A. and Karisiddappa, C. R. (2002). IIM Digital Library System: Consortia-Based Approach. The Electronic Library, 20(3): 211-214.

Patil, Y.M. (2014). Consortium Approach to Resources Sharing in an E-Environment. Scientific Publishers (India), Jodhpur.

Peek, R.P. and Pomerantz, J.P. (1998). Electronic Scholarly Journal Publishing. Annual Review of Information Science and Technology, 33 : 321-356.

Prior, A. (2001). Acquiring and Accessing Serials Information: the Electronic Intermediary. Interlending & Document Supply, 29(2): 62-68.

Prosser, D. C. (2004). Scholarly Communication in the 21st Century: the Impact of New Technologies and Models. Serials, 16(2): 163-167.

Reitz, J.M. (Ed.). (2012). Databases. Available at://www.abcclio.com/ODLIS/odlis_d.aspx#database.

Rowse, M. (2003). The Consortium Site License: A Sustainable Model? Libri, 53(1): 1-10.

Sanville,T. (1999). Use Levels and New Models for Consortial Purchasing of Electronic Journals. Library Consortium Management 1(3-4): 47-58.

Sasson, R. (2009). The Benefits and Advantages of E-Books.

Available at: http://www.successconsciousness.com/ebooks_benefits.htm.

Sloan, B. (2000). Understanding Consortia Better: What Vendors Can Learn? Library Journals, 125: 57-58.

Sreekumar, M.G. and Sunitha, T. (2005). Library Capacity Building through E-Journal Consortia: the Indian Scenario. 7th MANLIBNET Annual National Convention on Digital Libraries in Knowledge Management: Opportunities for Management Libraries held at Indian Institute of Management Kozhikode during May 5-7, 2005. Available at: http://dspace.iimk.ac.in/handle/2259/493.

Tedd, L. (2005). E-Books in Academic Libraries: An International Overview. New Review of Academic Librarianship, 11(1): 57-59.

Tian, X.Y. (2008). Disadvantages of E-Books. Available at: http://EzineArticles.com/?expert=Tian_Xiang_Yu.

Tripathi, A. and Lal, J. (2016). Library Consortia: Practical Guide for Library Managers. Chandos Publishing, Amsterdam.

University of Santo Tomas. (2008). Online Databases. Available at: http://library.ust.edu.ph/pages/onlinedatabase.html.

Varatharajan,N. and Ravi, B. (2004). Relevance of UGC-INFONET in Higher Education. In N.L. Rao and T.A.V. Murthy (Eds.): Proceedings of National Seminar on Library Consortia held at 22-23 March, Hyderabad. Pp. 63-67.

Vassiliou, M. and Rowley, J. (2008). Progressing the Definition of E-Book. Library Hi Tech, 26(3): 355-368.

White, M. (2001). Electronic Access to the Scientific Journals: Problems. E. Content, 24 (10): 66-67.

Wikipedia (2019). Stakeholder. Available at: https://en.wikipedia.org/wiki/Stakeholder_(corporate).

Wilson, R. and Landoni, M. (2001). Evaluating Electronic Textbooks: A Methodology. Fifth European Conference on Research and Advanced Technology for Digital Libraries (ECDL-2011). Darmstadt, Germany.

Wise, A. (2003). Are Digital Library Resources Useful for Learners and Researchers? Serials, 16 (1): 23-26.

5

Governance, Structure and Funding of Library Consortia

Organizational structure defines how activities such as task allocation, coordination, and supervision are directed towards the achievement of organizational aims. Organizational structure affects organizational action and provides the foundation on which standard operating procedures and routines rest (Wikipedia, 2019).

Organizational structure in the library consortium includes substantial committees facilitating participation at many levels among members to take a collective decision. Explicit financial arrangements underlying the procurement of information resources to be used by member libraries and operating the activities are necessary. Besides, the annual funding arrangements have a major impact on the governance and legal structure of consortia. Further, the collection management for information resources needs to assess the performance of use studies to decide whether to maintain a subscription or not.

5.1. GOVERNANCE OF LIBRARY CONSORTIA

Governance comprises all of the processes of governing – whether undertaken by the government of a state, by a market or by a network – over a social system and whether through the laws, norms, power or language of an organized society. There is need of organizational and managerial structures to successfully govern any organization.

The organizational structure creates an environment to take a collective decision through participation of all levels, through formation of committees which provide the opportunities for managerial and operational staff of member libraries to share knowledge with others. The managerial structure includes a staffing pattern to successfully run the consortium which is to be from the managerial level to the operational level.

5.2. TECHNOLOGY INFRASTRUCTURE

A long-range planning and spurting of the appropriate information technology and communication infrastructure conducive to proper delivery of information resources is a prerequisite. Thus, the consortium should ensure the following information technology infrastructure is available with the consortium and all participating member libraries, such as (Patil, 2014):

- Access to the Internet with sufficient bandwidth and World Wide Web (WWW) including provision of work stations; and e-mail service;
- Internet Protocol (IP) ranges for access to databases and full-text journal articles;

- Networking in the local area to share resources and linking local systems;
- Access to electronic resources, either by mounting them on local server or providing access to resources on other platforms;
- Develop infrastructure for archiving for back files in case of termination of subscription and provide access to the same.
- Develop home page and portal to access all subscribed titles under the consortium by the libraries.

Besides, the library consortia should facilitate new standards and protocols which help to manage usage statistics with Project COUNTER and SUSHI to standardize the transmission of statistical data. It should also work with the National Information Standards Organization (NISO), to promote SERU - the Shared Electronic Resources Understanding, where libraries and vendors working together can eliminate the need for a signed license altogether to reduce the overhead costs of licensing (Pesch, 2015).

5.3. STANDARDS AND PROTOCOLS FOR LIBRARY CONSORTTA

Interoperability - the technology driven library consortia environment is complex in nature which hosts relevant technologies, multipurpose data sets, various applications and many other networked resources. It is desirable to hide these aspects from access so that one may effectively search for information, communicate and perform other tasks (Pandian and Karisiddappa, 2004). However, there are following main key issues affecting interoperability among distributed libraries:

- Use of different library automation systems for multifunction or routines;
- Use of different search and retrieval protocols;

- Use of different metadata formats;
- Differences in cataloguing standards; and
- Differences in subject indexing systems.

But technically, the success of library consortia solely depends upon interoperability functions and application of standards and protocols, metadata formats, cataloguing rules and subject classification schemes. Thus, the consortium requires standards/protocols on several levels:

- Metadata standards - AACR2 and Dublin Core;
- Resource Exchange Standards - MARC, CCF;
- Protocol Standards for Resource Discovery - Z39.50; and
- Standards for Inter-Library Loan - ISO 10160/ 10161.

5.4. E-METRICS FOR MEASURING ELECTRONIC RESOURCES

The terms use, usage and users have different connotations as far as publishers, librarians and users are concerned. The measure of usage quantitatively is important to librarians as they invest large amount in purchase and licensing of e-journals from various publishers. This could also be useful to research administrators, funders and anyone concerned with the evaluation of research and researchers or their institutions. It is seen in the recent years that the publishers and other organizations are in the forefront in developing codes of practice, such as COUNTER and SUSHI where IT stands for usage aspects (Singleton, 2010).

5.4.1. Counting Online Usage of Networked Electronic Resources (COUNTER)

Libraries are shifting from print to e-products in the technology driven environment- thereby usage has become crucial and even more critical. Therefore, it has become more important to measure usage across heterogeneous collections and analyze and assess how library's collection budget is judiciously spent. The project COUNTER Code of Practice facilitates measure of usage of electronic resources (www.projectcounter.org) which was launched in 2002 and which serves librarians, publishers and intermediaries by setting standards that facilitate the recording and reporting of online usage statistics in a consistent, credible and compatible way. The first COUNTER Code of Practice, covering online journals and databases was published in 2003; and later its coverage was extended beyond journal with the launch of the Code of Practice for Online Books and Reference Works in 2006.

The body of COUNTER compliant usage statistics has steadily grown as more and more publishers and vendors have adopted the COUNTER Code of Practice. It has become mandatory for content providers to provide usage data to all users including consortia and libraries and one of the clauses in licensing agreement. This has contributed to the new discipline of usage bibliometrics and a great deal of work is underway to try to establish value metrics associated with the usage, in which the COUNTER compliant statistics play an increasingly important role (www.projectcounter.org). There are numerous benefits of COUNTER compliance, which are given below:

- Librarians are able to compare usage statistics from different vendors; derive useful metrics such as cost-per-use, make better informed purchasing decisions; plan infrastructure more effectively;
- Publishers and intermediaries are able to provide data to customers in a format they want; compare the relative usage of different delivery channels; aggregate data for customers using multiple delivery channels; and learn more about genuine usage patterns.

COUNTER code is a dynamic entity which keeps changing with technological advances. Its objectives fall under three broad categories, viz.

- To improve further the reliability of the core COUNTER data and extend scope of the code of practice beyond journals, databases and books;
- To continue to increase the number of COUNTER compliant publishers, vendors, and intermediaries; and
- To work with other information industry organizations to facilitate the implementation of COUNTER and develop metrics based on the COUNTER data that of practical value to both librarians and vendors.

Release 4 of the COUNTER Code of Practice for E-Resources has been developed with the input from vendors, librarians and intermediaries. This release is single, integrated code of practice covering journals, databases, and books as well as multimedia content. It supersedes both Release 3 of the Code of Practice for Journals and Databases and Release 1 of the Code of Practice for Books and Reference Works.

The aim of its Usage Factor (UF) Project is to explore how online journal usage statistics might form the basis of a new measure of journal impact and quality. Other specific objectives of the project are:

- To examine the ways in which journal quality is currently assessed;
- To assess whether the UF would be statistically meaningful measure based on usage data;
- Whether UF would be accepted by researchers, publishers, librarians and research institutions and its impact;
- Whether it would be statistically credible and robust; and

- Whether there is an organizational and economic model for its implementation that would be acceptable to the major stakeholders.

The project is being executed in three stages, from 2007 onwards, where stage-1 focused on market research into the overall feasibility and acceptability of the Usage Factor in principle. Stage 2 focused on modeling and analysis, in which real usage data from COUNTER-compliant publishers was used to test the formula for calculation of UF, as well as the processes for doing so on a sustainable, ongoing basis; and stage 3 of the project, which is commenced in October 2011, is now underway. COUNTER has been working actively with NISO on SUSHI, with the UKSG on the feasibility of developing a possible new UF measure for journals; and with UK JISC on the development of standards for recording and reporting usage at the individual article level.

5.4.2. Standardized Usage Statistics Harvesting Initiative (SUSHI)

The libraries are demanding that publishers should provide detailed usage statistical data to allow them to better manage their collections and purchases due to growth and proliferation of online products and their acquisition in the consortium. The project COUNTER was created to meet this demand, but it does not address the issue of automatic harvesting, storage and manipulation of usage data. Thus, the concept of SUSHI was introduced, in 2005, which addresses the issue of automatic import of usage statistics that would save the time of staff and shows a great promise as a protocol that simplifies the delivery of journal usage statistics (Pesch, 2007; Pradhan et al., 2012).

The COUNTER could give data on the usage of individual journal. As such the consortia or libraries subscribe hundreds of journals from various publishers. However, collecting data and collating for comparison is a daunting task. Thus, in order to overcome this kind of managing usage data, a number of library service vendors began developing a new type of application - the usage consolidation service consisting the following:

- To import the usage reports gathered from various contents providers.
- This usage data is stored in the application's database; and organized by titles, package, publisher, etc. and supplemented with cost and other information.
- When usage data is imported for a given month, the library uses the reports interface to create consolidated usage reports.
- These consolidated usage reports help to show what journals are being used, how often and at what cost.

SUSHI was created specifically to solve the very problem of retrieving and cleansing the usage reports, which meets requirements of all stakeholders. It is a standard designed to enable automation of the harvesting COUNTER Usage Reports. The need for SUSHI is even stronger today as it was in 2007 when it became a NISO Standard (ANSI/NISO Z39.93 - 2014). SUSHI Protocol defines an automated request and response model for the harvesting of electronic resource usage data utilizing a Web services framework. It is intended to replace the time-consuming user-mediated collection of usage data reports.

The protocol was designed to be both generalized and extensible that could be used to retrieve a variety of usage reports. An extension designed specifically to work with COUNTER reports is provided with the standard because these are expected to be most frequently retrieved usage reports. SUSHI has been successfully implemented in India by UGC-INFONET Digital Library Consortium (now e-ShodhSindhu), which has helped in easy and systematic harvesting of usage statistics and subsequent analysis at

INFLIBNET Center.

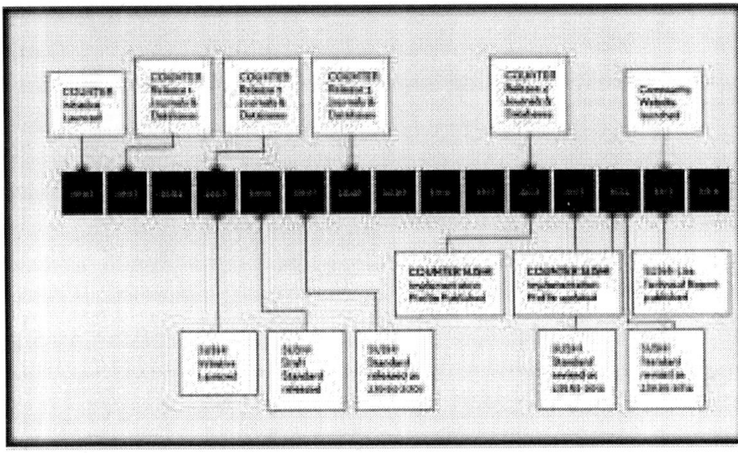

Fig. 5.1. Time Line of the Development of COUNTER and SUSHI

(*Source*: Pesch, 2015)

5.4.3. Publishers and Institutional Repository Usage Statistics-2 (PIRUS-2)

COUNTER facilitates reporting of usage for the individual journals whereas, SUSHI protocol provides the automatic consolidation of large volumes of usage data from different sources but there have been recent developments for recording, reporting and consolidation of usage statistics at the individual article level. So, in order to fulfill this task, PIRUS-2 Project was conceived and completed during June 2011, which builds on the work undertaken by the JISC-funded PIRUS project. This enables publishers, institutional repositories and other organizations to generate and share authoritative, trustworthy usage statistics for the individual articles and other items. It has the following objectives (Shepherd, 2006, 2011):

- To develop open source program to support the generation and sharing of COUNTER-compliant usage data for individual items from institutional repositories and subject repositories;

- To develop a prototype article-level publisher/ institutional repositories statistics service; and
- To define a core set of standard usage statistics reports both for external and internal usage.

PIRUS-2 has devised a draft version of an Article Reportl: Number of successful Full-Text Article Reports by Month and DOI, in MS Excel and XML formats in order to extend the COUNTER - compliant reports to the article level.

5.5. SHARED E-RESOURCE UNDERSTANDING (SERU)

The publishers and librarians have entered into their mature stage of experience in handling e-resources, where using license agreements for electronic resources has become a norm for librarians and publishers, who have shared common understanding and expectations for many licensing terms in many transactions. However, the annual license renewal process is more complicated, critical and taxes considerably on time and energy on both the parties but as a matter of fact, the process of licensing takes much of time as well costs, which is detrimental to early e-access. Therefore, both parties are looking for making standard or model licensing which is easier and acceptable keeping in view time and money and a better option for organizing the relationship between both the parties for electronic resource transactions in the form of model license (Hahn, 2007; Collins, 2007).

Shared Electronic Resource Understanding (SERU) that emerged during 2007 offers a mechanism that can be used as alternative to licensing agreement. It is a new tool available to both the parties, who are comfortable for going to a license agreement in an e-resource transaction. SERU statement expresses commonly shared understandings of the content provider; the subscribing institution and authorized users; the nature of the content use of materials; and inappropriate uses; privacy and confidentiality; online performance and service provisions; and archiving and perpetual access.

5.5.1. Aims of SERU

The major aim is to streamline and creating the licensing process a shorter process and certainly not in the process of creating another contract or license. It is very purpose is to provide a mechanism to do away with licensing. However, the other aims of SERU include the following:

- It has become an official NISO Working Group which has become a modest initiative and serves as a core document that large publishers would feel comfortable to reference in place of a license agreement.
- It could also serve as a basis around which a purchase order could be modified.
- No problem of negotiation, no investigation about whether license is required, just a simple statement, if registered with SERU, then set up the relationship between both the parties by outlining the various expectations of each and as a matter of fact, be the only document to choose to reference.

5.5.2. Shared Understanding

SERU approach addressed different areas of agreement, such as:

- Subscription;
- Subscribing institution and authorized users;
- Nature of the content;
- Privacy and confidentiality;
- Online performance and service provision; and
- Archiving and perpetual access.

NISO announces the publication of a new edition of

the recommended practice SERU: A Shared Electronic Resource Understanding in 2016 (www.niso.org/publications/rp/). Its 2012 updated version recognizes both the importance of making SERU more flexible for those who want to expand its use beyond e-journals, while acknowledging the fact that consensus for other types of e- resource transactions are not as well-established as they are for e-journals. Its 2015 version is related to Protocol for Exchanging Serial Content (PESC) and 2016 to the Outputs of the NISO Alternative Assessment Project.

5.6. INTERNATIONAL COALITION OF LIBRARY CONSORTIA (ICOLC)

International Coalition of Library Consortia (ICOLC), is a major step where various library consortia joined together to share information and to develop large scale agendas among themselves (Bostick, 2001). ICOLC first met informally as the Consortium of Consortia (COC) in 1997. The Coalition continues to be an informal, self-organized group whose active participants comprise over 230 library consortia in North and South America, Europe, Australia, Asia and Africa. ICOLC serves participating organizations by facilitating discussion among consortia on issues of common interest. It conducts meetings dedicated to keeping participating consortia informed about new electronic information resources, pricing practices of electronic information providers and vendors, and other issues of importance to directors, governing boards. During these meetings, the ICOLC meet with selected information providers, providing a forum for them to discuss their offerings and to engage in dialog with consortia leaders about issues of mutual concern.

Its membership includes consortia from all over the world. Further, its web page and an active listserv provide current information to members about membership which is free, although meetings have a registration fee etc. Thus, ICOLC endeavour is better communication between consortia, a sharing of mutual concerns and a stronger voice in policy and pricing structures, as well as enhancing the relationship between consortia and the vendors.

5.7. ORGANIZATIONAL STRUCTURE

The organizational structure of all consortia is more or less the same with differences in their nomenclature. However, the consortium should review its structures at an interval of a fixed period to ensure that they remain relevant in the changing environment. Various nomenclatures and their functions are observed in the literature for consortium organizational structure, and these are (Tripathi and Lal, 2016):

Governing Board : A board that manages the affairs of an institution. It provides leadership to all levels of organizational structure of the consortium. All member libraries are represented on the board.

Governing Body : This is a group of persons who make up a body for the purpose of administering something. This body appoints a steering committee. The chairman of the governing body has the authority to sign the license agreements.

Board of Directors : It is a body of elected or appointed members who jointly oversee the activities of an organization. A board of directors generally consists of the directors of the member libraries. Often the board of directors is on the top level of consortium management. Boards generally elect officers among themselves, and these officers comprise the governing council. They usually hire a coordinator or executive director. The board of directors sets the agenda for the consortium. This requires that the members of the board, who are usually the directors of the member libraries, be able to see more than just the needs of their individual libraries and look for the greater benefit of the entire group. Consortia tend to be governed by a board of directors. Sometimes, this board is a subset of another board, particularly if the consortium is part of a larger non-library group.

Governing Council : It is like a governing board but a smaller governing council that is elected by the full board and reporting back to them. Boards generally elect officers from among themselves, and these officers comprise the governing council.

Executive Committee : It is a senior-level management committee empowered to make and implement major organizational decisions.

Library Advisory Council : It is a body of senior librarians and non-librarians with relevant skills and an interest in libraries which advises regarding library services.

Advisory Committee : It is the body that is constituted from among the members of the library consortium and which advises the council on library matters and performance.

National Steering Committee : It is formed for a national level consortium which guides and steers the activities of the consortium. It is responsible for operational aspects of the consortium. The committee decides the e-resources to be subscribed to from various publishers and numbers and names of beneficiary universities.

Steering Committee : Steering committee is a key step in starting a cooperative venture which responsibilities include selecting and evaluating advisors to the group, determining the initial feasibility of a cooperative project, and building trust among potential members. This committee is responsible for the negotiations and running of the consortium. In many cases, members of the steering committee go on to serve as the interim board of directors also for the cooperative. However, the committee members should be representative, as much as possible, of the geographical area and demographic cross-section of the potential membership to avoid implications of favoritism. Steering committee members are expected to be responsive and articulate in answering questions from potential members and other stakeholders.

Committee of Library Director : The purpose of this committee is to promote library and information services in support of the purpose of the institution.

Coordination Council : This council makes corrections to and approves the strategic plan for the current year.

Negotiation Committee : It is constituted by the governing body of the concerned consortium as per the purchase rules of it for negotiating rates of subscription to e-resources.

Work Group : This group advises the institution on its role and priorities.

Systems Librarians Working Group : This group helps in maintaining and improving technological needs of the institution.

Document Delivery Working Group : This group helps in creating the database for providing document delivery services.

Electronic Resources, Acquisitions and Serials Working Group : This group suggests the higher authority regarding electronic resources and its acquisition.

Cataloging Working Group : This group manages the bibliographic control.

Circulation Working Group : This group manages the problems faced in circulation of documents.

Consortium Group : This group is responsible for more practical issues and consists of library directors from the library sectors.

Expert Group : This group consists of members with expertise in the various fields of science. Though the technological issues and the interests of end users are represented in the expert group, but the main task of this group is to submit proposals for resources to be licensed in the future and to develop portal services at the organizational level.

Technical Advisory Council : This council makes recommendations on appropriate technologies for smooth functioning of consortium.

International Advisory Board : This board includes publishers, intermediaries, industry organizations, libraries, consortia and others.

Advisory Board : A library advisory board is a group consisting of the library specialists, building administrators, teachers, etc. to develop a long-range plan.

Collections Committee : This committee makes recommendations on policies related to the organization, acquisition and the management of the information resources collections.

Collections Team : The collection team is responsible for the selection, management and promotion of resources.

Content Service Committee : This committee manages the content services to beneficiaries.

Inter-Library Loan Enhancement Committee : This committee proposes for convening the regional meetings for general inter-library loan training.

Special Collections Committee : This committee proposes the policy on special collections of the consortium.

Technical Issues Committee : This committee monitors and oversees the issues and procedures related to technical service activities.

National Review Committee : This committee is responsible for overall policy, monitoring, and coordination between the consortium and its funding body.

User Services Committee : This committee is

charged to investigate and develop effective and innovative programs that promote the use of library resources.

Strategic Management Team : This team is to coordinate strategic planning to make decisions to achieve the goal of organization.

Task Force : It implements the strategic plan as defined by the members and the board. This also looks for possible collaborative ways of tackling acquisition, retention, preservation, digitization and access etc.

Specific-task-oriented Team : This team focuses on specific functions to be done to elevate the rank of an institution among others.

Digital Interest Group : This group manages and implements access to and licensing of electronic resources in the member libraries.

Human Resources Group : This group helps the organizations with the human side of their requirements.

Interest Group : This group serves as a clearinghouse of sustainable community-based library projects.

Reference Interest Group : This group looks at how libraries continue to rethink; how they provide point-of-need services given changing patterns of access to and use of information.

Risk Management Group : This group offers a menu of human resources and safety and health services that control costs and improve services.

Resource Discovery Strategy Group : This group oversees the development of database of the consortium.

Resource Description and Discovery Steering Group : This group recommends changes in the rules and regulations and policies for the betterment of the organization.

Integrated Information Environment Committee : This committee looks into the policy issues related to access.

However, the members in consortia include a mix of library governance, such as publicly funded and privately funded university libraries. Thus, it is considered a good practice for a consortium board to develop a mission statement that articulates the philosophy of the group as well as a plan of action agreeable to all members. This in general will include a statement about the level of participation expectation of its members.

5.8. MANAGEMENT/STAFF STRUCTURE

It is observed that there is the need for operational resources for clear and frequent communication with the member libraries, for the coordination of the activities of members with the service provider, and for accountability to all parties with the joint provision of services. This requires the appointment of staff independent of any one-member library that designated staff more clearly identifies the costs of cooperation than the purely voluntary approach.

Staff of consortia which is set up as legal entities are generally not under the same terms and conditions as universities. This provides the consortia with a considerably more flexibility in staffing matters and also serves to reduce real staffing costs as compared with the consortia operating out of a university. It is seen that larger consortia often have staff reporting to the executive director. The staff may be as small as one part-time person. However, consortia office staff can include a number of people, some with specialization in areas, such as, the contract negotiation and member training programs. Further, some informal consortia recognize the value of having designated staff to focus on the needs of the group. Some appoint an executive director very early in their development where the responsibilities in consortia may vary but usually, they play a leadership role and work closely with the executive group. However, the description of responsibilities depends on the nature and needs of the consortium.

The designations of staff and their functions in a consortium may include (Tripathi and Lal, 2016):

Director of Governing Board : The Director of Governing Board is elected by the directors of the consortium who are the head librarians of member institutions. Directors of the consortium may meet twice in a year.

Executive Director : Executive Director is usually hired by the board of directors and is accountable to them, who manages the routine activities and coordinates the daily work. Executive director is in direct contact with all the member libraries and oversees the committee work and other activities performed by the staff of member libraries.

Assistant Director : Assistant Director oversees daily operations which encompass a wide variety of programmes and the services.

Regional Consultant : This provides consultancy services regarding library development.

Coordinator : This manages the routine activities and coordinates daily work.

Systems Librarian (Liaison) : This keeps the consortium portal up to date and offers a help desk to the members.

Systems Librarian (Implementation) : This helps in implementation advice for the consortium portal updating.

Full-time Executive Secretary : This manages the meetings of the governing board of the consortium.

Executive Secretary : This is responsible to the governing board.

Deputy Secretary : This manages the databases acquired.

Manager or Chief Executive Officer : This manages guiding the consortium in its development from a simple operation to a multifaceted operation.

Office Manager : This manages the office of the consortium.

Project Coordinator : This coordinates different projects running within the consortium.

Membership and Discount Manager : This manages the matter of membership and discounts to be received in negotiations.

Website Manager : This manages the website of the consortium.

Site Coordinator : This coordinates the website of the consortium members.

Operations and Grants Manager : This manages the operations and grants of the consortium.

Database Officer : This manages the databases acquired.

Administrative Assistant : This assists in managing the administration of the library consortium.

Program Staffs : This creates the program for the database of the consortium.

Support Staff : This supports the other staff of the consortium.

Volunteers : The volunteers work in the consortium on a volunteer basis for managing operations of the consortium.

Student Trainees : They may help the other staff of the consortium.

Newsletter Editor : This manages the publication of the organization's newsletter.

5.9. FINANCIAL MANAGEMENT IN LIBRARY CONSORTIA

Consortia vary greatly in terms of their funding

arrangements- some operate without any funding at all while others receive some grant funding. However, the majority have some sort of annual fee paid by the members which is generally on a sliding scale according to the size of a library's budget, sometimes offset by the library's loans in the reciprocal borrowing and inter-library loan agreements and/or size of collection.

Some consortia also include a base fee that allows for some equalization of costs between small and large institutions on the premise that the basic consortium activities benefit all members similarly. In some cases, this base fee is small and does not provide a major portion of total revenue. Generally, the annual fee levied covers staffing and the costs of the basic functions performed by the consortium and used by all members. Smaller and informal consortia often have no funding arrangement or agree to a very small contribution.

However, there is also a need for capital funding where, joint provision of services is involved in addition to annual funding. The funding of a consortium is based on multichannel financing consisting of fees from libraries, funds from the ministries and government, and grants from various organizations. Various funding sources for a consortium may be the:

- Parent organization
- Funding agency
- Government funding
- Membership fee
- Special membership levy
- Service fees
- Grants from a trust, and
- Financial assistances like, special grants from sponsoring institution or another member institution

All funds are transferred via the accounts of the consortium and are controlled by the consortium. Much of the money is spent on subscriptions. Subscription costs are covered partly by third-party funds and partly by membership fees. But the subsidy share varies from one resource to another and may also depend on the organization itself.

Kumbar (2004) has suggested a model funding formula for library consortia. In this formula, library members of a consortium decide upon annual target goals to fund their anticipated needs. Then an assessment is developed based upon these target goals, with each participating member assessing their cost share according to the following formula:

- Member Share = 25 percent of the target divided by the number of participating libraries
- Site Share = 25percent of the target divided by the number of sites of participating library
- Port Share = 50percent of the target divided by the number of active ports of participating library
- A library pays the member share × 1, the site share × 1 or more (for a branch or branches), and the port share × the number of ports it is using on the system.

Here, the participation means any library or group of libraries accessing the automated system for whatever purpose but the measure of participation is not the level of activity, number of functions accessed, or services utilized rather, rather it is the number of ports used by that library or group of libraries.

5.10. INFORMATION RESOURCES MANAGEMENT

The purchasing of a library product was simple by following a routine such as sending the order, paying the bill, receiving the item, cataloguing and marking it, and placing it on the shelf. There were no licenses, no passwords or "IP address" validation, no differential pricing options, no host platform decisions and no complex equipment compatibility issues. One person could often perform all the analysis required to make a subject selection decision. Now, due to the evolution of electronic products and all the above-mentioned points, it is necessary to handle purchases very carefully.

Arora (2011) has listed the following keys which are essential for considerations for consortia-based subscriptions for electronic resources:

- Lowest subscription rates for all consortium members.
- Archival backup or perpetual access to e-resources.
- Annual increase in the rates of subscription.
- Terms of license agreement.
- Provision of a single interface for access to the titles included in consortium.
- Research into the use of new technologies such as digital object identifiers, open URLs etc.

Further, the collection management for journals needs to assess the performance of use studies to decide whether or not to maintain a subscription. The publishers also package information into usable and buyable units (titles, series, and journals), market the product, and undertake or subcontract the physical production and distribution (Ball, 2004). Anyhow, the information resources in a consortium are managed by the following procedures.

5.10.1. Selection of Information Resources

The information supply chain includes creation, publication, aggregation, access, and use of e-journals. It is seen that major players are primary publishers, aggregators, consolidators, vendors, subscription agents, document delivery agencies, and e-printing systems. The supply chain from author to reader is characterized by two principal types of players: the publishers and the libraries. Each of the links adds, value to the information to a greater, or lesser degree, until it is used and the value is realized. Each link in the chain also has a greater or lesser degree of monopoly, which is particularly important for the information marketplace.

Librarians have to review multiple access options for online products, considering possible buying partners for services, and increasingly using more accountable differential pricing models. In addition, these new online products make it possible to customize and unbundle portions of product packages based upon local user profiles. This complex evaluation and selection process significantly change the roles of the selector and the subscription/purchasing agent.

The selection processes of e-journals revolve around the user needs, while the role of e-journals in university library collections raises many issues, meeting user needs remains the primary focus. Thus, as the increasing cost of subscribing to both print journals and their electronic equivalents leads to a movement toward electronic formats, the collection development decisions should be made against careful evaluation of user needs. Evaluating user needs involves usage statistics against which the provision of a service as a whole can be evaluated (Ashcroft and Mclvor, 2001).

However, the selection is a matter of experience, judgment and knowledge of subject although such a careful selection process is taken away from the librarian in the acquisition of many e-journal bundles. The selection process of information sources in UGC-Infonet Digital Library Consortium (now E-ShodhSindhu) of India was based on the print collection base available in university libraries. In addition, the requirements were accessed with a survey with an aim to identify and determine e-resources to be subscribed to. In order to understand the collection base in universities, meetings of librarians were held in different parts of the country and their views and feedback were obtained. Based on the feedback received from librarians, e-resources of various publishers were identified and evaluated before negotiating licensing arrangements. Keeping in view the diversity of academic programs offered by various universities, every attempt was made to subscribe to e-resources which are multidisciplinary in nature with wide scope and coverage.

Thus, the electronic resources to be selected for consortia-based subscription must be based on the following major criteria:

- On the basis of the usage/suitability of e-resources to universities;
- On the basis of the resources that are very important but highly cost intensive which should be preferred over those that are less important or less used but low cost;
- On the basis of the resources from scholarly societies, university presses, and not-for-profit projects should be preferred over commercial publishers;
- On the basis of the well-established multidisciplinary resources with broad coverage that should be preferred over highly specialized sources targeted for specialists;
- On the basis of the electronic resources which are already on subscription in the beneficiary universities, they should be preferred over those that are not being used in any of them;
- On the basis of the resources which are electronic-only that should be preferred over those that are print-based;
- On the basis of the resources where electronic versions are made available free on subscription to their print versions, they should be avoided as much as possible.

5.10.2. Procurement of Information Resources

Once the electronic resources proposed for

subscription are identified, proposals are invited from the publishers of e-resources/their authorized representatives for formal negotiations on their products, prices, and services. The competent authority; for example, Negotiation Committee in case of E-ShodhSindhu negotiates the lowest rates of subscription and favorable terms of agreement with the publishers/their authorized representatives as per the purchase rules of the particular consortium.

There are two types of patterns adopted in procuring information resources in consortia: purchase model (one-time payment); and subscription models (recurring mode of payment). Besides, there are three kinds of subscriptions (Shoba, 2011):

Standard Subscriptions : Subscription to as many journals in either electronic-only form or combined with a paper subscription.

Single-site License : If there are a large number of holdings from a particular publisher, for example, Kluwer, the institution may negotiate a single-user site license.

Multisite/Consortia Site License : Consortia may negotiate a license for all its member institutions.

However, library consortia can be powerful entities, particularly when they take a holistic view uniting procurement of both print and electronic resources. Thus, we can take control over suppliers, the publishers, by observing the standard procurement cycle, such as (Ball, 2004):

- Identify the need
- Prepare the specification
- Find the supplier
- Award the contract, and
- Measure and monitor suppliers' performance

This cycle, particularly through the specification and by monitoring performance against that specification, puts the purchaser firmly in control. Such control is easier too to achieve where there is competition between suppliers (for example, booksellers or serials agents) and not a monopoly as with publishers (Fenner, 2006). However, there must be one point of access to heterogeneous information coming from different sources with facilities for cross-searching journals from different publishers. This goal can be achieved by relying on solutions from one particular aggregator, by creating consortium solutions, or by implementing local solutions with the advantage of integrating journal information with other relevant local sources.

5.10.3. Selection of Suitable Pricing Model

The selection of consortia pricing model is quite complex in nature and the context in which pricing takes place. The pricing models could be considered in relation to sound library budgets, changes in the scholarly communication market, impact of technological changes, patron expectations. There are no standards developed for charging electronic products and content providers use many different pricing mechanisms which vary with the contexts. There is also no universally accepted pricing model available in the market (Gerhard, 2005). Only consortia approach could provide some alternative solutions which are to be accepted by all stake holdersas e-products are beyond the reach for individual libraries. Hence, the publishers are requested to quote best prices and invited for consortia negotiations, which should be economically viable for all participants (Sreekumar and Sunitha, 2005).

However, the pricing and business models depend on developing number of standards such as DOIs - to create metadata, economic and cultural issue of archiving. Some, new business models require predictable licensing environment. It is expected that novel forms of doing business will emerge based on the following factors (Cox, 2000):

- Advance payment for access at the article level;
- Subject wise package pricing;
- Payment with document delivery or pay-by-the-drink model;
- The database subscription model which provides access to a core collection including back volumes for a year - at the end of which continued access requires renewal of subscription;
- Micro-pricing in which a payment will become due every time an item of information is accessed, which could be a diagram, table or paragraph from an article.

There is seen a little change in business deals with consortia approach for big deals due to shift from print to electronic version. The business model also shifts accordingly in order to fit into new model keeping in view digital content licensing. Although 'big deal' did do a lot to overcome the serials crisis in the short term, but it could not fix the budget crisis. Further, the continued budget cuts forced re-evaluation of all practicing business models as major part of budget is spent on 'big deals' there will be libraries to think to unbundle and part with some of their 'big deals'.

Although, pricing models have been continuously evolving keeping in view technological changes but there have been no changes in libraries fiscal financial constraints. Librarians were compelled in dropping journals packages, and started using more pay-per-yiews (PpV) to deliver content and exposing more open access (OA) content to users. Article-level journal usage is now feasible and is used extensively thereby selectively going for subscribing heavily used titles. Usage metrics may help in increased use of PpV business models where libraries purchase articles on a need only basis.

5.11. OPEN ACCESS MOVEMENT

Open Access (OA) Movement has matured into a viable and alternate publishing channel, it may not put publishers out of business. Libraries use OA as a viable option for addressing growth in scholarly communications (Bosch, Henderson and Klusendorf, 2011). There are variety of pricing options offered, but it appears that the main lesson, at least from a publisher's point of view, is that customers appreciate the flexibility of picking and choosing articles (Berin, 2002).

Anyhow, the following are the concerns of publishers, scholars and libraries which are of great importance (Gerhard, 2005):

5.11.1. Publishers Concerns

These may comprise of the following :

- Pricing models are offered by publishers and how it effects on the sales and revenue generation and how to create a sustainable level of profit is a prime concern of publishers;
- Publishers who participate as fair-dealing partners in the scholarly communication system;
- What makes a fair reasonable deal, based on value for cost and usage within the context of library budgets;
- Inflation of e-journals is a prime concern for deciding a particular pricing models;

However, due to many variables involved fixing prices, it is difficult to ascertain whether an offer given is rational and fair.

5.11.2. Scholars Concerns

These may comprise of the following:

- Researchers do not publish papers for profit. They have wide range of communication channels for publishing for example, self-publishing, posting to an institutional repository or posting to a subject-based open access e-journals besides traditional communication channel for publications with the process of peer-review, etc.;

- The publishers pricing models are more on users centric, wherein as they rely more on financing from the individual or institutions supporting research work to be published. Such funding is essentially for wider dissemination of knowledge.

5.11.3. Libraries Concerns

It is a prime concern to get possible terms for users. However, the librarians closely look into this in order to meet institutional targets and priorities.

- How does one access to information?
- What makes reasonable pricing?
- What are those factors which distinguish a bad, fair, and a good deal?
- What are those parameters which make evaluating pricing structures?

Above points must be kept in view while going for subscribing to e-resources for a library consortium.

5.12. TYPES OF PRICING MODELS

There exist different pricing models for the procurement of information resources from various publishers depending on the customers. The offers from publishers are different for individual and institutional customers. Besides, the pricing models of commercial publishers are different from the society's publishers. But generally, the pricing models are based on the cost of the print publications (holdings) and the number of serials offered in electronic format. The consortia agreements of electronic journals are based on establishing a base price for the set of serials to which the member libraries will have access. The base price in principle is established fairly easily from the sum of the costs of the print collections subscribed to individually by the libraries participating in the agreement. However, the establishment of the base price is not always easy because one cannot always precisely establish what print collections are being subscribed to. Besides, the pricing also depends upon the total number of users in the member universities/institutes of the consortium, the number of participating institutions, and the number of campuses of the institutions of the consortium.

Use-based pricing is another option, where the advent of electronic distribution has allowed tracking of article use, making it possible to determine costs based upon actual use data because the tracking every use is not always difficult. Further, the new charging mechanisms need to be developed for these new selections and delivery options. The standard subscription approaches will no longer work when users build dynamic aggregations from materials across a variety of resources and services.

Tripathi and Lal (2016) has listed a number of pricing models in the contest of pricing:

Traditional Subscription or Site Licensing : Remote users can access a journal by using a site license. IP addresses of remote computers are recognized by the journal server. Most libraries prefer this model.

Priority Charges : Some publishers allow immediate online access to current issues for a fee, with older content available. However, there may be a delay in access for new issues that ranges from a few months to years.

Pay-Per-View (PPV) : The concept of PPV focuses more on individual papers than on a journal as a collection of papers. Users can choose only relevant content and pay for it.

These models are attractive for countries where the cost of airfreight is very high and print editions take a long time to arrive. But they can limit access to e-journals from off-campus even for readers with Internet access. Institutions in developing countries that may lack infrastructure and have slow or limited Internet connectivity face even greater problems. In addition to the subscription model, a number of methods exist to determine appropriate charges for specific organizations. Entirely new methods may also be developed to accommodate the new differential pricing and unbundled materials options. However, a detailed discussion on various models has already been made in chapter 3.

5.13. ADAPTATION OF BENEFICIAL LICENSING MODEL

It is tempting to think that a consortium might buy an electronic information item, mount it on a computer accessible to all, thereby saving the cost of buying numerous sets. Obviously, commercial publishers are conscious of the potential loss of revenue implied by an arrangement of this type. Thus, licensing arrangements have been developed that prevent this loss although consortia still benefit by mounting just one set of data for common use rather than several (Davies, 2001).

But the licensing model which is beneficial to the needs of a specific consortium of a specific country must be selected for signing the license agreement. Therefore, best license model is to be signed for library consortia purchase.

SUMMARY

This chapter provides detailed information on the governance, organization structure and financial management of the library consortium. It may be seen that organizational structure in a library consortium includes substantial committees facilitating participation at many levels among members to take a collective decision. Further, these committees provide the opportunities for managerial and operational staff of member libraries to share knowledge with others. However, the managerial structure includes the staffing pattern from the managerial level to the operational level.

Further, the funding of consortia is based on multichannel financing consisting of fees from libraries, funds from the ministries and government grants from various organizations. But all funds are to be transferred via the accounts of the consortium and are controlled by the consortium. The collection management for journals also needs to assess performance-of-use studies to decide whether to maintain a subscription or not. Once information resources and membership are finalized, the competent authority of the consortium places the order for subscription of information resources to the concerned publishers as per the purchase rules of the organization and licenses are signed for access of e-resources through the library consortium.

BIBLIOGRAPHICAL REFERENCES

ANSI/NISO Z39.93. (2014). ANSI/NISO Z39.93-2014 - the Standardized Usage Statistics. Available at: https://www.niso.org/publications/z3993-2014-sushi.

Arora, J. (2011). Managing Electronic Resources through Library Consortia: Examples from INDEST- AICTE Consortium. Available at: http://www.isical.ac.in.

Ashcroft, L. and Mclvor, S. (2001). Electronic Journals: Managing and Educating for Changing Culture in Academic Libraries. Online Information Review, 25(6): 378-388.

Ball, D. (2004). What's the Big Deal, and Why is it a Bad Deal for Universities? Interlending & Document Supply, 32(2): 117-125.

Berin, A. (2002). Unbundled Journals: Trying to Predict the Future. Learned Publishing, 15: 109-112.

Bosch, S., Henderson, K. and Klusendorf, H.(2011). Under Pressure, Times are Changing: Periodicals Price Survey-2011. Library Journal, 36 (8): 30-34.

Bostick, S, L. (2001). The History and Development of Academic Library Consortia in the United States: An Overview. The

Journal of Academic Librarianship, 27(2): 128-130.

Collins, M. (2007). SERU: An Alternative to Licensing-An Interview with Selden Durgom Lamoureux. Serials Review, 33: 122-128.

Cox, J. (2000). Developing Model Licenses for Electronic Resources: Cooperation in a Competitive World. Library Consortium Management, 2(1): 8-17.

Davies, B. (2001). Consortial Purchasing: A Feasibility Study for the UK Veterinary and Animal Health Field. Library Management, 22(8-9): 371-380.

Fenner, A. (Ed.). (2006). Integrating Print and Digital Resources in Library Collections. The Haworth Information Press,New York.

Gerhard, K. H. (2005). Pricing Models for Electronic Journals and Other Electronic Academic Materials: the State of the Art. Journal of Library Administration, 42(3-4), 1-25.

Hahn, K. L. (2005). Tiered Pricing Implications for Library Collections. Portal: Libraries and the Academy, 5(2): 51-163.

Kumbar, M. F. (2004). Consortia for Management of College Libraries in the E-Publishing Era: A Proposal. In Proceedings of the, 6th MANLIBNET National Convention, Janakpuri, NewDelhi. Available at: http://eprints.rclis.Org/archive/00003978/.

Pandian, M. P. and Karisiddappa, C. R. (2004). Emerging Role of Z39.50 for Library Consortia in India. CALIBER-2004 Paper. Available at: http://shodhganga.inflibnet.ac.in/dxml/bitstream/handle/1944/351/04cali_ 43.pdf?sequence=l.

Patil, Y.M. (2014). Consortium Approach to Resource Sharing in an E-Environment. Scientific Publishers, Jodhpur.

Pesch, O. (2015). A Brief History of COUNTER and SUSHI: The Evolution of Interdependent Standards. Information Standards Quarterly, 27(2-3): 5-11.

Pradhan, D.R., Rai, A.K. and Arora, J. (2012). Implications of SUSHI for Analysis of Usage Statistics of E-Resources: A Case Study of UGC-INFONET Digital Library Consortium. Annals of Library and Information Studies, 59: 187-193.

Shepherd, P T. (2006). COUNTER: Usage Statistics for Performance Measurement. Performance Measurement and Metrics, 7 (3): 142-152.

Shepherd, P T. (2011). PIRUS2: Individual Article Usage Statistics–

Developing a Practical, Global Standard. Learned Publishing, 24 (4): 279-286.

Shoba, J. (2011). E-Journals: Subscription Models and Access Modes. Available at: http://www. ncsi.lisc.ernet.in.

Singleton, A. (2010). Why Usage is Useless. Learned Publishing, 23 (3): 179-184.

Sreekumar, M. G. and Sunitha, T. (2005). Library Capacity Building through E-Journal Consortia: the Indian scenario. Available at: http://dspace.iimk.ac.in/bitstream/2259/249/1/09-mgs-sunitha-paper+new.pdf.

Tripathi, A. and Lal, J. (2016). Library Consortia: Practical Guide for Library Managers. Chandos Publishing, Amsterdam.

Wikipedia (2019). Organizational Structure. Available at: https://en.wikipedia.org/wiki/Organizational_structure.

6

Negotiations and Licensing

Negotiation is a dialogue intended to resolve disputes, to produce an agreement upon courses of action, to bargain for individual or collective advantage, or to shape outcomes to satisfy various interests. It is the primary method of alternative dispute resolution. There are many different ways to segment negotiation for a greater understanding of the essential parts of the license agreement. One view of negotiation involves three basic elements: process, behaviour and substance. Here, the *process* refers to the way in which the parties negotiate covering the context of the negotiations, the parties to the negotiations, the tactics used by the parties, and the sequence and stages in which all of these play out. *Behaviour* refers to the relationships among these parties, the communication between them, and the styles they adopt; and the *substance* refers to the agenda, the issues of interest, the options, and the agreements reached in the end by the negotiating parties (Jespersen, 2011).

There is another view of negotiation which comprises

four elements: strategy, process, tools, and tactics. *Strategy* comprises the top-level goals typically including relationship and the final outcome. The *process* and *tools* include the steps to be followed and the roles taken in both preparing for and negotiating with the other parties; and the *tactics* include more detailed statements and actions and responses to the statements and actions of others. Some also add *persuasion* and *influence* to this view, asserting that these have become integral to modern-day negotiation success, and so should not be omitted (Wikipedia, 2019).

Thus, negotiation is all about making, compromises between two parties with one on buying side and the other on selling side. It can be seen as a single event or it may be held in certain intervals till deal is materialized. It is done aggressively in a year though it may have impact on future years. Sustainable negotiation has the aim of reaching a mutually acceptable agreement. However, a good negotiation requires good communication skills.

6.1. WHY NEGOTIATION REQUIRED?

There are some obvious and compelling reasons as to why we should go for negotiations for an online subscription, such as:

- The terms in proposals may not match the needs of consortia;
- The buyer and seller need to maintain good relationship;
- The proposed cost may be prohibitive and other budgetary constraints;
- The consortia have to make decisions about whether to keep a particular subscription or to see the availability of comparative product elsewhere;
- The current prices are certainly different from past few years;

- The users' responses to particular product and comments thereon; and
- The product may be 'nice to have' and not essential.

However, it is rewarding and measurable in terms of reducing cost, yet the publisher gains some revenue and have more customers, where, previously the cost or terms had been a barrier to subscription.

6.1.1. Objectives of Negotiations

There is a consortia committee which has to negotiate with the publishers keeping in view fulfillment of set objectives, to derive maximum value and highest rate of return with investment made. Some of the contract objectives for negotiations are given below which should be based:

- On the total value of budget kept for the purpose;
- On the participants' requirements across publishers;
- On the broad definition of the term 'user';
- On the content and usage;
- On the wide usage rules;
- On the pricing based on volume;
- On the right contract terms;
- On the flexibility of usage and cancellation policies without financial liabilities; and
- On the proper support level from all levels in the consortium context.

Besides, developing own pricing model to negotiate with publisher's proposed pricing model may be the last but an important objective.

6.1.2. Process of Negotiation

Typically, in most cases, these types of deal are struck directly between the consortium and publisher. Senior librarians talking to key perspectives stated that they were somewhat surprised that subscription agents have not played a greater role in this process, particularly as the negotiation of consortial licenses is often a complex and protracted undertaking which impacts on the operational resources of both publishers and libraries.

However, it has not been unusual for negotiations to last for 1-2 years. The creation of a customized license for each new deal can slow things down, while securing the agreement of all consortium members can be time-consuming. Deals also may stick on certain clauses—most commonly those relating to inflationary increases over future years, or to archiving and back-file access. But the "process is greatly expedited by the adoption of model licenses which, according to key perspectives, are fast becoming the norms. It is partly due to the challenges presented by this process that consortial negotiation has tended to favour the medium and large publisher to date" (Rowse, 2003). Not only are the larger publishers able to offer the whole-list deals that provide rapidly increasing collections for libraries crucially, they also have the resources to dedicate to this intricate and time-consuming sales process.

Nevertheless, the negotiation process could be achieved during any phase of subscription period and service could start from calendar year but it is preferable to start negotiation with concentration on set objectives and contentious issues. Successful negotiations satisfy the interests of both the parties keeping in view the main concerns of contractual issues. But as a matter of fact, the negotiation across a table brings about win-win situation to both parties.

6.2. COMMUNICATION SKILLS

Negotiation requires soft skills like objection handling, assertive, presentation, credibility and good communication skills between consortia and publishers or the intermediaries. The communication channels available are: telephone, face to face meetings, e-mails, video-conferencing, letters or faxes. However, it is preferable to have face to face negotiation followed by other channels where small matters are to be discussed.

6.2.1. Consortium Negotiation

The consortium has a collective strength to negotiate and power in purchases of number of e-products. The publishers are also benefitted with offers at one point of contact thereby saving time, and money. A representative or the representatives from the consortium and from publisher's side, a representative or intermediary may attend the meetings for negotiation committee meeting.

6.2.2. Publisher and their Products

It is well known fact that the libraries know who are publishers/agents/intermediaries, their reputation and reliability, functionality and content of their products as well as their pricing models and customer relationship. But if not they should be aware of this fact. Also, it should be known what users are looking from a particular publisher's e-products.

6.2.3. Relationship between Publisher and Purchaser

Consortia negotiation committee members are required to deal with the dual functions in their dealings: to create/achieve favourable conditions during negotiations; and to maintain a good liaison and working relationship with the publisher or intermediaries. There has to be good working relationship between consortia coordinators and the publishers ensuring satisfactory and fruitful negotiation in order to achieve a win-win situation for both the parties.

6.2.4. Assertiveness

If both parties are passive during the meeting, then it is presumed that there exists no good communication and someone has to initiate the matter for discussion. If this is the case, then both parties will walk away with a feeling of dissatisfaction or distrust. On the other hand, if both parties are aggressive, then negotiation is unlikely to continue or collapse. If both parties come to a point of assertiveness, it will involve putting respective cases in a manner required where to give ground for open discussion, compromising on some issue and ultimately achieving something with the positive results.

6.2.5. Negotiating the Price

The publishers submit proposals keeping in view all the consortium requirements and the Negotiation Committee has to examine the proposal keeping in view number of consortia participants, whether it can afford prices quoted and also need to judge the sustainability of the pricing structure keeping in view the capping of expected future increase in prices. Negotiation is not only for getting reduced fair price, but it also looks critically into all contentious issues. It is also essential to be considered about publisher's situation so that good offers do come from publishers.

6.2.6. Language of Negotiation

Negotiation requires language skill and good communication in drafting the contract terms and conditions. A draft should be clear, brief, concise and to the context and without any ambiguity. It is more important to put across reason first and not the solution or demands. The good language skill comes into picture when negotiation is stalling but needs effective communication to get continue and finalize the deal.

6.2.7. Dealing with Emotions

Emotion is a human instinct which could reflect in the form of anger, frustrations or surprise and pleasure. In an ideal condition, strong emotions will over-ride logic and assertiveness, wherein both are required. Even, if emotions are strong during negotiations, it could be brought down with tact so as to get along with negotiation.

If, emotions and outburst override in a meeting on an issue, it is better to take off some time out or reconvene the meeting at a later date.

6.2.8. E-Mail Communication

Email is an important means of faster communication between parties discussing some issues which need not come across face to face meetings. This channel has to follow certain etiquettes: to read e-mail properly before sending reply which should be prompt; addressing e-mail - to whom to send; subject line to be clearly defined and not to be left blank. Besides, it should keep off using important, urgent, private tags; and be very concise but not curt; answer all questions without any room for ambiguity. Be confident about attaching any unnecessary files, if attaching file, consider the format - .doc, .pdf, .tiff; do not spell out an entire word in capitals; and use good language with proper grammar, punctuation and spelling. Further, structure the mail properly and sign off. If out of office - auto reply could be included, if required.

6.3. DETERMINING WHETHER IT IS THE BEST DEAL

E-mail communication either at the beginning of the deal or after negotiation committee meetings plays an important role either in initiating for the meeting or concluding meetings deliberations relating to smaller issues. However, one could be able to come to know whether best deal is brought from the replies.

6.4. MEETINGS

There may be several meetings to finalize a consortium negotiation. Here, some points are worth noting during meetings: schedule of meeting; venue of meeting; agenda drawn for meeting; introductions; test assumptions; make suggestions — coming up with ideas/ options; listen and take notes, proposals - counter proposals; reach an agreement and draw a conclusion by observing body language - eye contact, facial expression, style statements and the business objectives etc.

It is better on either side if all concerned departments in an organization are kept abreast of ensuing Negotiation Committee meeting like administration, legal and financial departments. The following could add the meaning to negotiations - where making people feel getting involved in the process and justifying subscription.

- Area of negotiation other than price;
- What if they refuse to negotiate?
- Common reasons for not wishing to negotiate.

Further, the consortium has to decide to carry out any addition or deletion in a particular stage of the negotiation process, which will depend on number of factors (Patil, 2014):

- **Contract Length :** Contract length is usually for a year but it may vary in time from 2 to 5 years.
- **Cancellation Terms :** Cancellation depends as per terms/conditions specified in contract about when the subscriber has to notify to the publisher if they wish to cancel, write a letter requesting to cancel.

However, some new initiatives are now seeking to redress this imbalance and to help the smaller and society publishers to participate. UK Association of Learned and Professional Society Publishers (ALPSP), is considering the development of a multi-publisher consortium that would help to bring clusters of smaller, society-publishers' journal lists to market. PCG, the Publishers Communication Group, a subsidiary of Ingenta, has recently launched *Consortia Link,* a service that similarly makes it possible for small and medium sized publishers to participate in consortia negotiations via multi-publisher packages and centralized professional sales negotiation.

6.5. AIDS FOR NEGOTIATION

Negotiation is a complex process in the consortia

environment which leads to mutually acceptable terms and conditions. But good negotiation keeps the consortium sustainable. As such, few dedicated professionals are involved in implementation of agreed terms and conditions. Some other specialists or experts may be called upon to provide technical, financial and legal advice in support of consortia implementation programmes.

If a model license is adapted, it saves lot of time, money and energy on both sides. It is beneficial to develop a common set of terms and principles that would be agreeable to both parties in an effort to move licensing agreement forward. As such, adaption of model license in hand signals content providers that consortia staff and participants are knowledgeable about legal and licensing issues and group willing to enter into serious negotiations to obtain what we view to be acceptable terms. Patil (2014) has given a list of what to do before, during and after negotiation process for a consortium:

6.5.1. Before Beginning Negotiation

There should be:

- Awareness of particular content keeping in view users' needs;
- Noting down all points needed for discussion in the meeting.

6.5.2. Be Prepared with Mindset

One should be prepared about:

- Institutional strategies and goals and what exactly we are looking for negotiation;
- Expectations from content owner?
- Mindset that negotiation is not an *"I-win-you-loose";*
- Relevant alternate options kept ready beside core points for negotiations;
- Clear in the perception about what we want and what we need; and

- Data in hand as to how much we are spending to license materials.

6.5.3. Plan Ahead for Negotiation

It may include the following points:

- Plan schedule of negotiation — decide when, where, who and how;
- Must know fully about publishers with their background information, financial status and where their interest lies; and
- Make sure that negotiation is done with concerned party, i.e., publishers, vendors or intermediaries.

However, it is better to succeed in the process to do negotiation direct with the publishers instead of intermediaries who may not be able to come out with terms required during the process.

6.5.4. During the Process of Negotiation

The following points need to be considered well during the process of negotiations:

- It is important to listen attentively as to what is being discussed and take note of crucial points;
- Open ended questions should be asked in order to get the other person to talk;
- Do not take things for granted and get cleared if any point is not replied clearly;
- Be assertive - not aggressive;
- Communicate clearly, precisely and to the point; and
- No compromise on the values and beliefs during negotiation.

6.5.5. Keep on Tracks

The following points must be kept in view:

- Take notes of all details which will help as reference point during license agreement approval;

- Check with pre-prepared notes while preparing for negotiations;
- Ensure that goals and needs are not diluted while negotiating; and
- Keep open mind and be honest while negotiating.

6.5.6. Buying and Managing Information

Consortium coordinating team as a whole is responsible for managing and purchase of e-resources keeping in view participants' requirements vis-a-vis the availability of information with different publishers. Thus, negotiators must know:

- Budget availability and information requirements of all participants;
- Currently available publishers' pricing models for their various products;
- Modalities for License Agreements; and
- Assessing whether getting the right value for consortium spending.

6.6. NEGOTIATING TOOLS - CONSORTIA CAN USE

It is simply good business practice to obtain the best agreement possible for all sides involved. Some salient, matter-of-fact points that consortia and libraries could utilize when negotiating an agreement, are listed below (McKee, 2014):

6.6.1. Though, the sale or publisher representative may start to inquire from the first day of meeting but it is important to understand that consortia have greater bargaining power nearer the end of the publisher's fiscal year. If the sales representative or company/publisher itself has 'had a rather lackluster selling year', they may feel more inclined to deal more aggressively. These circumstances could also aid the consortium in re-opening negotiations for a wanted brat never purchased product.

6.6.2. Ensure from the outset the main consortium

negotiator knows exactly who is the decision maker on the publisher's/content provider's side for approving packages and discounts. If it is known, at the beginning that the sales representative does not have authority to make discount approval, insist that the person who does have that authority be present at all negotiation meetings. This effectively eliminates the down time that can occur when, a sales representative must go back to his/her employer and consult about discounts.

6.6.3. It is also very helpful to ascertain, immediately who on the publisher's/content provider's side has final authority for approving licensing terms. This person may request to sit in on all license negotiation meetings as this also eliminates down time. Another option to request is that the commercial entity reads any and all documents the consortium has produced stating their required and preferred licensing language. Ideally, this information would be located in an easy-to-find tile on the consortium's web page. These can help to considerably shorten the negotiations on licensing.

6.6.4. Negotiate for agreements that do not carry a required "benchmark." These require many staff hours in contact time between the consortium and its members. Negotiate instead on discounts that increase as more members join in.

6.5.5. A negotiating point is that some alliances may try to now place in new agreements for the publisher/content provider to provide one free print copy for each title in the agreement. These can then be placed in an archive for use by all consortium members. If the publisher or content provider balks at this request, try to obtain a very deep discount for the paper copies.

6.6.6. Negotiate permission to extend the offer(s) to libraries outside your membership depending on your consortium's guidelines. A good bargaining tool is to demonstrate to the content provider the possible increased penetration of his/her material to a wider audience. These agreements also provide great public relations marketing tor the consortia.

Lastly, a small but important negotiation point is trying to arrange for the content provider to be the responsible party for mailing out the final licenses to all participants. It is a greatly-appreciated timesaver for the volunteer or paid consortial staff member that also saves the consortium mailing costs.

6.7. CONSORTIA APPROACH TO NEGOTIATIONS

The deals may cover various aspects covering structure of organization, objectives, participants' core requirements and budgetary provisions. The following could be to be right approach for negotiation:

- Prioritize the time with schedule with set objectives, future needs and critical nature of the issues to be addressed keeping in view that it may materialize at one sitting or may take longer period. However, prolonging on the issues, may lose credibility on either side.
- Gather information on prior usage/budget spent, supplier data, ongoing usage data, users' perception, which are critical to the process to keep fully prepared for negotiation;
- Set objectives into keeping in view what to "have to have" and which are "nice to have";
- Seek the advice on legal and contractual matters from legal experts in the organization; and
- What each party wants to achieve, try to know them.

Once the negotiation process reaches 'win-win' situation set schedules for tasks, responsibility and dates to implement if negotiation is successful. Then, sign the contract and later is the time for total implementation to access to information and rest of the related issues.

6.8. POINTS TO REMEMBER

The way of conducting the negotiations may be different depending upon the situation and time. Further, the skills of negotiation depend and differ widely from one situation to another. Basically, the types of negotiation can be divided into three broad categories, which may include: managerial/ day to day negotiations, commercial negotiations and legal negotiations (Shah and Shah, 2011). They are briefly described in table 6.1.

Table 6.1. Types of Negotiations

Types	*Parties Involved*	*Examples*
Managerial / Day to Day Negotiations	1. Different parties of management 2. In between colleagues	1. Negotiations for pay, terms and working conditions. 2. Description of the job and fixations of responsibility.
	3. Trade Unions	3. Increasing productivity.
	4. Legal advisors	
Commercial Negotiations	1. Management	1. Striking a contract with the customer.
	2. Suppliers	2. Negotiations for the price and quality of goods to be purchased.
	3. Government	3. Negotiations with financial institutions as regarding the availability of capital.
	4. Customers	
	5. Trade unions	
	6. Legal advisors	
	7. Public	
Legal Negotiations	1. Government	1. Adhering of the laws of the local and national government.
	2. Management	
	3. Customers	

However, the major points to be covered in negotiation are as follows (E-Shodhsindhu, 2019):

Coverage : It includes the total number of journals/ records covered in resources/databases.

Journals Offered : It includes the total number of journals offered in the proposal.

Subscription Rates : It means the lowest rates of subscription for all consortium members as compared to its list price. But they must be in decreasing order with increase in number of subscribers/members.

Cancellation of Subscription : Subscriptions must be cancelled if there is no proper balance between quality, relevance, use and the price.

Back Files : It means the extent of coverage of back files with current subscription.

Archival Access Provision : It is to provide perpetual/CDs/print/other media plus one additional year on each renewal of subscription each year.

Open Access Policy : It means the policy regarding permission of self-archiving of articles by authors through institutional repositories.

Trial Access : There should be the availability of trial access for new members.

Besides, there may an annual increase in rates of subscription in subsequent years, so provision of such effect must be there. The rates for associate members may also be quoted, if acceptable. Further, resource sharing/inter-library loan provision in using soft copy/ print copy and provision of inclusion of associate members must be there.

6.9. LICENSING

The licensing is concerned with the agreement between the originator and the user with certain terms and conditions applicable to both the parties. It requires being strictly adhered to at the time of implementation. Licensing stipulates viable terms and conditions vividly which needs to be thoroughly outlined in writing. The provider and the beneficiary are expected to have a soft study of the terms and conditions before agreeing in principle which can be materialized by putting signature. So, a set of rules and regulations are required to govern license which needs to be accepted in principle by both the provider and acceptor. However, any contravention to the terms and conditions by both or any of the party must be put on to the court of law. The resources may be of any kind that includes, goods, learning resources, publications etc. which allow the subscriber through licensing to use the products and for that, an agreement established through writing mode between them is followed strictly by both the parties. Licensing especially in library connotes to the use of intellectual materials produced by the publisher or vendor who is licensed by a group of publishers to market their products and the library who uses the resources acts as a consumer. Though, the consumers may differ from library to library, but the library being the social institution is meant to impart service without any profit as the basic principles of the library is that, it is non-profitable.

Therefore, the library being a service institution use the resources created by the publisher and provides the same to the users. The library, thus, acts a facilitator of resources. However, the publisher may directly supply the intellectual resources to the library or supply the same through any established organization under terms and conditions. Library as an individual member also can go for subscription directly from the publisher when the resources are not available through any other mode and are essential for the users. Especially, the library in such a situation goes for subscribing to the electronic resources where, the provider allows access directly from their site by giving the user name and password. In this perspectives, the library as a body goes for making an agreement with the publisher through internet so as to impart service to a multiple number of users and the publisher after agreeing in principles as would be stipulated by the library allows to use the resources by giving link to access the same including downloading on internet.

However, the library pays the charge to access the resources which seem to be high for an individual member. Therefore, the library acquires the e-resources through any established organization designated as a body that is responsible to acquire the e-resources on behalf of the member libraries. In this perspective, the designated body require a group of libraries to be the member of such organization so that, collectively the resources can be acquired by the body to disseminate the common resources to the individual library through the networking effectively. In this situation, the individual library has to go for licensing agreement with the provider of such resources which will be used strictly by the users of the library. Thus, licensing stipulates strict regulations and it is a legal document for the library to use the resources.

6.10. WHAT IS A LICENSE?

A 'license' is a physical or virtual document between two or more parties that allows digital content owned by one party (the licensor) for a fixed period of time, usually one or more subscription period. It highlights the conditions of use of digital content as well as specific price and time period of the agreement. It is a permission given by publisher to engage in an activity that would otherwise be unlawful, without the presence of license.

While, the 'licensing' is an act performed by the licensor (the publisher), giving that permission to the licensee (the consortium or the library). A licensor does not give ownership of copyright of the content rather it only allows using the content according to a set of agreed terms and conditions in the form of license.

According to Patil (2014), the licenses can be negotiable or non-negotiable but both the parties agree upon to a set of terms and conditions for content use in the process of negotiation. A *Non-Negotiable License* is one where one party sets forth the terms and conditions of the agreement and other party have to accept these in order to use the content. While, *Negotiating Licensing Agreements* include settlements from both parties on the terms and conditions of the agreement and then license in finalized.

However, copyright and licensing are two important components for the use of resources in library consortia. A library in the print environment, purchases a document to which users have potentially unlimited access and owns document forever. Copyright prohibits indiscriminate use of document for commercial purpose and thus, protects ownership. Copyright does not allow reproduction, electronic storage or otherwise rather one must get permission from content owner for any means of reproduction for commercial use.

But, a library in the digital environment, is to buy access to the electronic copy for a specific period of time and use under carton, set terms and conditions, where the access is provided only through a license which is mostly regulated by contract law. However, the degree of access to and use permitted for an electronic journal depends solely on the terms and conditions negotiated in the license for that specific product. When a publisher who is copyright holder sends a proposal for license agreement, it is an open invitation to negotiate terms and conditions under which the product may be used. The basic aspect of the copyright is ownership and owner has right to say 'No' for any reproduction by any means. So, a license is an agreement under which the copyright owner says 'Yes' to certain defined uses in return for payment and those licensed uses override the exceptions provided in (Cox, 2000).

6.11. LICENSE AGREEMENTS

A license agreement is the meeting of minds or evidence of mutual accord or understanding between two or more legally competent parties about their relative duties and rights regarding current or future performance. Although a binding contract can (and often does) result from an agreement, yet an agreement typically documents the give-and-take of a negotiated settlement and a contract specifies the minimum acceptable standard of performance (Business Dictionary, 2010).

A license grants permission to do something that, without such permission, is illegal. A license for e-content is a contract that presents the terms under which a vendor, publisher, or distributor grants access to a library or sells e-content to a library. A contract is a formal and legally binding written agreement between two or more parties (Johnson, 2013). He further adds that license for e-content is a matter of contract law which takes priority over the copyright law. Once a license is signed, fair use and other rights granted under copyright law are superseded by the terms of the contract.

Thus, license agreements are a fact of life in conducting business in the electronic environment. The providers of electronic information resources are employing licenses as a legal means of controlling the use of their products. In the electronic environment, where the traditional print practice of ownership through purchase is being replaced by access through license, libraries need to be aware that licensing arrangements may restrict their legal rights and those of their users. The librarians as responsible agents for an institution, must negotiate licenses that address the institution's needs and recognize its obligations to the licensor.

However, the legal environment is complex because of constantly changing technologies, new business models, and new offerings from the vendors, publishers, or distributors. Libraries are challenged to make the best deal possible when negotiating e-resources' licenses. It is an agreement between the publisher and the user wherein the publisher transfers the nonexclusive and nontransferable right to use materials to the user or licensee. All electronic resources are governed by license agreements. License lists the terms and conditions for using the resources. But in the electronic world we do not buy and own a physical product; rather we buy generally a time-limited license that confers certain rights of access to the content. Such licenses do not necessarily offer archival rights, implying that our users do not have continuing rights of access to material beyond the term of the license. However, the content to which we buy rights may change. The titles, imprints, and companies may be bought, sold, and transferred but there is no guarantee of continuing access to content. Further, licenses may restrict access to content to a particular class of users and our freedom to determine who may have access to our resources has been forfeited (Ball, 2004).

Thus, it is in the interest of both the libraries and publishers to reach a fair and useful compromise. A useful and user-oriented agreement requires that publishers use open standards and provide access to their files in such a way that a seamless integration within the local and national infrastructure is possible. Though, the publishers use licensing as a legal method for controlling the use of their products and services but it is important to ensure that all issues concerning consortia licensing, of e-content that go into publishers/vendors' licensing agreements are reviewed and understood thoroughly by the consortia negotiation committee and the agreement signing authorities.

6.12. LICENSING MODELS

Various licensing models exist for library consortia purchasing. Some of them are elaborated as under (Tripathi and Lal, 2016):

6.12.1. Nationwide Academic Site Licensing Model

These are site licensing arrangements that involve a great number of libraries across a country and are not confined by geographic proximity. It often involves government and large-scale collaboration and also has the potential to solve many problems in the complex licensing world.

6.12.2. Cooperative Purchasing (Co-Purchasing) Model

Here, two or more libraries agree that everyone will have certain areas of "primary collection responsibility" and that they will exchange such materials with one another free of charge.

6.12.3. Institutional/Organizational Site License sold to Libraries/Corporations

The subscription rate varies according to type of institution in this model.

6.12.4. Individual/Member Subscriptions

License agreement in this model is done for an individual member and not for the whole consortium.

6.12.5. Access Modes Authentication via User ID/ Password and IP Address or Authentication via IP Address

The use of resources under license is done either by ID/password or by IP address in this model.

6.12.6. Multiyear Agreements with Fixed Annual Price Cap

License agreement is done for multiyear basis with fixed annual installment in this model.

6.12.7. Pilot Site License Model

This model makes academic journals cheaper and more accessible for academics and students.

Some other models may include the following

6.12.8. Title by-Title Subscription Model

Most of the libraries subscribe the journals especially in print form. The only concession library uses to get through this model is for special issues or package. In such case, a special discount price is being offered by the publisher for those libraries which subscribes few journals in package.

6.12.9. Print Plus Model

Print plus model operates in the situation where the publisher along with the print version also brings out the electronic version of the documents. In such cases, the pricing of the electronic journal product is expressed as an "add-on" to the price of the print product or the price quoted is linked to a "no-print cancellation" clause in the contract.

6.12.10. Electronic Plus Model

Electronic journals are supplied as the base price and the price for print copies are added to that base price. ICOLC argues for keeping the purchase of the print copies as optional, the best price for the electronic content is not more than 80 percent of the price for the electronic-plus-print, and the combined electronic and print price is hot higher than current print-only prices.

Besides, national electronic site license initiative model is there which retains the benefits of a single national negotiation and access to a wide range of journals but reduces the overall cost by adopting an "opt-in" model. Individual universities could decide to buy or not to buy the deals negotiated nationally according to their local needs. But the license is updated every year to reflect changing academic needs.

However, different models may also be seen in chapter 3.

6.13. MAJOR POINTS IN LICENSE AGREEMENT

The following points are important from the viewpoint of consortium members to be included in the licensing agreement (Jhonson, 2012; E-ShodhSindhu, 2019). Thus, agreement should:

- Provide choice of cost-effective model.
- State clearly about the access rights being acquired by the licensee whether the access rights are for permanent use of the content or rights only for a defined period of time.
- Recognize and not restrict the rights of the licensee or its user community permitted under copyright law. The licensee should make the terms of the critical uses to its particular users including printing, downloading, and copying clear to the licensor.
- Recognize the intellectual property rights of both the licensee and the licensor.
- Not hold the licensee liable for unauthorized uses of the licensed resource by its users, as long as the licensee has implemented reasonable and appropriate methods to notify its user community of use restrictions. Licensee should be willing to undertake reasonable and appropriate methods to enforce the terms of access to a licensed resource.
- Fairly recognize those access enforcement obligations which the licensee is able to implement without unreasonable burden. Enforcement must not violate the privacy and confidentiality of authorized users.
- Responsible for establishing policies that create an environment in which authorized users make appropriate use of licensed resources and for carrying out due process when it appears that a use may violate the agreement.
- Require the licensor to give notice to a licensee of

any suspected or alleged license violations that come to the attention of the licensor and allow a reasonable time for the licensee to investigate and take corrective action.

- Not require the use of an authentication system that is a barrier to access by authorized users.
- Allow the licensee to copy data for the purposes of preservation and/or the creation of a usable archival copy when permanent use of a resource has been licensed. If a license agreement does not permit the licensee to make a usable preservation copy, a license agreement should specify who has permanent archival responsibility for the resource and under what, conditions the licensee may access or refer users to the archival copy. It should provide guarantees on the permanent storage and archiving of the information and the conditions for access in perpetuity.
- Consider fixed at the time the license is signed by both parties. If the terms are subject to change (for example, scope of coverage or method of access), the agreement should require the licensor or licensee to notify the other party in a timely and reasonable fashion of any such changes before they are implemented, and permit either party to terminate the agreement if the changes are not acceptable. A license agreement should also include flexibility to remove the duplicate titles.
- Require the licensor to defend, indemnify, and hold the licensee harmless from any action based on a claim that use of the resource in accordance with the license violates any patent, copyright, trademark, or trade secret of any third party.
- Include freedom to choose the members of a consortium and the provision of access to the electronic information by nonregistered users on-site.

- Include availability of different access mechanisms for the members of a same consortium and the provision for seamless linking between bibliographic data acquired from intermediaries and the full-text from different publishers in order to provide integrated access to heterogeneous information.
- Provide the use of the electronic files to generate electronic copies for electronic document delivery to other university libraries.
- Provide the provision for separation of electronic data and the applications because several publishers desperately want to provide access to their material only in their preferred manner or form.
- Not require the licensee to adhere to unspecified terms in a separate agreement between the licensor and a third party unless the terms are fully reiterated in the current license or fully disclosed and agreed to by the licensee.

Besides, the routine collection of use data by either party to a license agreement should be predicated upon disclosure of such collection activities to the other party and must respect laws and institutional policies regarding confidentiality and privacy.

6.14. RESTRICTIONS IN THE LICENSE AGREEMENT

License agreements include clauses for licensee regarding what to do and what not to do. What to do clauses are referred to as permitted, including (E-ShodhSindhu, 2019):

- Viewing, downloading, copying, printing, and saving a copy of search results;
- Viewing, downloading, copying, printing, and saving individual articles;
- Using e-resources for scholarly, educational, or scientific research, teaching, private study, and clinical purposes;

- Sending a copy of an article to another authorized user, i.e. the current faculty, students, or staff; and
- Posting the URL to the publisher's version of the article on a class website, i.e. the publisher links will allow only authorized users access.

What not to do clauses are referred to as not permit. Most of the license agreements entered into by the consortium and publishers specify items that users are prohibited to do. Some of them are as follows (E-Shodhsindhu, 2019):

- Use of robots or intelligent agents to do systematic or programmatic downloading, retention, printing of entire journal issues or volumes, and large portions of other e-resources is prohibited. For example, a user cannot download an entire issue of a journal or print out several copies of the same article.
- Electronic distribution of content is also restricted although the specific restrictions vary from publisher to publisher. It may be permissible to forward an article to another colleague in the same institution by e-mail; however, transmitting an article to someone outside of the institution, or to a large group of recipients, a mailing list, or an electronic bulletin board, is not allowed.
- Faculty in a university can print out a copy of an article from an electronic journal and include it in their course pack. However, multiple copies should not be made for circulation. Copyright laws protect published material in any format so that it cannot be copied except in accordance with fair use. However, access to material for educational purposes falls within the realm of fair use.
- Subscribed e-resources should be used for educational and research purposes and not for commercial purposes.

- Providing electronic links to the licensed resources on the course Web pages is permitted but it is not permissible to post a PDF or otherwise an article on a website. However, a researcher can post a preprint of an article that they have written.
- A researcher can use phrases or quotes from other articles and cite the source of information. as with any kind of scholarly communication. However, a researcher is prohibited from using large chunks of information (paragraphs and chapters) from an article or from a chapter in a book.

If these restrictions regarding uses are violated, the publisher may track the usage, inform the institution and seek action, and suspend access to all of its resources for the entire institution.

6.15. TYPES OF CONSORTIA LICENSING DEALS

Consortia licenses are agreed for 3-5-year periods or as agreed between consortia and publishers depending upon the context. However, consortia license deals may be divided into two basic types of package (Patil, 2014).

6.15.1. In the first type, 'Big Deal' model was initiated by Elsevier and Academic Press and offered later by many publishers consists of bundled package to a consortium of libraries on a one price, one-size-fits-all basis. The pricing is essentially based on historical subscriptions, and a publisher may supply a whole list for a price of the sum of the original print subscriptions of a library consortium, with an electronic premium added generally in the range between 5 percent and 15percent. However, members of the consortium gain considerable access to expanded pool of content for relatively little more cost.

But Big Deal is the most debated, and discussed themes in the literature about consortia and purchase of electronic resources. However, Frazier (2001) mentions that "Do not buy the 'Big Deal' and stated that, 'the push to build an all-electronics collection cannot be undertaken at the risk" of:

- Weakening that collection with journals we neither need nor want;
- Increasing our dependence on publishers who have already shown their determination to monopolize the information marketplace.

It is binding on libraries that big deal contract does not allow to cancel active individual subscriptions, and is a main obstacle in the library collection development policy. Libraries are the strongest marketing place for publishers who clinch a deal for sale of unwanted titles and bundles. However, there are following three main issues with big deal:

Enhanced Royalty : the indispensability of the big packages offered allows publishers and aggregators to add, cancel and modify the contents of the package without contacting this with libraries.

Disintermediation : largest commercial publishers have chances to control terms and conditions of the information market;

Changing the Rules : the academic reward system is changing, where libraries have to support the change by investing in new emerging systems of scholarly communication.

Thus, there have been several studies to find new pricing models (Anglada and Cornelias, 2002). It is believed that in the short term the 'big deal' may have been positive for large and small libraries and for large publishers but in the long term, it is necessary to find alternative purchasing models to guarantee better deals overcoming short comings of big deal but it is also important for libraries to have the scaling benefits (Friend, 2003).

6.15.2. In the second type, member libraries get access to journals on a publisher's list that other members of the consortium are already subscribing to. While in not a 'whole list' deal, the individual member library's holdings are increased to total the sum of all other members' subscriptions to that publisher's content. Again, consortia pricing in this arrangement tends to be based on the sum of existing subscriptions, plus an electronic access premium.

Broadly, there are two types of license (Fowler, 2005), such as:

End User Agreement : This is the most common type of license where a piece of software could be utilized by licensee. For end users, a given piece of software could be installed on a particular machine in a library or it could alternatively be installed oh multiple workstations in the library as long as a maximum number of users (single, two or more) have not been exceeded beyond set terms and conditions of usage. 'Shrink-wrap' licenses, which are licenses that came into force when a piece of software is opened, are usually grouped within this category;

Site Licenses Agreement : Site license agreements are taken by consortium wide access to an electronic resource, via IP - range access so that logins will be completely transparent to the end users. It differs from publishers to publishers and may require negotiations between the vendor and licensee. The license usually set a negotiated price based on size of the consortium in return for specific services from the vendor, viz. campus-wide access to their product, which may include usage statistics linking additional features and other terms and conditions.

6.16. STRATEGY OF CONSORTIA LICENSING

Today's, the libraries have to change their strategy and implement a number of changes in order meet the current crisis because no additional funding is available and at the same time take advantage of the new opportunities offered by scientific publishing and consortia licensing. So, the library in cooperation with other libraries must develops and implements a strategy consisting of a combination of the following features:

- Reducing the paper work and adapt to the situation of handling the information electronically and change the mind setup to acquire the electronic mode of information.
- Preparing an adjustment among the in-source technical staff not only in carrying out varied functions of the library in electronic mode but also create an environment of minimum paper works.
- Imparting training in skill development among the library staffs to work in the new environment.

Besides, taking initiatives by the management authorities in consortia building with the other libraries in the region thereby, needs opening a scope of the library for recognition in national and international level.

6.17. ADVANTAGES OF CONSORTIA LICENSING

Licensed based consortia have a multiple advantage for the member libraries. Some of the advantages can be highlighted as follows (Komrelli, 2003).

- Licensed based consortia act as a single-window service with multiple electronic resources for a large number of universities / institutions with their diverse research and academic interest;
- Consortia with its collective strength of participating institution libraries attracts highly discounted rates of subscription with most favourable terms of agreement for a wider range of e-resources.
- Consortia allow the users instant access to a wide dimension of e-resources both current and archived without any incremental costs; and also improves the existing library services and reduces the subscription cost of library resources;
- Consortia trigger remarkable increase in sharing of both print and electronic resources amongst

participating library through various programmes;

- Consortia does not have any binding to enroll the regular universities or the educational institutions but also allows the private universities and other institutions to join in the programme with same discount rate of subscription;
- Subscribed resources are accessible online in electronic format; thus, the beneficiary institutions have less pressure on space requirement for storing and managing print-based library resources.
- License allows access to all types of users provided it is defined clearly in the agreement regardless of the location of the licensee;

Besides, license provides easy user-friendly interface to download, print the e-resources. Further, the research productivity of beneficiary institutions may also be expected to improve with the increased access to international databases and full-text resources.

6.18. DISADVANTAGES OF CONSORTIA LICENSING

There are also associated some disadvantages with the consortia licensing. Thus, the library after being agreed to access the consortia-based e-resources encounters multiple problems, such as: libraries have to depend upon the technician or the computer professionals for rescue in networking failure:

- When the publisher from his side does not provide link to the databases, the librarian feels helpless. Only option left out for the librarian is to send the request through e-mail to provide links. Further, the publisher at any point of time may discontinue providing the links;
- Sometimes, the publishers discontinue publishing a journal that may be both print and electronic form. In such case, before expiry of the period of license for a particular e- journal, the publisher may request

the librarian either to stop access and or may request the librarian to access some new journals that may be irrelevant to the users which may to create chaos in the library and affects teaching and research.

- Lack of permanent structure makes it difficult for a consortium to establish a long- term relationship with the third party.
- Unavailability of user-friendly interface creates problems in accessing the e-resources, which is required to be provided by the publisher;
- License needs to be clearly mentioned about the provision of the extension of new technology adopted by the publisher and access to the same requires being provided to the beneficiaries i.e, the licensee failing which, the users get stacked in accessing and downloading the information.
- Content stability both in single and in aggregated resources are not guaranteed; thus, libraries may face various problems such as: the customer needs notification in case of some changes.
- The library also confronts problems when the privacy is not protected and duly respected and is intervened by the intermediaries or the information provider. The problems faced by the library are also due to the non-receipt of the usage (as opposed to user) data from the networked information provider as per the agreement.

Besides, the bandwidth problems may also lead to in-accessibility of e-resources. When the license does not cover the provision for affordable, perpetual access to the licensed information by some suitable and workable means, the library come across with other problems.

6.19. FACTORS MOTIVATING CONSORTIA LICENSING AGREEMENT

Today most electronic information is transmitted

through the Web and not in a tangible medium. It is delivered via remote access and there is no object to own. Therefore, publishers prefer to license rights of use. Publishers and vendors are willing/eager to lease large, costly e-resources to library consortia under a single negotiated agreement. Further, the technology revolution has increased expectations of users and they want rapid access independent of location and time. Now, there are available numerous brand-new electronic materials as well as electronic versions of traditional print materials. Thus, there are hundreds of databases to license and negotiating with multiple institutions at once which can save the time and money of publishers and information providers.

However, the licenses for electronic resources impose two types of restrictions on its usage, namely (i) who can use these resources and (2) how the resources can be used. The first restriction defines authorized users for e-resources, which generally includes students, faculty, staff, and onsite visitors of a subscribing institution. While, the second restriction deals with how these resources can be used (Ramaiah, 2013). It is the responsibility of individual users to ensure that e-resources are used for personal, educational, and research purposes only.

SUMMARY

This chapter discusses about the negotiations for purchasing e-resources. Further, various pricing models of information sources, factors influencing pricing models, license agreements for the consortia are dealt in details. However, it is clear that some models are appropriate for some disciplines but not for others. It is not yet sure how these new models will impact the economics of the entire journal system, reader information seeking patterns, and the ultimate consequences of reading on research, teaching and other purposes.

Thus, depending upon the situation and time, the method of conducting the negotiations differs. However, the skills of negotiations depend and differ widely from one situation to another. Further, the publishers use licensing as a legal method for controlling the use of their products and services. So, it is important to ensure that all issues concerning consortia licensing of e-content that go into publishers/vendors' licensing agreements are reviewed and understood thoroughly by the consortium negotiation committee and the authorities that sign the agreement.

BIBLIOGRAPHICAL REFERENCES

Anglada, L. and Comellas, N. (2002). What's Fair? Pricing Models in the Electronic Era. Library Management, 23 (4-5): 227-233.

Ball, D. (2004). What's the Big Deal, and Why Is It a Bad Deal for Universities? Interlending & Document Supply, 32(2): 117-125.

Business Dictionary (2010). Licnese Aggrement. Available at: http://www.businessdictionary.com/definition/licensing-agreement.html.

Cox, J. (2000). Developing Model Licenses for Electronic Resources: Cooperation in a Competitive World. Library Consortium Management, 2(1): 8-17.

E-Shodhsindhu, (2019). Available at: ess.inflibnet.ac.in.

Fowler, D.C. (2005). Licensing: An Historical Perspective. Journal of Library Administration, 42 (3-4): 177-197.

Frazier, K. (2001). The Librarian's Dilemma: Contemplating the Costs of the "Big Deal". D. Lib Magazine, 7 (3). Available at: http://www.dlib.org/dlib/march01/frazier/03frazier.html.

Friend, F.J. (2003). New Intermediaries or the Old Intermediation in a New Guise. Serials, 14 (1): 41-45.

Jespersen, C.B. (2011). Intermediation of Insurance and Financial Services in European VAT. Wolters Cluwer, the Netherlands.

Johnson, P. (2013). Developing and Managing Electronic Collections: the Essentials. American Library Association, Chicago (USA).

Komrelli, P. (2003). E-Resources in UGC-INFOENT Digital Library Consortium: A Profile. International Journal of Digital Library Services, 4 (3): 263-275.

McKee, A.E. (2014). Consortial Licensing Issues: One Consortium's Viewpoint. In K. Rupp-Serrano (Ed.): Licensing in Libraries: Practical and Ethical Aspects. Routledge, New York (USA). Pp. 129-142.

Patil, Y.M. (2014). Consortium Approach to Resource Sharing in an E-Environment. Scientific Publishers, Jodhpur.

Ramaiah, C.K. (2013). Electronic Resources Management in Libraries. Allied Publishers Private Limited, New Delhi.

Rowse, M. (2003). The Consortium Site License: Is It A Sustainable Model? Health Information and Libraries Journal, 20: 104-107.

Shah, K. and Shah. P.J. (2011). Negotiating Skills. Available at: http://www.laynetworks.com/TYPES-OF-NEGOTIATION-IN-ORGANIZATIONS.html.

Tripathi, A. and Lal, J. (2016). Library Consortia: Practical Guide for Library Managers. Chandos Publishing, Amsterdam.

Wikipedia (2019). Negotiation. Available at: https://en.wikipedia.org/wiki/Negotiation.

7

Management Issues and Challenges

It is a fact that information sources are much expensive and the budgets of libraries are limited. Thus, the libraries are finding it difficult to develop good collections and opting new other ways, among which library consortium is one of them. However, the library consortium activity is a complex process that involves the wholehearted support and concerted efforts of the librarians, their management, and the publishers. They form an important trio in the new scholarly information environment. But there are innumerable issues like zeroing in and identifying the resources, uninterrupted online access, perpetual access to back issues, pricing, licensing, subscription payment, copyright and archival solutions, etc. related to consortia. Besides, the planning and implementing the right kind of information technology infrastructure is yet another pressing issue.

However, resource identification, stability of contents, vendor communication and embargo periods, quality concerns and publisher concerns etc. are some important points to be considered for management of library consortia. Each of them from 7.1 to 7.8 (based on Brooks and Dorst, 2002) are discussed below:

7.1. INCREASING EXPECTATIONS AND STATIC BUDGETS

Though library consortia render electronic information services to the patron, they may expect their libraries to maintain traditional print collections in addition to new e-resources until their electronic resources are fully stable. The libraries may not be able to meet user expectations with stable budgets, and no additional funding. Here, library consortia must use information communication technologies effectively to facilitate increased information delivery and to make electronic information more generally, readily and flexibly accessible than its print counterpart.

7.2. RESOURCE IDENTIFICATION

Resource identification refers to the unambiguous reporting of various resources such as organisms, tools, and reagents which are to be reported within publications with enough information so that reviewers and subsequent researchers can identify the exact strain or reagent used. It is more or less a difficult proposition to identify the most suitable product that is agreed upon by all the members of the consortium. This is mostly due to the fact that each and every member will have his or her own wish list of information products and services, though the overlap between the products will be on the higher side in the case of an ideal homogeneous group.

7.3. STABILITY OF CONTENTS

It is observed that every librarian cites stability of content as an important quality for a full-text database. 'Stability of content' refers to the ability of a full-text database to maintain existing titles and it is a main factor for renewals. But the unfortunate fact is that some databases have lost hundreds of full-text journals as a result of publishers deciding not to renew licenses with database vendors. A common reason for this database content turmoil is the database vendor's inaccurate representation of full-text resources as they correlate to equivalent print and e-journal formats.

One of the biggest concerns librarians have with database aggregators is that the content that is available today may not be available next week. However, the IDAL (Illinois Digital Academic Library) provided databases are remarkably stable in this area, with consistency of journal availability and as members of the IDAL group, the quality and stability of the full-text titles included. Other, the database vendors like EBSCO are offering a major advantage if they can continue to offer stability of full-text content. But in lot of cases, this full-text aggregator has not informed the titles that have been discontinued, and libraries are forced to constantly monitor the discontinued journals in their databases. Thus, the stability of content is a real concern.

7.4. VENDOR COMMUNICATION

It is noticed that although information may not be readily apparent on database coverage lists, it is those titles which have been halted unnaturally in databases (at the publisher's request) that are causes of concern and should be examined. Thus, the lack of communication by vendors continues to pose problems for academic librarians. As turmoil (full-text titles halted or removed completely by publishers) appears with greater frequency in many full-text databases, libraries find it increasingly more difficult to maintain complete collections.

However, the database used prior to IDAL was excellent until a few years ago—possibly related to a company merger, and consequent service deterioration. IDA: preselected subheadings for subject headings facilitate searching when students approach a very broad topic; therefore, it is a good database. But it happens in most of the cases.

7.5. EMBARGO PERIODS

Embargo period that is the length of time for which an author has to wait to make material open by their publishers is another problem. It is noted that many full-text journals in aggregated databases have embargo periods. This means that the publisher requires the aggregator to delay the release of full-text for a particular journal for a specific period of time. Though, the length of embargo periods varies by publisher and by publication, but tends to range from three months to a full year. Embargoed sources in databases tend to be the highest quality, most expensive journals available in full-text databases.

EBSCO, the full-text database vendor selected by IDAL, chooses to display this information as a component on the coverage lists of academic databases, as it is very important to subscribing libraries. Thus, when institutions select databases, and manage collections, all vital information pertaining to these full-text databases is available to them, including coverage dates (both full-text and indexing and abstracts), ISSN, Publisher, Peer-Reviewed status, etc. but it does not necessarily mean that the publisher has not levied an embargo just because a journal is not listed (by some vendors) as having an embargo period. For example, the journal 'Science' is found in many full-text databases with a mandatory one-year embargo. However, most aggregators do not provide this information on their title lists.

7.6. PRICING ISSUES

The price of e-publications depends on the production cost and profit, but the rising price of some journals puts them beyond the reach of libraries. The result has been cancellations; hence, decreasing access to information. Basing prices may aggravate geographical and also institutional disparities and may widen the digital divide. Further, the maintenance is a major cost associated with the e-journals. Open-access journals incur these costs without support from subscriptions but it is difficult to estimate future costs for maintenance because of the speed at which technology changes.

Consortia are advantageous to libraries since they supposedly provide greater bargaining power and e-resources are offered at lower prices. However, they are more likely to be helpful to publishers in maximizing their revenues through bundling, site licensing, and consortium pricing. The low marginal costs of providing digital information make it possible to distribute that information widely. Scholarly publishers such as Elsevier and Springer are consolidating and bundling their electronic journals into single packages, with no chance for purchasing access to a subset. One can expect prices of e-journals to be settled by negotiations, which is manageable with the consolidation of publishers as well as libraries through consortia. Nevertheless, the market power of publishers may be counterbalanced by the rise of library consortia.

However, there are no standard practices or processes being followed by a majority of the publishers of scholarly literature and hence this is a gray area all together. Some publishers complicate pricing of e-resources by linking the cost of the electronic information directly to the cost of the print version. In most cases, costs of the journals are out of reach for many of the libraries and only a consortia approach could provide some meaningful and practical solutions to these issues. Thus, publishers are invited for negotiations and asked to offer their best prices to the consortia. Several methods of pricing are followed. However, what is important is that finally the price offered by the publisher should be economically viable for the participating libraries. Besides, the publishers should also ensure uninterrupted and perpetual access to the resources.

7.7. PUBLISHER CONCERNS

It has always been EBSCO's position that full-text databases should be viewed as a complement not a replacement to the core print and electronic journal collections in academic libraries. However, they have halted or embargoed their content in these databases as publishers have experienced cancellations of current (print or online) journal subscriptions due to the inclusion of their content in other companies' aggregated databases. It is also expressed that the issue caught the attention when enough librarians said they had cancelled print subscriptions because the journal appeared in an aggregated database. This causes enough to re-evaluate the inclusion of some press journals in these products and their reservations are echoed by a growing number of publishers.

7.8. QUALITY OF CONTENTS

The quality of the contents is another concern; therefore, the libraries have to only focus on full-text peer-reviewed journals. The more peer- reviewed content included in full text databases, the better it may be. However, the flip side to peer-reviewed journals is the contrasting inclusion of inappropriate titles in full-text databases. It means assuming that "academic" databases contain only scholarly materials may be a premature conclusion because many times, some database vendors include hundreds of inappropriate full-text titles such as: *Radio Control Car Action* and *Humpty Dumpty's Magazine* in their "academic" database.

It is seen although the general consensus is that peer-reviewed content is of utmost importance, but it is interesting to note preferences and needs of individual libraries. Thus, many times, a mix of both trade magazines and scholarly business journals is preferred in the libraries.

7.9. LINKING AND SEARCHING

Now a day, users like a seamless, integrated, transparent network that allows searchers to link quickly and painlessly to any document they seek. Users want easy access to full-text, and content providers are also continually breaking new ground in their attempts to give users what they want.

Mouw (cited in Brooks and Dorst, 2002) echoed their sentiment, offering, "linking is very high on our list of importance. One of, if not the greatest value of aggregated databases is their ability to provide links to full-text from licensed databases". Links are valuable facilitators in working with licensed databases such as *CINAHL, PsycINFO* and *Sociological Abstracts.* They can also tremendously enhance research by seamlessly interacting with a library's OPAC's or e-journal collections. As full-text periodical databases are often looked upon as a primary reference tool in academic libraries, it makes sense for these databases to also act as the catalyst or "hub" for linking. It is seen that the aggregators are providing more and more linking capabilities. EBSCO offers a myriad of linking capabilities dubbed EBSCO *SmartLinks,* which have played a large role in increasing the value of the (nearly thirty) licensed databases offered through *EBSCOhost.*

However, an interesting point of contention was raised when distinguishing between a librarian's perception of a full-text search service and a student researcher's view of the same resource. Kassel (2001) points out that it goes without saying that professional searchers think differently from the patrons, clients, or the end users whom they serve. Keyword searching is better than subject, or vice versa as this relates to searching? But it is noted that subject searching may need to be brought more to the forefront as most of the users choose broad topics for papers. Subject heading searches facilitate gathering and sorting of relevant information.

Again, better access to subject searching in the interface may, in fact, be more of a librarian's issue than a student preference because in the age of the Internet generation, students are most certainly keyword searchers. Thus, this debate hinges primarily on preference.

Further, the expectations and attitudes have changed for both librarians and users. A variety of viewpoints has been depicted for the need for proper instruction, regardless of the resource utilized. However, instruction must have several aspects, including critical examination of the accuracy and reliability of content, search strategies for Boolean logic and relevance ranking systems, and the ability to deal effectively with a variety of interfaces and systems. But a large database is needed that may cover specific areas in great detail. This way, users can use one search engine and one step to access this vital information.

This idea of an enormous database covering all subjects in tremendous detail may be splendid to imagine, however difficult or impossible for vendors to maintain. There are, indeed, "mega" databases available, but lacking in areas of major concern such as percentage of peer-reviewed full-text content. Thus, 'linking' offers the most viable option for this 'utopian' search environment. It is the components being linked that must be appropriately addressed. Further, it is summarized, stating, "companies such as EBSCO' that offer sophisticated linking capabilities, as well as scholarly full-text databases with thousands of peer-reviewed full text journals, are leading the way" (Brooks and Dorst, 2002). With these linking capabilities, a single search system allows users to access a variety of databases from a single interface.

7.10. ACCESS AND ARCHIVING-RELATED ISSUES

Due to the transient nature of electronic information, consortia and the collaborating libraries should be allowed to archive the content they purchase to make backup copies. Even consortia and their constituent members should provide electronic information services with perpetual archival access to information to users when it exists in electronic form. Therefore, agreements with information providers to procure electronic information must include provisions to purchase and not just to lease or provide temporary access.

The archiving of information is an area that needs careful attention and unfortunately this is yet to be the case with the consortia in India. Long- term preservation of the invaluable wealth of information being accumulated by many of the consortium is to be archived and preserved for posterity. It is high time that these costly information resources are carefully archived and preserved on a long-term basis as the technology is fast progressing and also becoming obsolete almost at the same pace (Srivastava and Verma, 2014).

When an information provider gives access to data from its website rather than through local mounting of data, the provider should assure perpetual availability and access to the content, or the consortia or libraries wishing to mount information locally should be authorized to do so. Hence, the consortia should have the flexibility of choosing the format, such as real PDF, HTML, and SGML, in which they desire to retrieve and store the information.

7.11. LICENSING AND COPYRIGHT ISSUES

A license agreement is a legal contract between the information providers and libraries, which gives each of them a legal duty towards each other and also the right to seek a remedy in case of breach of those duties. Electronic information service of library consortia is being carried through the licensing of electronic information on behalf of their patrons. Electronic information providers employ licenses as a legal means of controlling the access and use of e-resources they offer. Though, the purchasing options that information providers offer may be print plus electronic or electronic access only but the libraries must choose the appropriate options and negotiate licenses that address the needs of the institutions as well as those of the patrons and also recognize their obligations to the licensors.

Libraries as the members of the consortia should consider the following principles that respect the rights and obligations of both member libraries and content providers (Tripathi and Lal, 2016):

- License should permit the "fair use" of information by authorized users including unlimited browsing, downloading and printing, complying with the provisions made under the copyright act, as applicable in the country of origin.
- License agreements must not place liability on the consortia or its member libraries for the misuse of content or an e-product by an individual user since neither the library nor consortia assist in breach of terms.
- A license agreement should state clearly what information access and use rights are extended to the licensee, i.e., whether perpetual use of the content or access rights only for a definite period of time.
- A license agreement should allow the licensee to copy data for the purpose of preservation and/or the creation of a usable archival copy when the rights are for permanent use of a resource. If a license agreement, does not permit the licensee to make a usable preservation copy, it should specify who has permanent archival responsibility for the resource, and the terms and conditions under which the licensee may access or refer users to the archival copy.

- Both parties should fix the terms of a license agreement at the time of signing the memorandum of understanding. If these terms are subject to change; for example, for scope of coverage or access methods, the agreement should require the licensor or licensee to notify the other party before such changes are implemented, and permit either party to terminate the agreement if the changes are not acceptable.

Last, but not the least, a license agreement should provide termination rights that are appropriate to each party.

7.12. SUSTAINABILITY ISSUES

It is observed that almost all library consortia try to rationalize the building and use of information resource collections through sharing and by granting access more than ownership in many libraries. Perhaps, the designing and launching a library consortium is perhaps the easier part as compared to its long-term sustenance and longevity. The management and the members of the consortium have to strive hard in formulating and establishing robust models toward achieving the previous goals.

Though, the library consortium is perceived to be a panacea to the extent that they attempt to solve the economic problems of sustaining adequate traditional comprehensive collections in traditional campus-based academic institutions by moving operations onto a larger scale, but it is bound to fail in the long run unless technological change transforms the game (Darch, 1999) Thus, the technology allows us to do what we want, but the economics of the technology may prevent us from doing it.

7.13. CUSTOMIZATION AND STATISTICS

Single search interface acts as a common searching

point for a multitude of electronic resources, it must still offer options for searching. Therefore, as Tenopir and Ennis (1998) mention, librarians must still find the best resource and searching features for every researcher and each question, but can do so from a single access point. Thus, it is best for librarians and users alike to have search options available to them. This customization is a critical element in adapting resources to meet the differing needs of individual libraries, and falls into the categories of content and software functionality with equal importance. It alludes to the fact that customization is not simply a matter of better customer service, but of control as well—control over information—and librarians must scrutinize these resources as a priority for users.

The customization and administrative capabilities can include such features as the ability to select default screens – basic, expert etc., add local notes and holdings information in addition to OPAC and ILS linking, choose number of items displayed on result list, select detailed versus basic result display, utilize multiple retrieval options, and include web links, incorporate options for document delivery and forms for inter-library loan, choose on-screen search limiters and expanders, and also may include the personalization options for individual users, initiate alert functionality, etc. However, the degree to which libraries use these administrative components varies greatly because some one may use the administrative component to "add individual journals to holdings information, change note fields, generate statistical reports etc."

There are the *Guidelines for Statistical Measures of Usage of Web-based Indexed, Abstracted, and full Text Resources* set forth by the International Coalition of Library Consortia (ICOLC) where it is mentioned that: "the use of licensed electronic information resources will continue to expand and in some cases become the sole or dominant means of access to content. The electronic environment, as manifested by the World Wide Web, provides an opportunity to improve the measurement of the use of these resources. In the electronic arena, we can more accurately determine which information is being accessed and used. Without violating any issues of privacy or confidentiality, we can dramatically enhance our understanding of information use".

Thus, for viewing usage statistical reports is a necessity. However, it is a long-standing debate that the statistical measurements deemed necessary and important for electronic databases to provide statistical reports or not? Vendors such as EBSCO are working closely with ICOLC and other "standards" organizations in order to provide the most complete and useful representations of the usage of full-text databases, in both individual libraries and across a consortium. Thus, these statistical measures are an effective means for gauging the value of consortia-provided resources.

7.14. USAGE AND USABILITY ISSUES

It is noted that neither libraries nor information providers have sufficient experience or data to determine the effective economic model to determine the unit cost of information, effective return on investment, or charging/ paying for electronic information. Hence, the libraries and publishers or vendors in coalition must develop and agree upon a strategy for measuring the effective use and value of electronic information so that members of the consortia demonstrate better return on investment (ROI) that is measured in terms of the increased usage and usability of the costly information products, and which is ultimately reflected in the scientific productivity of the host institutes. It ultimately enables libraries to secure additional funding for the procurement of e-resources. Thus, ROI is the earnest efforts of the consortium, the management, the researchers, the faculty, and the librarians that determine the success or otherwise of any consortium.

Fair use is a general principle lawfully permitted by a society for copying or citing of copyrighted material in the course of education, scholarship, advanced learning and other societal goals. Fair use can be made either without paying a specific fee or needing to seek permission from the copyright owner by the user. Thus, the providers should allow electronic information to be used to generate copies either in print or electronic form for non-commercial sharing of information between two academic libraries in support of learning and research. Though, there is seen no empirical evidence that fair use causes undue harm to content providers, but many information providers are seeking to cease the principle of fair use especially in the e-environment. However, fair use continues to be relevant and must be retained in the electronic environment.

Further, the plagiarism can be a problem for both print and e-journals because it is more acute with e-journals because of the ease of copying and pasting in an electronic document. However, the plagiarism can be avoided by following the guidelines in style manuals, and using a number of software packages that help to detect the plagiarism. For example, the Urkund that is also recommended by University Grants Commission, New Delhi for all universities in India and Turnitin etc. Besides, there exist many other software - free or subscribed for detecting plagiarism (Dhiman, 2015, 2018) which may be used to make the text plagiarism free.

7.15. CUSTOMER SUPPORT AND DATABASE ENHANCEMENTS

It is also noted that some resources were largely considered "supplemental" and not looked upon as replacements to existing databases because of two main factors-unfamiliarity with newly acquired resources and uncertainty surrounding the permanence. However, the statistics show that the database provided by some databases is most used in the library; therefore, it is justified to say that if libraries were to choose between the provided resources and those previously used in the library, but at this point, should not be forced to choose between them.

These comments reflect the increasing acceptance and reliance upon these resources as librarians and users become more familiar with them. However, it is the quality of resources, as well as the service and support offered by the consortium and participating vendor that helps first to instill the confidence in these resources that eventually leads to familiarity. Thus, over and above providing resources, consortia sometimes offer a layer of service and support in addition to that of the vendor, which increases the value of this body.

Further, in addition to customer service and support, the databases must incorporate regular enhancements to both software functionality and the content. Though, stagnancy was determined to be a factor in librarians' deteriorating confidence in a given resource but in light of the loss of many full-text sources in the other databases used. It has been noted in a study that "the IDAL provided resources have grown steadily. By making journals available in these databases that are not available as e-journals, the library and its users experience a great benefit" (Brooks and Dorst, 2002).That is why that the consortium is always looking into the possibility of upgrading to the expanded version of the database concurrently.

7.16. NEW CHALLENGES

Some new challenges are confronting due to the shift from physical form to electronic form where the impact of ICT has boosted resource sharing to a large extent. It has become possible with introduction of web to discover more resources and web-based resource sharing become a reality. It has also become possible to enhance inter-library loan with introduction of e-journals and e-products.

Hence, some new challenges have appeared in the scenario, which include (Patil, 2014):

- Shift from print to electronic form enhances ILL;
- Union catalogues of library holdings enhances ILL;
- The request for an article by scanning the same and sending to indenter quickly is met by support of technology and consortia licensing agreements;
- Physical collection is exposed through OPAC where as electronic collection through knowledge basis and A to Z lists. But such efforts do not indicate embargo periods or who is actual supplier and publishers prohibit electronic supply.

Therefore, as such, the publishers have allowed access to e-journals articles with many restrictions (Sachin and Prasanna Kumara, 2018):

- It is required that supplier library to print the article and send it either by fax or mail;
- Others require the library to print the article and then scan it for electronic transmission;
- However, the terms and condition are not explicit in licensing contracts.Further, different tools were introduced like Facebook, iTunes, iPads, You Tube, Flickr and e-journals in place of CDs, films, photo albums, etc.

Thus, many challenges are emerging in the domain of resource sharing and efforts continue to find new solutions for older problems (Goldner and Birch, 2012), likewise:

- We should work to find a solution for the problem of distributed knowledge bases;
- We need to work together, as a professional and with all players in the industry to support for libraries the same rights to e-journals that we had prints for decades; and
- We need to promote copyright legislation that serves

the interest of information seekers as well as publishers.

Last but not least, we should continue to work with resource sharing system suppliers to ensure to improve and accommodate both the shift from physical to electronic materials and the growth in buying resources in place of borrowing when appropriate.

7.17. CONSORTIA CONSTRAINTS IN CONTEXT OF INDIAN LIBRARIES

Inspite of the electronic publishing of scholarly journals that has emerged due to technological developments, the libraries even in the present situation prefer to own the materials, rather than accessing them from other libraries or a network. They do not think of increasing their information base by adding the item that is not available with other libraries. Hence, some of the constraints of consortia to libraries compromising, especially in India, are given below (Sachin and Prasanna Kumara, 2018).

- There is a fear of losing an identity which is one aspect because they feel they have to follow the guidelines set for a group of libraries.
- There is a centralization of activities and services under a network that is still not preferred or accepted by many libraries.
- The benefits gained through participation in consortia are hard to explain or convince the authorities, particularly in the beginning stage.
- There is a lack of a well-tested mechanism of transfer of document or information to build confidence in the end users, which requires timely delivery of required information in an efficient manner.
- There is a lack of awareness about consortia and its benefits.

- There is a slow acceptance of e-resources by the users.
- There is a lack of maintenance and balancing both physical and digital library.
- There are rigid administrative, financial and auditing rules, including inadequate funds and single point payment.
- There is uncertainty about the persistence of digital resources.
- There is a lack of infrastructure for accessing electronic sources.
- There is a lack of appropriate bibliographic tools, and
- There is a lack of trained personnel for handling new technologies.

Besides, unreliable telecommunication links and insufficient bandwidth hinder the use. Some other barriers are also there such as geographical, legal, administrative, etc. but they can be sorted out easily.

SUMMARY

This chapter deals with the management issues and several challenges which authorities face in managing the library consortia. Several challenges are there which include the increasing expectations of users and static budget provisions, identification of information resources useful to users, rapidly changing technology and infrastructure, issues regarding pricing of information resources, access- and archival-related issues regarding information resources, problems in licensing the resources and uses, and usability of information resources subscribed to/purchased by the library consortia.

So, there are various issues related to library consortia acceptance but they can be tackled tactfully. Thus, it is high time that these costly information resources are carefully archived and preserved on a long-term basis as the technology is fast progressing and also becoming obsolete almost at the same pace.

BIBLIOGRAPHICAL REFERENCES

Brooks, S. and Dorst, T.J. (2002). Issues facing Academic Library Consortia and Perceptions of Members of the Illinois Digital Academic Library. Portal: Libraries and the Academy, 2 (1): 43-57.

Darch, C. (1999). Academic Library Consortia in Contemporary South Africa. Library Consortium Management: An International Journal, 1 (1-2): 23-32.

Dhiman, A.K. (2015). Research Methodology: Basics of Research Methods, Tools and Techniques. Avon Publications, New Delhi.

Dhiman, A.K. (2018). Basics of Research Methodology. S.K. Book Agency, New Delhi.

Goldner, M. and Birch, M. (2012). Resource Sharing in a Cloud Computing Age. Interlending & Document Supply, 40 (10): 4-11.

Kassel, A. (2001). Power Searching Strategies for Success. Searcher, 9 (4): 36-42.

Patil, Y.M. (2014). Consortium Approach to Resources Sharing in an E-Environment. Scientific Publishers (India), Jodhpur.

Sachin, Y. and Prasanna Kumara, B. M. (2018). E-Journal Consortia for Academic Libraries. International Journal of Information Studies, 10 (2): 53-61. Available at: http://www.dline.info/ijis/fulltext/vl0n2/ijisvl0n2_l.pdf.

Srivastava, J.P. and Verma, V.K. (2014). Library Consortia: Issues and Challenges with Special Reference to INDEST-AICTE Consortium. PLANNER 2014 Paper. Inflibnet, Ahemdabad. Pp.103-112. Available at: https://ir.inflibnet.ac.in/bitstream/1944/1790/1/11.pdf.

Tenopir, C. and Ennis, L. (1998). The Impact of Digital Reference on Librarians and Library Users. Available at https://trace.tennessee.edu/cgi/viewcontent.cgi?article=1136&context=utk_infosciepubs.

Tripathi, A. and Lal, J. (2016). Library Consortia: Practical Guide for Library Managers. Chandos Publishing, Amsterdam.

8

Nationwide Single Library Consortium : The Merging

It is worth to mention that Library Consortia have been developed world-wide for sharing of electronic resources as the agreement, combination, or group to undertake an enterprise beyond the resources of any one member. However, library consortia vary in their type, goals, structure, membership and funding (Woodsworth and Wall, 1991). A consortium may be a formal or informal agreement between libraries based on a common principle. For example, a consortium may be based on library type - academic, special or public. A regional consortium may be based on a geographical principle. A statewide or nationwide consortium may incorporate all its libraries, government-funded and those in private institutions.

Now, they have improved considerably for access to licensed materials while merger could provide much more secure operating environment for participants. One has to look into analysis of current scenario and objectives of each consortium covering practical, financial and institutional/participants and legal aspects of merger of groups of consortia. It is needless to say that before merger, one has to look at various collaborative options and whether merger of consortia are viable options to achieve better access to large number of e-resources.

8.1. WHY THE URGE TO MERGE?

The following could be the attributes for the merger of library consortia:

- Understand mechanisms as to why consortia should merge and what better opportunities are there for the third sector, i.e. the new consortium; and
- To decide whether the options looked into merging are right for constituent consortia/participants/ institutions based on feedbacks of all concerned.

8.2. BEST PRACTICE

The following could be best practices for merger of consortia:

- Review with business techniques what steps are needed for implementation of merger of consortia;
- What could be merged consortia partner look like?
- Look into financial decisions that need to be made with consortia merger; and
- Make a feasible study of merged consortia which could be a better reference point to go ahead.

8.3. APPROACHES AND IMPLEMENTATION

The following could be the approaches and parameters for implementation:

- Study the market and make appropriate approaches afterthe strategy for merger of two or more consortia is decided;
- Facilitate initial discussion and meetings between

consortia/participants;

- Draw up proposal with complete details of merger;
- Develop feasibility study reports with next step and recommendation strictly outlining time schedule; and
- Arrange any financing and legal services as appropriate.

But be sure that under any circumstances the merger should not disturb existing access by users.

8.4. MEMBERSHIP AGREEMENT

The mission of the merged consortium is to create and sustain a rich, supportive and diverse knowledge environment that enhances teaching, learning and research through the sharing of large and enhanced collections, expertise and programme. It does not replace an institution's obligations rather further enhances library collections and technological infrastructure. Each member retains autonomy over its staff, operations and budget. However, it is mandatory on the part of participants to collaborate and firm commitment to new consortium. To be a member in newly formed consortium, the participants should agree to (CARLI, 2019):

- To abide by the bylaws of the Consortium of Consortia (C of C) and the common policies, protocols, rules and regulations adapted by the consortium;
- To pay promptly all financial obligations arising from membership and participation in services offered through the consortium;
- To follow with all terms and conditions of contractual agreements made by the new consortium on behalf of its members and accept responsibility for the acts or omissions of its own users related to such agreements;

- To freely and fairly share its information and library resources with the students, faculty/staff of other members in new consortium;
- To maintain current awareness of new consortium programs and services, technology, policies and best practices, in order to meet the library's responsibilities to its fellow members;
- To play an active role in the consortium, including the provision of consultation, advice, and expertise to colleagues in other member libraries; and
- To support for staff participation in consortially provided forums, workshops and support appropriate staff to serve on new consortium committees, task forces and working groups.

Failure to comply with these terms and conditions may lead to the imposition of sanctions of membership termination as specified in consortium's bylaws/policies and other obligations with vendors and service providers as may be appropriate.

8.5. BENEFITS OF CONSORTIA MERGING

The merger is a collective, cooperative and collaborative efforts among participating consortia. Thus, various benefits of merging of consortia into a new consortium may be enumerated as follow (Patil, 2014):

- Merging is the long-term development for its participants as it enhances and increases the services that members will have access to;
- Participants will have choice of vendors for electronic resources and library supplies;
- Libraries hit hard by funding cuts and depend more on collaboration and discounts to access of electronic resources;
- Merging considerably reduces the operating costs and continues to provide critical services to libraries and their users;

- Merging enhanced resource sharing on a grander scale;
- Archival materials of each participant can be kept in offsite storage, closed or open stacks;
- Merging will enhance services to collective membership;
- Merger leverage buying power, preserve region's rich cultural heritage, strengthens each member's ability to serve and lead its community in the creative and effective use of information resources;
- Merging of consortia that is caused by economic crisis, is the matching of merging of publishers - making it possible to critical mass necessary for negotiating from the strongest possible position; and
- Helps to develop and support new initiatives that will save the members time and money that is driven by the need to save our staff and financial resources.

Besides, it is expected to deliver enhanced savings on services such as group licenses and to expand resource sharing options for users across large track of geographical area.

8.6. IMPACT OF MERGER/MIGRATION

Various advantages and disadvantages are associated with the merger/migration of library consortia with each other. Patil (2014) has discussed its advantages and disadvantages as under:

8.6.1. Advantages

- With combined strength, more buying capacity, more negotiating power and more flexibility with more members;
- Informal to formal that means protection under law;
- Enhances combination of more products for subscription;

- Facilitates better-negotiation with the publishers/ vendors;
- Interests of small libraries is protected by subscribing costly titles;
- Facilitates e-access to all products subscribed;
- Publishers are happier to negotiate at a single point with a consortium committee thereby saving time and money of the consortium; and
- Some professional societies are privileged to get access to some core resources free of charge as user population is considerably small in number.

8.6.2. Disadvantages

- Purchase bundled offer in the consortium is redundant to some participants – 'all you cannot eat';
- No flexibility to choose titles of interest by individual participants for which subscription is to be done at institution level;
- Absence of flexible licensing models;
- Staff time is spent to manage consortium activities which is additional work and pressure on staff;
- Additional fund may be required to support the merger which is additional burden to libraries; and
- Non-uniformity of access to content by participants.

Besides, there is a need to maintain print plus e-subscriptions by individual participants for some resources and further all members may not use some resources provided in the consortium.

8.6.3. Problems in Merging Consortia

It can be cited that a new consortium – E-ShodhSindhu has come out after merging of UGC-INFONET and INDEST-AICTE and NLIST programme. Another merging takes place in between CSIR and DST and a new consortium - National Knowledge Resource Consortium has come out. However, the following problems may be encountered in merging of two consortia (Patil, 2014):

- Participants are from different subject areas and background;
- Participants have different journals collection policy;
- Duplicates of journals to be retained;
- Mode of subscription cannot be altered;
- Likelyhood of disruption of subscription period;
- Total subscription of print to be maintained;
- Participants' collection policy is diluted with addition of the journals of marginal or no interest;
- Requirement of training program for access to additional contents; and
- Less usage of contents of marginal interests but cannot drop titles.

8.6.4. Negotiation by Merged Consortium

The following points need consideration for negotiating for new consortium:

- For negotiation, participation by both the consortia members is desirable;
- To follow administrative and financial procedures in a merger works well as two departments representing in the same consortium;
- Requirement of formal committees with hierarchy and procedures;

Besides, it is essential to have series of meetings for selection of materials and negotiation which require more time. Further, requirement of proper name after merger and consensus among all participants. For example, National Knowledge Resource Consortium and E-ShodhSindhu.

8.6.5. Access and Usage

The access and usage need following points for consideration :

- Contents of publishers have to be identified for new consortium and be provided to members based on actual requirements;
- Access to the content can be made through IP authentication, or password / identification wherever needed;
- Access has to be monitored by each institute and review of usage statistics at the time of renewal; and
- Each member has to arrange training for all new products and awareness of products among users.

Further, a nodal officer at institute level has to monitor all activities related to the consortium and liaise with the new consortium headquarter.

8.7. NATIONWIDE LIBRARY CONSORTIUM AND NATIONAL CONSORTIUM SITE LICENSING

Nationwide purchasing of e-resources through consortia is of recent origin in many countries. Despite the differences in their political, social and cultural environment, these consortia in general share many common characteristics (Shachaf, 2003). Through consortium approach, libraries have to negotiate with the publishers and vendors individually or collectively for purchase of e-resources. A few consortia have come together in different countries and taken a lead in getting different licensing models, i.e. National Site Licensing (NSL), involving government agencies and large-scale collaboration at national level, as it has the potential to overcome many obstacles in the complex nature of licensing.

The idea of a "National Site Licensing Model" appeared as early as in 1992, when "site licensing" was widely adopted in electronic journal practice. The initial vision of NSL was for it to be a model for publishing serials, with which end-users received issues of serials on a regular subscription basis but at a far lower price (Hunter, 1992). Over the times, the definition of NSL changed, but it was not always clear. As Turner (1999) said "a National Site License is one of those simple concepts that are never quite as straightforward as it might appear at first sight".

ICOLC established in 1998 put forth a resolution and adopted, "Statement of Current Perspective and Preferred Practices for the Selection and Purchase of Electronic Information", which was drafted by ICOLC leaders and sets forth concerns for "current electronic information environment, the desired environment for the future, and their preferred practices for library consortia and their member libraries to achieve the desired outcomes". The document goes on to identify and discuss in detail a list of current problems and needs for the future and preferred practices in the emerging electronic information environment, contract negotiations, pricing, access, archiving, licenses, management data and authentication. Thus, ICOLC has given new directions to consortia licensing at different levels with set guidelines.

8.8. NATIONAL CONSORTIUM

There are several National Consortium or Federation of Consortia at national level formed with the sole aim to have National Site Licensing (NSL) for various e-resources. Licensing is a tedious job with many issues of the multiplicity of licenses offered by publishers and intermediaries. After merging, a single national model license is a necessity and would be universally welcomed by libraries and consortia (Ball, 2003). Looking into a few national consortia, six parameters could be identified, viz. participating libraries, core program, reason for formation, sources of funding, involvement of large academic libraries in the state/region, and structure of governance (Potter, 1997). Van de Ven, et al. (1975) has proposed another set of criteria for analysis of inter-organizational analysis, viz. homogeneity, domain consensus, awareness of other parties, stability, resource distribution, number of resource sources, size of the network and overlap in membership.

A comparative study of standard NSLs was made by Zhu (2011) and a preliminary model is proposed for adoption. The basic parameters that support a country's adoption of NSL are given below:

- Need for new institutions;
- Centralized educational policy and funding;
- Supportive bureaucratic/political trends;
- Cooperation or partnership tradition.

Further, the factors potentially preventing the adoption of NSL may include:

- Decentralized educational policy and funding;
- Diversity and magnitude of institutions;
- The 'Big Deal' and monopoly concerns.

However, different approaches in adopting NSL have been made. But two approaches are important and they include:

- NESLI in UK has adopted NSL - viewing it as top-down changing process.
- CNSLP adopted from a consortia base, which could be seen as a bottom — up changing process.

8.9. INSTITUTIONAL PERSPECTIVES

NSL is a new institution created in practice and adopted by a few countries. Scott (2001) stated that "the seeds of change are lodged both within and outside institutions." However, the practices of the UK and Canada show that the "seeds" of change and creating new institutions lay both within the existing institutions—the deficiency of individual libraries and the need for collaboration—and outside the institutions— the pressures from technology, the publishing industry, and increasingly complicated copyright issues. Libraries in various countries are still facing the same pressures, problems, and needs; therefore, NSL as a new form of institution has the potential to be diffused to other countries. But the comparisons of Canada, the UK, and the US suggest that the decision of whether to adopt NSL also depends on other variables, such as government support, a cooperation tradition, and concerns about monopoly (Zhu, 2011).

- First, is there a source of strong regulative support? Government is often essential in large-scale reform. The analysis of the UK and Canada cases reveals that the central governments played important roles in implementing NSL, though the roles varied. The government's stance and political trends always influence public affairs, all more in national-scale cooperation. Both CNSLP and NESLI fit with the government policies; therefore, they got enough resources and support from their central governments, which was a significant factor to the successful creation of the new institution. However, in the US, the lack of regulative support was one of the obstacles to the adoption of the NSL model.
- Second, the support of a normative pillar is also required. Even, there is a deep-rooted tradition of cooperation that might be a key factor to successful adoption of NSL. Working on a national scale, usually involves significant challenges in decision making, communication, and mutual understanding far beyond the challenges for smaller groups. These challenges call for a cooperative manner of all participating institutions which is usually built on long-term cooperation activities. Without the support of this pillar, the problems arising from national-scale cooperation may counteract the benefits achieved from such activities.

However, last but not least, whether or not adopting NSL depends on whether NSL is suitable for the particular social context. The problems of NSL, such as having to accept the Big Deal and the potential to create a monopoly, indicate some limitations of this model. These problems could be more severe in some countries with diverse educational institutions and varying user needs such as the US, while they may be less severe in countries with smaller and relatively homogenous research and educational sectors. Therefore, the applicability of NSL relies much on the specific social and political conditions in specific countries. However, it should be pointed out that NSL as a new institutional form is not stagnant rather it has the ability of adaptation. For instance, in spite of their different problems, the NSL programs in the UK and Canada still work well and customization has become one of their future directions.

8.10. INTITIATIVES AT INTERNATIONAL LEVELS

There are several initiatives in forming national consortia/ national site licensing. It is sufficing to take a representative NSL - i.e. the UK's National Site Licensing Initiative (NESLI), Canadian National Site Licensing Project (CNSLP), and the United States. Further, it is appended with the case of Netherlands, New Zealand, Turkey and Korea etc. Various initiatives at international levels are briefly discussed below which are mainly based on Patil (2014):

8.10.1. The National Electronic Site Licensing Initiative (NESLI)

NESLI is a national consortium of UK for site licensing, with single aim to achieve pricing models for e-resources. It is a part of the Joint Information Systems Committee's (JISC) Distributed National Electronic Resource (DNER) which includes all the UK universities and institutes of higher education. NESLI is committed to unbundle totally print journals from e-journals. NESLI mention "what is most noticeable about the majority of pricing policies is that very few publishers offer electronic-only access - libraries are still expected to maintain print-based subscriptions with the 'added bonus' of electronic access". JISC appointed a Managing Agent (MA) - Swats Blackwell to administer the license, to negotiate with publishers and to provide access to the licensed materials through a proprietary system. NESLI's terms of references are such that it is only empowered to deal with electronic journals. NESLI's salient features are:

- It aims to separate the electronic component from the paper;
- The means, of access is part of the deal;
- The MA negotiates a deal on behalf of all members;
- Payment is from the individual members direct to MA who also handles the subscriptions for electronic content and arranges for access through the NESLI system; and
- NESLFs arrangements are completely independent of existing or fixture UK consortia arrangements with publishers and agents.

Under NESLI, the negotiator is the MA, who is charged with negotiating for the libraries. If the MA is to negotiate for libraries, the MA needs to be paid directly by them as a fee for the service - which is covered from publisher's discount and from the library in terms of a small flat fee per subscription. Thus, the MA tasks (Bley, 2000) may include the following:

- Negotiation with scholarly publishers;
- Handling transactions/orders that emanate from any take-up of NESLI deal;
- Exploration the use of new technologies; and
- Providing single interface for the negotiated content of various publishers.

NESLI2 in the year 2003, was formed as the second phase of NESLI for 2003-2006. Although, day-to-day activities undertaken by the MA included negotiating deals with publishers, handling subscriptions, providing a single interface for access, and encouraging use of NESLI Model License, yet unsuccessful bid of MA after the initial phase, the values and roles of NESLI were reconsidered, and the management structure was changed. Further, in 2002, the negotiation task was separated from the managing role: JISC replaced the MA (Swats and Blackwell), and Content Complete Limited was appointed as the negotiation agent for NESLI2.

8.10.2. Canadian National Site Licensing Project (CNSLP)

CNSLP is a national consortium of 64 university libraries to provide access to full- text electronic journals and the number of member libraries was enhanced to 74 by 2005. It was a three-year pilot project beginning from 2001 but after the pilot project, the Canadian Research Knowledge Network (CRKN) was incorporated as a not-for-profit organization in order to continue the work of the project. CNSLP signed Pan-Canadian Licenses with 7 vendors and a Steering Committee was formed to control the CNSLP's activities.

Canadian Foundation for Innovation (CFI) is a Government nodal agency for CNSLP, whose goal is to strengthen the capability of Canadian universities, colleges, research hospitals and other not-for-profit institutions to carryout world class research and technology development. It is noted that the total budget for the three-year CNSLP Pilot Project was 50 million Canadian Dollars, with CFI contributing 40 percent and remaining by participating institutions. All university libraries were committed to sustaining the project beyond the initial three-year pilot project period as a free condition of CFI seed funding.

In March 2000, the CNSLP Steering Committee

approved a formal two-step license procurement process, consisting of:

- An open Prequalification Bid, to elicit general content, functionality, technical and pricing information from vendors, followed by-
- A detailed Request for Proposal (RFP) issued to pre-qualified vendors.

In May 2000, the said committee approved the principles for licensing electronic resources. Negotiations Resource Team evaluated bids and 23 vendors were short listed in July 2000 and the Team presented the final results of the RFP evaluation to the Steering Committee on October 16, 2000. Further, agreements for three years license (2001 to 2003) were reached with 7 vendors, who were agreed to set terms and conditions, such as:

- Sign the CNSLP Model License agreement, with unique or specific amendments dealt with in separate amending letters;
- Offer a three years' agreement, with fixed pricing in Canadian Dollars;
- Hold annual price increases significantly lower than prevailing rates;
- Commit to a price increase cap in year 4, at license renewals;
- Offer an 'unbundled' pricing model, i.e. unbundling print subscriptions from electronic access. Several vendors implemented, for the first time, an electronic based pricing model, with print subscriptions treated as an optional add-on at deeply discounted rates.

Keeping in view the achievements of power of collaboration and the fitness of the NSL model in Canada, CNSLP was selected as one of the ten worlds 'success stories' by IFLA in 2003.

8.10.3. The United States: the Non-NSL

USA is a federal form of government, where education is considered to a large extent, a local and regional or state concern and hence, small funds are made available by the federal government for education. The federal government enacts the laws and administrative regulations in respect of higher education policy. As such, American higher education system is largely state-based decentralized system which is an obstacle to form nationwide library cooperation or consortia in the US. So, it is not possible for licensing on a national basis in spite of close collaboration and cooperation exists amongst libraries. However, there was a boom of consortia in the mid-1990s, and by mid 2000s, there were more than 100 consortia have been formed to deal with electronic resource licensing.

Consortia activities in US provided a strong basis for large scale cooperation. The 'Big Deal' and monopoly were increasingly prevalent which might have created barriers for NSL adoption. Later on, some libraries felt that the "Big Deal" serves only the big publishers and stopped buying the "Big Deal" purchases. There is wide variation amongst higher educational institutions in respect of diversity in scale, type, funding, focus, number of students and faculty members etc. Thus, libraries had different emphasis on their collection development; and therefore, one form of licensing could hardly fit all. Further, diversity and number of higher education institutions were important factors that prohibited acceptance of the 'Big Deal' and NSL adoption in US.

Anyhow, the US Council on Library and Information Resources (CLIR) and the Digital Library Federation (DLF) released Liblicense Standard License Agreement, which was prepared keeping in view librarian's perspective with emphasis on academic library community on a wider basis. This model has been adopted by various consortia, such as: Northeast Research Libraries Consortium (NERL) and

New England Library and Information Services Network (NELINET). California Digital Library that was established in 1997 has adopted CLIR/DLF license to support the assembly and creative use of the world's scholarship and knowledge for the US Libraries. MIT also borrowed this model license to create pilot project for licensing journals. Thus, majority of publishers had accepted the standard license in some form, either outright or with some minor modifications by the end of 2003. As such, this model license was exploited by many local, regional and large networks of libraries. New England Law Library Consortium, Virtual Library of Virginia (VIVA) and OhioLink were the most successful consortia. However, in US, there is nostandardized national site licensing.

NSL strategy was adopted by many other countries also around the world. Some of the other representative of them are discussed below:

8.10.4. The Netherlands

In Netherlands, the current licenses are offered by SURF, the collaborative organization of Dutch higher education and research in the field of network services and ICT. Formerly, a Covenant was offered between scientific and professional publishers of the Dutch Publishers Association and the cooperative body Innovation Scientific Information Supply.

Dutch National Licensing Organization is serving universities, research institutions and public libraries and their library consortia UKB and SHB. SURF diensten is a partner in SURF, the collaborative organization in which research universities, universities of applied sciences and research institutions aimed at innovative ICT facilities operate at a national and an international level.

14 Universities, 46 Colleges, 140 Research Institutes, 100 Public libraries are participating in this venture.

8.10.5. New Zealand

In New Zealand, a National Library Survey that was conducted in 2002 showed that there the libraries were interested in forming a self-funded consortium for the purchase of electronic content. Hence, two multi-sector working groups were set up which has made recommendations on a possible consortium structure, funding arrangements and content.

Later, a concept project was started in 2003. Its initial focus was on a Request for Proposal (RFP) process to identify and select possible vendors and products. The key principles emphasized were:

- collaboration in the national interest;
- model with the potential to include any New Zealand library;
- expanded access to e-resources for all users;
- financially self-sustaining consortium after set-up; and
- partnering approach with e-resource providers.

The outcome of the RFP was a proposed all-of-country deal, meaning every person in New Zealand could access the resources through a consortium member library. The deal was put to libraries in November 2003 and commitment was gained to form the consortium, which now known as Electronic Purchasing in Collaboration (EPIC). It is a consortium of libraries which license packages of electronic resources to be used in New Zealand libraries. Its vision is to provide access to high-quality electronic information for all New Zealanders. It provides access to electronic resources through a consortium of member libraries, which is the Ministry of Education funded access for all New Zealand schools.

EPIC has over 150 members drawn from all library sectors. However, the organizations must be based in New Zealand and providing the library/information services to be eligible for EPIC membership.

8.10.6. Turkey

In Turkey, Anatolian University Libraries Consortium (ANKOS) is there which is a vibrant national consortium that was established with its main mission to provide cost effective solutions for electronic products to Turkish Universities and access to researchers of global information network. ANKOS's Steering Committee entrusted the task of creating the Turkish National Site Licensing (TRNSL) to a group.

Lindley (2003) mentions that this group studied Academic Consortia Model (ACML)/CNSLP/NESLI and commonly used US Models and developed TRNSL incorporating local environment. TRSNL and the statement of licensing principles have greatly facilitated the negotiations between the vendor representative and the ANKOS negotiators by making what ANKOS wants to see in a contract transparent to both sides.

8.10.7. Republic of Korea

In Korea, the Korean Electronic Site License Initiative (KESLI) Consortium was started in 1999 for joint buying of scholarly e-journals. It has grown up to one of the largest consortia around the world. Government support this consortium, and there are currently 355 libraries are its members. In order to meet ever growing demands, KESLI is trying to meet:

- Working to develop KESLI Standard License Models and use it instead of license agreement of publishers; and
- For perpetual access and long-term preservation of subscribed licensed materials.

Besides, KESLI is on the move for construction of National Digital Archival System.

8.11. INITIATIVES AT NATIONAL LEVEL

In India, there are over a dozen consortia either big

or small, formed which are dynamic and running on a sustainable basis. They cover wide range of subjects and institutes which fall under different departments of Government of India. All consortia, in effect, face various obstacles/problems as well as various issues like uninterrupted online access, perpetual access to back files, pricing, licensing, copyright and archival issues. But there are no concerted efforts to solve problems with a single approach by forming a National Consortium (NC) with the aim of creating National Site Licensing (NSL).

However, some studies have been made to develop a National Consortium (Arora and Agarwal, 2004; Rani and Dhiman, 2011), where a need over to integrate various consortia into one single consortium with truly national site licensing provision, which is feasible if the competent authorities come together willingly to cooperate and coordinate for developing NSL, is stressed.

8.12. WHY NATIONAL CONSORTIUM?

In a larger consortium at National Level, large number of participating libraries is essential as it serves national interest. It is a powerful tool to bargain with the publishers for better rates of subscription and terms and conditions for licensing. The total cost for National Site Licensing comes down as compared to multi-consortia cost put together.

In the Indian scenario of education and research, more than 75 percent is being funded by Government of India; thus, it is very conducive for developing National Consortium with the following benefits:

- Combined National Site Licensing for much more resources;
- Reduce duplication which otherwise is prevalent with multi-consortia approach;
- Considerably enhances purchasing power;
- Can better handle archival issues, which is the most

crucial aspect in consortia environment; and

- Can enhance collection building across the participating institutions.

8.13. HOW INDIAN CONDITIONS ARE SUITABLE FOR NSL?

Keeping in view different consortia formed in India, their parent organizations fall under the purview of different government departments/ministries of Government of India. The positive point is that the funding resources are made available from the Central Government. To look into creating NSL, it is essential to know three basic factors: education policy, extent of library cooperation and 'Big Deals' concerns (Patil, 2014).

- Education system in India is highly centralized and all major institutes of higher learning and universities are directly funded by central agencies for education, and research. Keeping this in view, creating NSL is feasible.
- Resource sharing in the digital environment has been practiced by many institutes/universities by developing library networks. With recent spurt in proliferation of electronic resources and steep hike in prices, library professionals are joining hands to share resources through groups or consortia negotiations to deal with dual functions - try achieving savings and facilitating access to more information with optimum payment. Many consortia in India are successful and running on a sustainable basis which have played an important role in license negotiations as well as many other library cooperation activities. As such, active cooperation traditionally practiced by Indian libraries and expertise gained in forming various consortia, strongly support for adoption of NSL in India.
- The 'Big Deal' and monopoly concerns are there in

many Indian consortia purchase models. 'Big Deals' are preferred for the reason that consortia are negotiating licenses for the whole higher education sector/major research organizations. Generally, 'Big Deals' enable to serve organizations with access to wide range of electronic resources. It is observed that in Indian consortia context, there are some issues about monopolies, which needs to be tackled under NSL.

So, it is feasible to create NSL having one coordinating agency, to be identified from the existing consortia and constituting a National Coordination Committee with subcommittees to deal with the resource selection, availability of funding, negotiation and licensing, monitoring and evaluation, as per the needs. The goal of the National Coordination Committee could be, "to achieve in line with the principle that intellect is an investment and information is an asset, considering both as national property".

8.14. PROPOSAL FOR A NATIONAL CONSORTIUM IN INDIA

National Consortium (NC) means the support for higher education and research would act as a central agency to coordinate acquisitions and access to information in digital format. Coordinating Agency of NC would get full government support of both administrative and funding for subscription to core collection of electronic resources synchronizing requirements to both education and research and training in the country. There are few existing bigger consortia, such as: E-shodhSindhu, NKRC, CeRA, MCIT, DAE and DeLCON which could serve as a nucleus based on which national consortia could be built.

8.14.1. Logic Behind It

The following logic may work well behind the formation of nation-wide consortium.

- Educational and research in India are mostly funded by the central government;
- Most of educational /research institutes fall under different departments/ministries of central government; and
- Integrating existing consortia with large number of consortium members will enhance greater bargaining power to the consortium and greater benefits to its members by bringing all consortia under NSL.

8.14.2. Strategy

Ministries/Departments may constitute a National Coordination Committee representing all members of consortia:

- Expanding existing resources of national level consortia by and identifying additional resources of common interest;
- Negotiate with the publishers for the best rates of subscription and terms of reference with Committee Members; and
- Expand structure of representative consortia to function as a National Consortium and NSL.

However, more sub-committees may also be formed as per requirement.

8.14.3 Financial Resources

Further, financial resources are also required which should also be kept in mind. Thus:

- Ensure the availability of sufficient bandwidth and network connection to all participating institutions;
- Establish physical and computer infrastructure for the consortium; and
- Provide funds for subscription to core electronic

resources that would be used by the institutions under a given ministry/department.

However, it should not be forgotten that the consortia-based subscriptions to electronic resources not included in core subscription that will be borne from participating institutions. Thus, amount involved in consortium-based subscription to electronic resources be diverted directly from funding agency to the National Consortium.

National Coordination Committee will work for various types of guidelines. Some of them may include the guidelines on the access, administration, archiving, documentation, governance, statistical measures, infrastructure development, information etc. Besides, there may also be the guidelines on the licensing, management, monitoring and evaluation, operation of the consortium and also the pricing & purchase and staff training.

8.15. CASE STUDIES

There are two entities: migration and merging which look differently in consortia aspects.

- Migration in consortia takes place where existing consortia members, not satisfied with resources made available to them will see requirements elsewhere and migrate to that consortium laterally and subscribe the requisite resources at concessional rate as applicable without disturbing activities of existing consortium.
- While in case of merging, a consortium or loose constituencies of consortia or a group may join another consortium and form a new and larger consortium, where they can have strong purchasing power and access to large amount of information.

Some example or case studies are illustrated on the above aspects in the following paragraphs.

8.15.1. Migration to Another Consortium

Forum for Resource Sharing in Astronomy (FORSA) was started in the year 1981 with twelve members as a cooperative venture like ILL, combined union catalogue of serials holding, etc. The forum was matured over a period of time to adapt the consortium approach on cooperative acquisitions, access to large amount of information, which otherwise not possible at an individual level. FORSA had formed informal consortium for about half a dozen publishers' journals facilitating cross e-access to all combined number of titles (Birdie and Patil, 2010).

However, it was not possible to purchase some costlier journals, which otherwise required by some participants of the consortium. Thus, three members could migrate to other consortia laterally for availing access to required titles without hampering activities of the FORSA Consortium. RRI could join INDEST-AICTE Consortium for IELXplore Datebase; IUCAA could join UGC-Infonet (now E-ShodhSindhu) for many of physics related journals and TIFR could work with DAE Libraries consortium for titles of mutual interest.

8.15.2. Merging Two Different Consortia: CSIR and DST

DST has 25 institutes including FORSA Members but DST was contemplating forming a consortium since 2006. CSIR had already established its own consortium called CSIR E-Journals Consortium, which falls under Department of Scientific and Industrial Research (DSIR), Ministry of Science and Technology, Government of India. DST also falls under the Ministry of Science and Technology and forming yet another consortium for its 25 institutes that was a useless exercise. Thus, it was decided that the group of 25 institutes of DST could join CSIR E-Journals Consortium instead of forming a parallel consortium within the frame work of Ministry of Science and Technology. Hence, 25 DST institutes (including five

FORSA Members) merged with CSIR E-Journals Consortium.

The new consortium has 64 members (CSIR -39 and DST -25) and after merging the new consortium has been named as - National Knowledge Resource Consortium (NKRC) with Coordination Committee - members of which are drawn from both CSIR and DST. The merger that took place during 2009 is working on a sustainable basis, providing access to wide range of e-resources.

8.15.3. Merging Two Different Consortia: UGC-INFONET and INDEST AICTE

INDEST-AICTE and UGC-INFONET Digital Library Consortium along with N-LIST have been merged to form E-Shodhsindhu in the year 2016 on the recommendation of an Expert Committee of MHRD, New Delhi. It is now being executed by INFLIBNET, Gandhinagar (Gujarat) and all the resources of both the consortia are now available with this new consortium.

E-Shodhsindhu can also be cited as a good example of nationwide single library consortium to some extent because it is providing access of e-resources to technical institutes, universities – private and government both and also to the colleges at nominal prices.

8.16. THINGS TO BE SORTED OUT

Various points are to be taken into consideration before merging two or more than two library consortia together. However, at least following points must be kept in view before the merger of library consortia into a single consortium as discussed by Patil (2014):

Federation of Indian Consortia : It is to be formed to suggest ways and means for electronics resources subscription but it should have representatives from all major consortia in the country.

Online only Journals : It has to ascertain agreed to go for subscription of 'online only' version directly with publishers as major publishers are having their offices in India and as far as possible to avoid services of vendors/ consultants. It should also be agreed to pay subscription charges to publishers in advance as per prevailing international practice.

Archival Access : It is to be agreed to avail the services of service providers like PORTICO to ensure complete and live perpetual access to subscribed content even after termination of contract with the publishers. Also, it is suggested to compile a list of content subscribed through all major consortia to access archive through PORTICO or other Digital Repository System.

Bibliographic Content of Databases : It is also to ascertain to have a bibliography of database of the resources subscribed by all consortia along with a federated search engine for effective document sharing among institutions. This can be out sourced to a third party by inviting tenders.

Model License : A model agreement/license is to be executed between publishers and consortia. It is to be prepared to ensure/protect the interests of all stake holders.

Negotiation : The formation of a National Negotiation Committee to negotiate with the publishers on behalf of all consortia members is also needed. This committee needs to work for national license for common interests like reference books and journals like Nature, Science, Scientific American and the databases like JSTOR etc.

Usage Data : It is proposed to share usage of journals subscribed and other methods used to assess the value and relevance of content among consortia.

E-Group : It is suggested to start an e-group for effective communication among consortia at national level at any other appropriate place.

However, further meetings may help to concretize the Federation of Consortia and help in realizing National

Site Licensing to many of e-resources of interest to many of consortia members across the country e-mail communication. Thus, NSL has created great benefits for the countries that adopted it and has the potential to continue in contributing to licensing solutions in these and other countries for nationwide access of e-resources.

8.17. LIFE CYCLE OF LIBRARY CONSORTIA

Each consortium is affected by several levels of the environment at different stages of its development, from its founding to its disbanding. However, the general environment (legal, political, social and cultural) and the task environment(libraries, consortia, publishers, vendors, and patrons) influence the consortium's formation, development and disbandment. Further, consortia face the need to manage boundaries as an ongoing process, especially at specific developmental stages. Successful boundaries management is achieved through a balance of differentiation and integration. On one hand, a consortium must differentiate itself from its environment, as a unique organization, with a unique definition of goals, funds, and members. But unsuccessful differentiation threatens the consortium's viability. On the other hand, the consortium must aim for integration with its environment, in order to coalesce with publishers, vendors, and libraries. Further, too little integration results in to isolation, reducing consortia effectiveness and perhaps leading to eventual dissolution.

Thus, consortia have a life cycle, which is developmental that consists of several stages, common to all consortia, despite social, political, cultural and technological differences. But more commonly there are four stages: embryonic, early development, development and maturation.

Shachaf (2003) has discussed them briefly with examples from different consortia all over the world. These are:

8.17.1. The Embryonic Stage

This stage is characterized by informal, voluntary networking activities and inter-library loans. However, attributes of this pre-establishment stage are based on the cases of Italy, Micronesia, and Spain. The recognition of the need for collaboration is the initiating force, whether internal or external to the later established consortium. Further, sporadic efforts for cooperation are evident throughout the country for single-type library consortia, as in the case of Italy and Spain. These efforts provide the basis upon which a committee of academic library leaders and other stakeholders can begin to work towards establishing formal mechanisms of national cooperation.

Italy, Brazil and China exhibit this transition but another aspect of this committee work is collection of data and best practices from other consortia worldwide. The cases of China and Italy can be cited with efforts to obtain funding and to create awareness of the need for library collaboration. Ultimately, it is governmental funding and approval that enables the foundation of a formal library consortium, which leads to the next developmental stage. However, at this point, consortia need strong internal leadership and are affected strongly by external forces in the task environment.

8.17.2. Early Development

The early developmental stage is characterized by the transition from embryonic to development stage, towards an independent, self-defined and self-supported maturation stage. Usually, this state is mentioned as the first phase or the trial period. Brazil's case study provides an example of this stage while the information also derived from the cases of China and Israel. Recently established consortia are composed of a group of member libraries, which are using the external funds to implement the plan approved at the embryonic stage. The consortium at this stage defines and cultivates its processes and member relationships.

First, the consortium gains understanding of the best structure, budgets, relationships, and services that fit within its specific context. Then, the consortium also employs intensive assessment of its predecessors and works through the funding arrangements. It must achieve the primary goals of its charter and demonstrate benefits that will reach fruition in the development stage. The consortium at this stage might provide several shared subscriptions beyond the bibliographic network and inter-library loan services. Some of these subscriptions are international bibliographic and full-text databases' subscriptions, and some are local services. However, differentiation and integration efforts are evident at this stage, when the consortium is creating its unique identity and cultivating outside relationships. This phase may last for from one to three years and appears to be a prerequisite for the next developmental stage.

8.17.3. Development

This is third stage which is characterized by tension between confidence and uncertainty. Success through the first developmental stages suggests sustainability, but there is uncertainty regarding the consortium's future. Consortium works to secure its viability by seeking funds from external sources and to suggest internal membership commitment. These funds are used to enhance operations, increase membership, and expand services. For example, the Chinese consortium devised a business economics model for their services, and the Israeli consortium planned to increase library membership. However, both described the process of extending the number and range of services.

Another example may be cited for the UK, where JISC in 1999 approved three years funding for NESLI, which is projected by that time to be a self-financing management agent on the basis of its service revenues.

In this phase, the number of subscriptions shared between consortia members grows and some services are added. This stage lasts up to five years, where efforts are focused on the consortium's effectiveness and efficiency.

8.17.4. Maturation

This stage was observed only in the case of the Australian consortium, which was just embarking on the maturation phase (Costello, 1999). However, US statewide consortia suggests some characteristics of mature consortia. Therefore, the characteristics of this stage are based mainly on the state-wide consortia and the Australian consortium.

Consortium activities in this stage usually include: union catalogues and inter-library loan, access to electronic resources through shared subscriptions, supporting Internet connections, and sometimes, providing hardware for that purpose. Membership is expanded and services are extended beyond the publicly supported academic libraries. Nationwide consortia at this stage are expected to be independent from most external funding, government or otherwise, but statewide consortia vary in their funding resources and mechanism. Some were funded as part of the state budget on an ongoing basis, and others received ad hoc funding. Consortia might still get support from their parent funding agencies, at a lower proportion of support. The membership fees and service fees are a significant part of the budget at this stage.

However, the size of the consortium is generally established at this stage, and most potential members are partners in the stable consortia. The consortium operates as an independent organization and is perceived as the primary conduit and negotiation agent for electronic licensing subscription. Consortium at this stage is supposed to performing in full operation and works to streamline its processes. Though, competition from other consortia may now increase the pressure to maintain organizational boundaries and identifying improved services by collaborating with other consortia but now the consortium can be said stable, with a clear identity and clear boundaries. This stage can exist for many years, during which minor changes in membership, services, goals, and budgets may occur.

It should also be noted that although a consortium may perform at a maturation stage for long time, it may develop further in one of two directions but its first direction is disbanding or termination of the consortia activities, which may occur at any stage of development if consortia viability weakens to that degree. However, so far this path is not common and hardly mentioned in the previous literature. Examples of consortium failure at the nationwide or statewide level may be cited for the Farmington Plan in the US and CISTI (Canada), NCLIS (US) and USBE (International).

A second possible path may lead to Meta Consortium, which is a consortium of consortia, founded on the basis of cooperation among several consortia to achieve shared goals. International Coalition of Library Consortia (ICoLC) and the eIFL consortium are the best example of meta consortium. This cooperation among several consortia at the international level is now at the embryonic stage. For example, ICoLC first met at 1997, and continues to be an informal, self-organized group comprising nearly 150 library consortia from around the world. It facilitates communication and discussion among library consortia. A Meta Consortium as a new consortium can be expected to follow the development stages already identified for the nationwide consortia life cycle.

Thus, it is concluded that organizational growth and change can be conceived of in terms of life cycle development, which suggests that organizations are born, grow older, and die (Adizes, 1979).However, unlike the business dynamic, for nationwide consortia, size is driven by context rather than by organization age. Furthermore, the growth rate dimension of the business model does not apply to the nationwide consortia development. These differences may be due to the fact that these consortia are not-for-profit organizations. Universal life cycle approach most closely mirrors as compared to other business development models of library consortia developmental stages, but it is none-the-less a poor fit.

Lastly, it can be said that nationwide purchasing consortia emerged during the last decade in many countries around the world. Despite the differences in their political, social and cultural environments, these consortia share many common characteristics and a universal developmental sequence.

SUMMARY

This chapter deals with the concept of nation-wide single library consortium. There are two ways of formation of new consortium: migration into new consortium that takes place where existing consortia members, not satisfied with resources made available will see requirements elsewhere; and secondly is the merging where two or more than two consortia are merged to form a new consortium. Besides, national site licensing is also discussed with the examples from international and national levels.

Further, a frame of reference for the development of nationwide library consortia and details on a universal life cycle at the inter-organizational level of analysis are also discussed.

BIBLIOGRAPHICAL REFERENCES

Adizes, I. (1979). Organizational Passages – Diagnosing and Treating Life Cycle Problems of Organizations. Organizational Dynamics, 8(1): 3–25.

Arora, J. and Agarwal, P. (2004). Building Digital Libraries in a Consortium Mode: towards A National Consortium. In DRTC-INDEST (IIT, Delhi)-USEFI Joint Symposium on Consortia held during 6-8 October 2004. DRTC, ISI, Bangalore. Paper E.1-29.

Ball, D. (2003). Public Libraries and the Consortium Purchase of Electronic Resources. The Electronic Library, 21 (4): 301-309.

Birdie, C. and Patil, Y.M. (2010). Migrating from Informal to Formal Consortium-COSTLI Issues. In E. Isaksson, J. Lagerstrom, A. Holl and N. Bawdekar (Eds.): Library and Information Services in Astronomy VI: 21st Century Astronomy Librarianship, From New Ideas to Action. Vol 433. Astronomical Society of the Pacific, California (USA). Pp. 332-335.

Bley, R. (2000). NESLI: A Successful National Consortium. Library Consortium Management, 2 (1): 18-28.

CARLI (2019). CARLI Membership Agreement. Available at: https://www.carli.illinois.edu/membership/memagree.

Costello, D. (1999). More, Better, Cheaper: the Impossible Dream? Information Technology and Libraries, 18 (3): 154–159.

Fullan, M. (2001). The New Meaning of Educational Change. 4th Ed. Teachers College Press, New York.

Hunter, K. (1992). The National Site License Model. Serials Review, 18(1-2): 71-72, 91.

Lindley, J.A. (2003). The Turkish National Site License (TRNSL). Serials, 16 (2): 187-190.

Patil, Y.M. (2014). Consortium Approach to Resource Sharing in an E-Environment. Scientific Publishers, Jodhhpur.

Potter, W G. (1997). Recent Trends in Statewide Academic Library Consortia. Library Trends,45(3): 416-434.

Rani, Yashoda and Dhiman, A.K. (2011). Why Not a Nationwide Single Library Consortium? In Satyaprakash Singh (Eds.): Digital Library Management and Challenges. Asian Books Private Limited, New Delhi. Pp. 404-410.

Shachaf, P. (2003). Nationwide Library Consortia Lifecycle. Libri, 53: 94-102.

Scott, W. R. (2001). Institutions and Organizations. 2nd Ed. Sage Publications, London.

Turner, R. (1999). National Site Licensing and Consortia Purchasing. Library Consortium Management: An International Journal, 1(1-2): 33-40.

Van de Ven et al (1975). Framework for Interorganizational Analysis. In A. Nagandhi et al (Eds.): Interorganizational Theory. Kent State University Press, Kent (Ohio). Pp. 19-38.

Woodsworth, Simpson A. and Wall, T. B. (1991). Library Cooperation and Networks: A Basic Reader. Neal-Schuman Publishers, New York.

Zhu, X. (2011). The National Site Licensing of Electronic Resources: An Institutional Perspectives. Journal of Library and Information Science, 9 (1): 51-76.

9

Evolving Roles of Library Consortia

The consortia which are the agreement, combination or group are formed to undertake an enterprise beyond the resources of any one member, usually involve collaboration among direct competitors. Zhang (cited in Ossai, 2010) notes that while consortium building often expresses itself in resource sharing, it could also include a planned process of getting libraries to share human resources, bibliographic data and various other services found in each of the operating libraries that are part of the sharing group.

It is already seen that the library consortia vary widely in their type, goals, structure, membership and funding. Their organizational framework and structure may be a formal or informal agreement between libraries based on some common principle or principles. They may also take the form of a cooperative arrangement among several libraries that could involve the loaning of books, inter-library exchange of staff, or an electronic network interconnecting different libraries for shared access to resources. Most commonly, a library consortium encompasses similar types of libraries: academic, special (such as medical or corporate), or public. A consortium may also be geographically based and include several types of libraries. However, what remains unclear in some of the professional literature is a precise distinction between a library consortium and a library association, other than the connotation that a consortium may be a more closely-knit group and created for some specific purpose.

9.1. MISSION OF CONSORTIA

Generally, the mission of a consortium is to fully utilize and develop the information resources of their libraries for the purpose of promoting education, research and lifelong learning. A vision should be thereto create a virtual library by linking together participating organizations via electronic networks. An overview of some of the principal library consortia reveal that their mission includes the following (Ossai, 2010):

- Establishing a formal relationship between the members of the consortium in order to foster cooperation and communication.
- Supporting the information needs of clients through regional cooperation, while encouraging each member to build good, basic collections sufficient to meet out the needs of its clients.
- Promoting resource sharing and enhancing access to information, formulating appropriate collection development and acquisitions policies among members, and exploring opportunities for cost savings.
- Facilitating access to information through shared computer systems and networks.
- Utilizing appropriate and current technology and keeping abreast of new technological developments.

Besides, library consortia may also be used for

improving information literacy among clients and sharing training resources and expertise where appropriate.

9.2. OPEN ACCESS AND LIBRARY CONSORTIA

Open access (OA) is a mechanism by which research outputs are distributed online, free of cost or other access barriers. However, the main focus of the open access movement is "peer reviewed research literature. Historically, this has centered mainly on print-based academic journals. Conventional (non-open access) journals cover publishing costs through access tolls such as subscriptions, site licenses or pay-per-view charges" (Wikipedia, 2019). Open access can be applied to all forms of published research output, including peer-reviewed and nonpeer-reviewed academic journal articles, conference papers, theses, book chapters and monographs etc.

Read (2010) mentions that library consortia have proven that a collective voice succeeds where a solitary one fails. Through advocacy, education and institutional repositories, consortia are utilizing collaborative relationships to effect change, yet consortia may also be helpful in promoting open access. Talking with faculty about open access, Malenfant (2010) says that open access requires knowledge of its principles and technology, as well as preparation and strategy. Many librarians agree with an advocacy role, but carrying the torch alone or even as a team can seem as daunting as confronting the steep increases in journal costs. Some consortia have created informational packets, policy statements, written negotiation tools and brochures for both librarians and faculty. The Scholarly Publishing and Academic Resources Coalition (SPARC), a division of the Association of Research Libraries, is a pioneering effort in this direction. In existence since 1997 and now supported by over 800 alliance members, SPARC furthers the open access movement by educating, advocating, and assisting with the creation and proliferation of open access publishing.

Canadian Association of Research Libraries (CARL), a 29-member consortium, is another vocal advocate for open access. CARL advocates for both institutional repositories and authors' rights with its "Transform Scholarly Communication" project. CARL has worked with SPARC to create a Canadian Author Addendum to aid faculty and researchers in retaining the rights to their writings. Most recently, CARL has initiated an Institutional Repository Pilot Project Harvester, which makes searchable the contents of CARL member libraries' repositories to increase accessibility of open access content.

Boston Library Consortium, with 17 members, supports the open access movement via advocacy and education. Massachusetts Institute of Technology following the lead of its member library, the consortium adopted an "Agreement to Extend Author's Rights." By advocating for authors' rights and institutional repositories, the Boston Library Consortium hopes to inspire its members to prioritize open access efforts (Corbett, 2009).

Some library consortia have taken a role in creating and maintaining institutional repositories in addition to advocacy and education efforts. Consortia can put institutional repositories within reach of even very small institutions by sharing the cost of infra-structure, such as staffing, hardware, and networked storage space. OhioLINK, consortium for 89 member libraries, has done just this. Though its larger member libraries could build institutional repositories on their own, OhioLINK saw the need to aid its smaller members, for whom creating an institutional repository would be cost-prohibitive (Smith, 2009). Seventeen OnioLINK libraries have their own institutional repository through its Digital Resource Commons.

Contributing financially to broader open access efforts is another way for consortia to participate in the

OA movement. OhioLINK and the Pacific Northwest's Orbis Cascade Alliance are among fifteen library consortia that purchase a membership with the Directory of Open Access Journals (DOAJ) which facilitates identifying and using peer-reviewed scholarly and scientific open access journals.

Besides, Colorado Alliance of Research Libraries has an institutional repository system similar to that of OhioLINK - their Alliance Digital Repository Service (ADR) uses open source software, centralized hardware, and shared staff to power individualized repositories for its member libraries. Seven of the ten Colorado Alliance of Research Libraries institutions have repositories through ADR.

Inflibnet, Gandhinagar (Gujarat) also has a digital repository known as Shodhganga which is a reservoir of the theses and dissertations submitted to Indian universities. The repository has a collection of 2,10,661 theses which are contributed by member libraries (http://shodhganga.inflibnet.ac.in/). However, on the top five, in terms of the numbers of theses submitted, are the Punjab University, Aligarh Muslim University, Jawaharlal Nehru University, Karnataka University and Anna University.

OA initiatives sponsored by consortia can also mitigate the strain on library budgets. Consortia have successfully procured savings for libraries by negotiating with publishers. Those that actively support OA models have the potential to greatly reduce libraries' costs because OA models are much cheaper for libraries than traditional journals. Suber (2007) rightly states that "open access journals are economically sustainable because the true costs of peer review, manuscript preparation, and open access dissemination are considerably lower than the prices we currently pay for subscription-based journals. ... Moreover, as OA spreads, libraries will realize large savings from the conversion, cancellation, or demise of subscription-based journals".

Thus, by sharing resources, ideas, expertise, and funding, consortia with open access initiatives can lead the transition to more sustainable and equitable forms of scholarly communication. Library consortia are uniquely poised to further the ideal of equitable access to information. Maskell (2008) states that this view of library consortia "supports the belief that consortia have a responsibility to address social issues such as the widening gap between the information rich and the information poor."

9.3. CONSORTIA AND DIGITAL PRESERVATION OF E-RESOURCES

The main stakeholders, viz. publishers, consortia and users have important role in digital preservation and facilitating perpetual access to subscribed content. In the process of licensing and negotiating, the consortia should take concrete steps to ensure perpetual access of subscribed content for future use. The following aspects should be taken into consideration (Bhattacharjya, 2017):

- While negotiating deals with publishers, consortia must ensure the modalities of access to archival information of the subscribed content in the process of licensing;
- There should be an archival unit within the consortia or institution to take care of archival aspects; and
- The consortia should get involved in participation with existing international Digital Preservation Systems.

Further, the publishers' archival policies should be considered on the following lines:

- Archiving policies for long term digital preservation and perpetual access;
- Access post cancellation;

- Transfer of e-journals from one publisher to another and policy matter thereon;
- Publishers getting merged, taking over by one over another and
- Breakdown of publishers' servers due to natural calamities.

Thus, the publishers should be asked to host their content locally. The preservation matter to be sensitized amongst libraries and policy makers; and the adequate manpower in this area be trained and made available at each institute and consortia location.

Therefore, there is a need to have access to subscribed content from publisher's platform but there are inherent limitations to publisher's archiving models. There is an urgent need for long-term perspective as technology keeps changing rapidly with risk of obsolescence requiring constant migration of contents to new platforms. It is seen although that publishers facilitate perpetual access to subscribed content, but guaranteeing perpetual access suffer from trust factor with the following aspects (Satyanarayana, Krishnan and Arora, 2004):

- Archiving is a new function for publishers, but they never engaged themselves in the past although they owned the content.
- Large number of medium/small publishers cannot afford archiving as it is cost prohibitive.

Hence, the survival of publishing companies is questionable in the age of economic crisis and competitive environment. A wide variety of other organizations are developing "Digital Preservation Systems" (DPS) to overcome the above problems. Their strategy involves a comprehensive approach to preservation, including standards, migration, replication, emulation, metadata attachment and building trustworthy digital object repositories.

Besides, consortia subscribe huge amount of information contents from different publishers with provision to access back files. With passage of time, consortia may add or drop titles as per need or the consortium may itself stop continuing or join with yet another consortium that may create access problem to content. In order to mitigate problem of access to subscribed content, many developments have emerged in recent years to provide services to publishers' past contents. Therefore, consortia should make every effort to participate or to become member of any of the DPSs. The following selective DPSs are briefed from the point of view of consortia archival interest (Patil, 2014; Dhiman, 2016).

9.3.1. PORTICO

Portico is a digital preservation service for electronic journals, books and other contents which is provided by ITHAKA, a non-profit organization with a mission to help the academic community to use digital technologies to preserve the scholarly records and to advance research and teaching in sustainable ways. It was created in 2002 as a project funded by the Andrew W. Mellon Foundation to further its seminal E-Journal Archiving Program. Today, Portico is among the leading digital preservation services provider in the world.

Fig. 9.1. Portico Logo
(*Source* : https://tinyurl.com/tjkeran)

(i) Access to Archived Content : Publishers and libraries have entrusted e-journals, e-books and other content to Portico. Participating libraries gain access to preserved/archived content when specific conditions or 'trigger events' occur which causes titles no longer available from publisher or any other source. The 'triggered events" may include:

- Cessation of publisher's operations;
- Discontinuation of a title by a publisher;
- Back issues no longer offered by a publisher; and
- Catastrophic and sustained failure of a publisher's delivery platform.

(ii) Post Cancellation Access : The majority of titles in Portico are available for post cancellation access, if needed. Upon receipt of a claim from a participating institution and confirmation of the past subscription status by the publishers, campus-wide access is provided.

(iii) Portico's Certification : Portico becomes the first digital preservation service to be independently audited by the Centre for Research Libraries (CRL) during 2010. CRL has certified that Portico is a trusted, reliable digital preservation solution that serves the needs of the library community.

(iv) Archives Facts and Figures : Portico is one of the most comprehensive digital preservation archives in the world, which holds more contents than other available archives. The data given below provides regular updated figures on content, including details about various files and formats as well as global library and publishers participation. Upto December 2019, 1.7 billion files have been preserved in PORTICO comprising of:

- Journal articles preserved:88+ million
- Books preserved:1+ million
- Digital collection items preserved:4+ million
- Triggered titles:122

- Participating libraries: 1,014
- Participating publishers: 659

(v) How Portico saves Time and Money : With reliable digital preservation service solution in place, libraries can move their collection more rapidly from print to electronic formats, freeing up precious space in their libraries and storage facilities and reducing purchasing costs. Publishers can also reduce costs related to printing and mailing by transitioning to greater reliance on electronic sales of their publications. Both libraries and publishers can save the time by participating in Portico in handling both archival and post-cancellation access.

Besides, the libraries and publishers participating in Portico have reliable, secure access to archived content under specifically defined circumstances. Faculty, staff and students at participating institutions can access the archive to use content that has experienced a 'trigger event' or that fulfills a post cancellation claim. It can be contacted thorough its website www.portico.org.

9.3.2. LOCKSS

LOCKSS that stands for Lots of Copies Keep Stuff Safe, is a free and open software developed under the auspices of Stanford University started in the year 1999 with a vision to empower communities to steward for themselves the content that mattered to them. It works on the principles like replication, format migration and repair through a polling mechanism. When LOCKSS is downloaded and installed on an individual system, it automatically becomes part of a LOCKSS network comprising of hundreds and thousands of nodes. Each node connected to network share information with one another as a result of which multiple copies of information gets produced at different geographical locations. LOCKSS includes a unique polling and repair mechanism. If particular information on a node gets deleted or reports a difference in comparison to other nodes, it is automatically pulled out odd in the network and the deleted information is replaced or the difference found is neutralized thereby keeping the data secure for long.

Fig. 9.2. LOCKSS Logo

(*Source* : https://en.wikipedia.org/wiki/LOCKSS)

LOCKSS possesses various features – some of them are:

- Support format migration i.e. if the information is available in the format which is no longer valid; LOCKSS automatically changes it to the usable or current format.
- The requests through LOCKSS for material are sent to the publisher, and if the content is not retrieved for any reason, the LOCKSS copy is provided with one exception of dynamic content i.e., the advertisements or graphics that change with each screen display, remains static.

(i) Participating Libraries and Publishers : There are about fifty publishers who are currently participating in LOCKSS program, and most of these have agreed to allow their subscribers to use LOCKSS as a backup system. LOCKSS is a "light Archive" i.e. it provides access to archived information even in case of temporary loss of access to publisher or publishers' website.

(ii) LOCKSS Fee : Though LOCKSS is open and free software, but its members have to join an alliance called LOCKSS alliance. The participation fee tiers for institutions in the United States are based on the Carnegie Classification but international institutions can also join.

Its annual fee ranges between Rs. 77000.00 to 762000.00 (Shah and Gul, 2019) but pricing information can be confirmed through JISC.

9.3.3. CLOCKSS

CLOCKSS that stands for Controlled Lots of Copies Keep the Stuff Safe, is a "not for profit joint venture" of the leading scholarly publishers and research libraries whose mission is to build a sustainable, geographically distributed dark archive with which to ensure the long term survival of Web-based scholarly publications for the benefit of global research community. Contents no longer available from any publisher ('triggered content') are available free. It uniquely assigns the abandoned and orphaned contents with a Creative Commons License to ensure they remain available.

There are the following reasons for choosing CLOCKSS:

- It is nonprofit organization governed by, and for, its stake holders — publishers and libraries, who have equal say in deciding procedures, priorities and when to trigger content;
- It is decentralized, geographically disparate preservation model that ensures that the digital assets of the community will survive intact. It satisfies the demand for locally situated archives with 12 archive nodes;
- Low operating costs make it possible for institutions of all sizes and budgets to participate in it;
- Orphaned and abandoned electronic scholarly contents are permanently preserved in it; open access contents no longer available with publishers are available for free;
- Its participants have the opportunity to be deeply involved in all aspects; and
- Libraries and publishers want a choice of archiving

solutions; therefore, some institutions may prefer to participate in multiple archives.

Though it has an endowment that is built and asks libraries, publishers and other participating institutes to contribute but it has goal to have lower participation fee. As libraries migrate from print to online only publications, they expect assurances from publishers that their shared investments are protected and preserved for generations to come. CLOCKSS archive provides this assurance via its secure network of content that can be accessed when a "trigger event" is deemed to have occurred. This archive is unique because it makes all content triggered from the archive freely available.

(i) Contribute to CLOCKSS : Libraries and publishers around the world are invited to contribute to help to build an endowment, which is intended to lower participating fee over time. Lower operating costs make it possible for institutions of all sizes and budgets to participate in CLOCKSS.

(ii) Participating Libraries and Publishers : Today, with 310 supporting libraries and 250 participating publishers, CLOCKSS preserves the authoritative versions of 33 million journal articles, over 26,000 serial and 183,000 book titles, and a wide array of supplementary materials and metadata information, with regular checking of the validity of stored data and preserving it for the long term.

CLOCKSS is committed to keeping fees affordable, to allow libraries and publishers of all sizes and budgets to participate in CLOCKSS. Thus, the participation is affordable and anticipating still lower costs over a time. It can be contacted through its website: www.clockss.org.

9.3.4. JSTOR

JSTOR was conceived in 1994 by William G. Bowen, the then President of the Andrew W. Mellon Foundation to help the university and college libraries to provide adequate space for an ever-increasing amount of published scholarship. Later, in 1995, following a pilot launched under the direction of the University of Michigan, JSTOR was established as an independent not-for-profit organization to help the scholars, researchers and students to discover, use and build upon a wide range of contents in a trusted digital archive of over one thousand academic journals and other scholarly contents. In 2009, JSTOR merged with and became a service of ITHAKA that works to advance and preserve knowledge and to improve teaching and learning through the use of digital technologies.

(i) Collaboration : JSTOR collaborates with hundreds of publishers and content providers to preserve and broaden access to their scholarly contents. It connects libraries, researchers and students around the world with vital scholarly contents in more than 50 disciplines.

(ii) Content and Collections : JSTOR offers high quality, inter-disciplinary content to support scholarship and teaching. It currently offers more than 10 million academic journal articles, 50,000 books, and 2 million primary source documents in 75 disciplines.

Its contents are expanded continuously with a current emphasis on international publications as well as pamphlets, images and manuscripts from libraries, societies and the museums. However, the ultimate aim of JSTOR is to make available to everyone who wants access to it, while doing so in a way that ensures sustainability of the service.

Scholars, teachers and the students around the world are making use of JSTOR daily, searching JSTOR directly or locating articles and other content through search engines and specialized portals. New initiatives are coming up to support innovations in scholarship such as using the content for text mining and enabling the pre-publication sharing of ideas among scholars, which are also underway.

JSTOR also includes scholarship published in over one thousand journals of the highest quality academic journals as well as monographs and other materials. New collections are developed continuously, expanding JSTOR's international depth and disciplinary range, and including content types such as letters, oral histories, pamphlets, plant type specimens and 3-D models. It can be contacted through its website: www.jstor.org.

9.3.5. Astrophysics Data System (ADS)

ADS, the Astrophysics Data System of NASA which have the largest freely available Archive of scanned literature in the world is an abstract service and full-text articles in a central facility of bibliographic research in astronomy. One major part of this archive is to provide access to the full-text of the historical astronomical literature. This covers almost all major astronomical journals and many smaller journals accessible online from issue number one.

Established in the year 1992, it has completed its twenty-seven years of its existence and acts as central discovery engine for access to wide range of astronomy and related literature and continues to serve astronomical community at large. It began as a data system, became bibliographic system and is now the coordinating mechanism for publishing, data, ontologies, bibliometrics, scientometrics and other tools and services using astronomical information. ADS maintain three bibliographic databases containing more than 13 million records covering publications in Astronomy and Astrophysics, Physics, and the arXiv e-prints. Abstracts and full-text of major astronomy and physics publications are indexed and searchable through the new ADS modern search form as well as a classic search form.

In addition to maintaining its bibliographic corpus, the ADS tracks citations and usage of its records to provide advanced discovery and evaluation capabilities. Integrated in its databases, the ADS provide access and pointers to a wealth of external resources, including electronic articles available from publisher's websites, astronomical object information, data catalogues and data sets hosted by external archives. It currently has links to over 13.3 million records maintained by its collaborators. This depth of information has enabled a number of publications (refereed, non-refereed) in fields such as bibliometrics and information science.

However, there are two main parts of ADS: the abstracts and full article service. Its *Abstracts Service* provides access to four databases- Astronomy and Astrophysics; Instrumentation, Physics & Geophysics and the Los Almos preprints in astronomy. Each database is separately searchable through different interfaces, allowing user to easily identify the information in which they are interested. *ADS Article Service* provides access to scanned images of astronomical journal articles in a variety of formats and resolutions. The project initially focused on the scanning last years major astronomical journals, seeking permission from the copyright holders and publishers. Subsequently, and as a result of the project's success, both smaller journals and older volumes started being digitized and made available. Later, it moved to place all the historical astronomical literature online.

Besides, ADS Users Group (ADSUG) is also there who advises the ADS on the operations of the project, and recommends changes and improvements to both its services and procedures in order to maximize the scientific productivity of the community it serves. It can be contacted through its website: http://ads.harvard.edu/.

9.3.6. Mirror Sites of Publishers

It is a publisher extended facility, which can be hosted locally. This is an archiving model by the consortium where the publishers make available their entire content and related software to the consortium for mirroring locally. Updates are sent for local uploading by FTP of CDs. This is an advantage for the publishers as arrangement eases traffic to publisher's site.

9.4. LIBRARY CONSORTIA AND KNOWLEDGE MANAGEMENT

Knowledge management (KM) is a quite timely technique of organization theory and management. The knowledge-based organizations are the organization of the future and libraries have much to learn from industry and business for once more. The rules and the tools of KM may contribute to the information and knowledge sharing and delivery throughout the world, as the globalization has facilitated the communication. Consortia, consisted from libraries of various strength, power, age, collection, staff experience and specialization can operate according to these concepts of KM in order to enhance effectiveness and efficiency as well as to expertise the services of the member- libraries (Katsirikou, 2012).

Swan et.al. (2000) states that there are three modes of knowledge development that facilitate the value-creating knowledge processes:

Generative : Knowledge developed and created through joint activities involved with solving problems;

Productive : Knowledge developed and accumulated through the creation of products and services. This knowledge is reproductive in the sense that it may be applied repeatedly but within a different guise; and

Representative : Knowledge made available to suppliers for example, concerning their own value creating processes.

Thus, knowledge mobilization depends upon an organizational culture that promotes overlapping behaviours such as information sharing and joint experimentation. Anyhow, knowledge management philosophy is managing the balance of people, processes and technology that determines the organization and its relationship with its environment. Beneath this, there are layers of values and attitudes that determine whether the organization is a knowledge environment. It is about creating an environment where knowledge is valued and where the difference between information and knowledge, and their interdependence, is understood, an environment that values creativity and innovation, encourages a variety of working patterns and facilitates communication between people in different locations and from different departments.

Further, knowledge management philosophy creates an organization that encourages ideas, rewards success, allows people to fail and learn from failure, enables people to admit problems, reflect on and share failure, success, problems and solutions, and encourages people to ask for help. It creates an organization that is aware of its environment, developing a corporate instinct that allows it to react quickly and make informed decisions.

Thus, a model of the knowledge management system of consortium is given by Katsirikou (2012) as shown in figure 9.3.

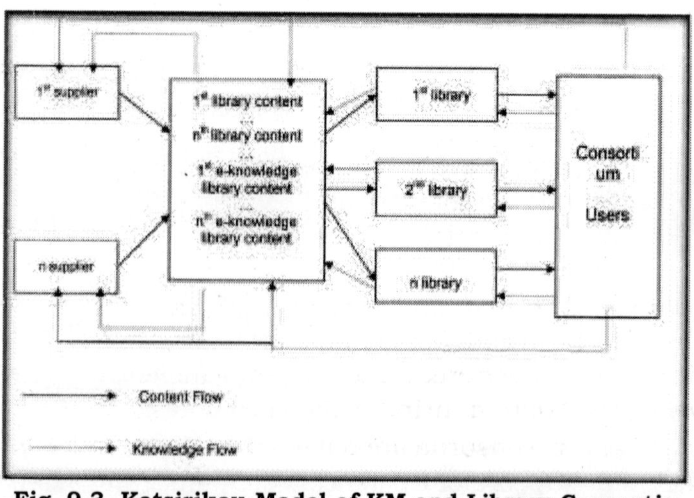

Fig. 9.3. Katsirikou Model of KM and Library Consortia

It is consisted by four major integrated parts: the first part is the knowledge resources, such as publishers, database providers, websites, R & D organizations (industries, universities, research institutions, etc.), digital media and information technology. Its first part directs its content to the second part, which is consisted by the libraries' content and e-knowledge database of every library as a unique integrated and distributed system. This new two-part information and knowledge system is diffused to the libraries - members, which play the role of wholesalers and are the third part of the systems, as the fourth one is the users of libraries members.

However, the crucial point here is the second part, which consists of an entirely integrated body regarding resources. Consortium members face so that the suppliers and the users are equally common. Otherwise, if the model would be one-library centered, the collaborating libraries would be considered as customers and would be included in the users.

9.5. FUTURE OF LIBRARY CONSORTIA

Consortia are having to negotiate the ever-changing serials landscape in the 21st century. Consortia are formed around an array of common interests, be they geographic, institutional size, or disciplinary in nature, among many others. Consortia have occurred as a consequence of libraries which have a long history of cooperation, and the advent of the Internet and the explosion of digitized resources have not only intensified the need for such cooperation but the concerns of consortia are more complex than ever, and consortia are having to reinvent themselves. In addition to traditional issues such as group licensing for electronic materials, educational and training ventures, shared print repositories, and cooperative cataloguing, consortia are having to navigate new things, including support for Open Access materials and emerging metrics for evaluating shared collections.

Consortia have a unique opportunity to affect the economic and social life of information distribution and delivery. In the digital world, the very distinctions between "monograph" and "serial" have become less and less meaningful. For example, is not a subscription to a collection of e-books a serial? Even one-time purchases of digitized materials require extended maintenance in ways unforeseen in the print world. Libraries, publishers, vendors, subscription agents, book jobbers, and the content and service providers are struggling with how best to adapt services and workflows for maximum efficiency while concurrently fulfilling the vastly different missions. The libraries are able to work with all others in the serials chain in order to expedite the implementation of such efficiencies by working together through consortia.

Thus, since the growth of library consortia during 1990s, it has become a major force in acquisition of electronic resources to all its participants. During the same period, publishers marketed the so called 'big deal' to consortia with large package of e-journals. So, the consortia have become focal points in marketing and large-scale sale of database aggregation from various vendors. With technological changes, consortia are looking ahead for newer aspects and show more sustainable ways to provide resources to library patrons. It is time for thinking beyond books and journals and think of how that information might access and used in electronic environment, for example, the impact of mobile technology has given the way for access to articles and book chapters. New technologies and methodologies are emerging to measure self-publication repositories or in an open access publishing model. Thus, a new pricing models at articles level or book chapters or pay-per-view models are emerging which might supplant subscription models.

However, in spite of emergence of open access system which is alternative to the commercial publishers' model, there still exists a need for libraries, consortia and publishers to work together and to look beyond what they have so far achieved together. Library consortia are strong advocates on behalf of alternate models due to unsustainable economics of current publishing models.

Besides, the consortia have promoted collaboration and move beyond 'buying clubs' for purchase of electronic resources, support for digitization, preservation projects and cooperative collection-development. They also assisted libraries to move print resources into storage to create more public services and creation of print repositories. Consortia have become more important than ever before as library budgets shrink and old ways of operating become economically untenable. Perry (2009) in his international survey revealed that two new issues have become the highest priorities for most consortia for the immediate future: budget management and license renegotiations. Out of necessity, library consortia will be focusing a great deal of attention on managing their budgets in this time of economic uncertainty.

EBSCO studies which were conducted during February 2010 and 2011 also reveal that more than 80 percent of librarians responded indicated that they were likely to move print plus online subscriptions to online only in order to achieve budget goals. It is also to be noted that pricing models are evolving in response to prevailing business conditions and expects the next generation of pricing likely to be based on some forms of tiers to be arrived in the coming years keeping marked improvements over existing pricing models. Even if, the pricing models are changing, will not they alter library's fiscal constraints? However, the librarians will be using more pay-per-views (PPV) to deliver articles to users in addition to dropping large journals packages.

The launch of iPad in 2010 created a stir in the publishing and reading communities as tablet devices showed their e-content potential and publishers responded making their content increasingly available on mobile devices. How does the move to mobile services affect the periodicals pricing and libraries? It is said that libraries will continue to struggle to meet the demands for mobile support and built into library acquired products. In order to remain competitive, they must offer mobile options. But new technology will not come without price. In order to survive during the next phase of coming years, the library community has to locus on the much more difficult task of finding new opportunities. Libraries, publishers and vendors will all shed some legacy process, where information packaging pattern will change leading to the inevitable new pricing models. Thus, the times are changing, and to survive, libraries will need to be more proactive (Bosch, Henderson and Klusendorf, 2011). Nevertheless, the librarians and consortia will continue to explore new answers to many of their problems. However, in the years to come, consortia may be able to provide access to entire requirements of the library and libraries have to carry out services to users based on products made available to them (Alexander, 1999) but what will be the future?

Thus, the near future may see a contraction in the number of consortia, a broadening of the services offered by the consortia, more inter-connections between the consortia and a trend toward a formalization of their structures in order to take the pressure off the range of volunteers. With these developments, there will be the need for further skill development on the part of librarians and the consortia staffs to learn how to work this new environment most effectively. Librarians at all levels will need to develop new skills and middle-management will need to be able to work effectively across different organizational structures while achieving results. Senior managers will have to learn new power relationships, to become able to negotiate for results where they do not have total control.

Besides, there exist ample opportunities for the consortia to expand beyond the well-trodden ground of resource sharing and electronic resource purchasing in order to help member libraries strengthen their respective contributions to student success and advance their institutions' missions (Arch and Gilman, 2017). However, to do so, consortia and their members must be prepared to experiment with new types of collaboration and develop more significant levels of trust within the group.

SUMMARY

This chapter discusses the evolving roles of library consortia. It starts with the mission, and further expands the role of Library Consortia in open access initiatives. For archiving of the e-resources, various initiatives of Digital Preservation System (DPS), like PORTICO, LOCKSS etc. are also briefly described. The chapter ends with the role of library consortia in knowledge management and the comments on the future of the library consortia.

BIBLIOGRAPHICAL REFERENCES

Arch, X. and Gilman, I. (2017). Innovating for Impact: The Next Evolution of Library Consortia. Collaborative Librarianship, 9 (4). Available at: https://digitalcommons.du.edu/collaborativelibrarianship/vol9/iss4/4.

Alexander, A.W. (1999). Multi-Consortial Obligations: Too Much of a Good Thing. Library Consortium Management: An International Journal, 2 (7). Doi:10.1108/lcmij.2000.24702gaf.001.

Bhattacharjya, S. (2017). Digital Preservation of E-Resources in Library Consortia Environment: Publishers Perspective. IOSR Journal of Humanities and Social Science, 22 (4) Ver. 4: 92-98.

Corbett, H. (2009). The Crisis in Scholarly Communication - Part I: Understanding the Issues and Engaging Your Faculty. Technical Services Quarterly, 26(2): 125–134.

Bosch, S., Henderson, K. and Klusendorf, H. (2011). Under Pressure, Times are Changing: Periodicals Price Survey-2011. Library Journal, 36 (8): 30-34.

Dhiman, A.K. (2016). Assuring Access of E- Journals: Some Models for Digital Archiving. In Sangita Gupta (Ed.): Future of Libraries: Trends, Issues and Challenges (NOSOFOL-16 Proceedings). Black Publications, New Delhi. Pp. 95-105.

Katsirikou, A. (2012). Consortia and Knowledge Management: the Functional Context and an Organizational Model. Available at: https://docs.lib.purdue.edu/cgi/viewcontent.cgi? article =1578&context=iatul.

Malenfant, K.J. (2010). Leading Change in the System of Scholarly Communication: A Case Study of engaging Liaison Librarians for Outreach to Faculty. College and Research Libraries,71 (1): 63–76.

Maskell, C.A. (2008). Consortia: Anti-Competitive or in the Public Good? Library Hi Tech,26(2): 164–183.

Ossai, Ngozi Blessing (2010). Consortia Building among Libraries in Africa and the Nigerian Experience. Collaborative Librarianship, 2 (2): 74-85. Available at: https://digitalcommons.du.edu/collaborativelibrarianship/vol2/iss2/5.

Patil, Y.M. (2014). Consortium Approach to Resources Sharing in an E-Environment. Scientific Publishers (India), Jodhpur.

Perry, Katherine A. (2009). Where are Library Consortia Going? Results of A 2009 Survey. Serials, 22 (2): 124–25.

Read, Kim (2010). Collective Voice for Collective Good: Library Consortia, Open Access, and the Future of Scholarly Communication. OLA Quarterly, 16(3), 23-28.

Satyanarayana, N.V., Krishnan, S. and Arora, J. (2004). Library Consortia and Resource Sharing Initiatives in India: A White Paper. Rajiv Gandhi University of Health Sciences, Bangalore.

Shah, U.U. and Gul, S. (2019). LOCKSS, CLOCKSS & PORTICO: A Look into Digital Preservation Policies. Library Philosophy and Practice. Available at: https://www.researchgate.net/publication/332464326_LOCKSS_CLOCKSS_PORTICO_A_LOOK_INTO_DIGITAL_PRESERVATION_POLICIES/citation/download.

Smith, K.L. (2009). Open Access and Authors' Rights Management: A Possibility for Theology? Theological Librarianship, 2(1): 45–56.

Suber, P. (2007). Open Access Overview. Available at: http://www.earlham.edu/~peters/fos/overview.htm

Swan, W., Langford, N., Watson, I. and Varey, R.J. (2000.) Viewing the Corporate Community as a Knowledge Network. Corporate Communications: An International Journal, 5(2): 97-106.

Wikipedia (2019). Open Access. Available at: https://en.wikipedia.org/wiki/Open_access.

10 Important Library Consortia

Now, it is very clear that the rising costs and decreased purchasing power have forced libraries to share their resources to meet out the informational needs of their users. However, there are many reasons why libraries are turning to the consortium model, many of which relate to 'saving a buck'. The other are may include the following (Lowe and Feighan, 1999):

- It provides consistency of resources to guarantee equity of access amongst a particular group of libraries, where consistency means both in terms of information access, and also technological development or advancement.
- It provides more cost-effective solution for the library, with lower administration costs for the vendor, hence lower running costs overall.
- It can lead to benefits of shared knowledge, skill and experience among the libraries.
- It provides the libraries with increased lobbying power with vendors for product development.

- It provides an increase in end user autonomy and reliance on remote mediated reference services especially in poorly resourced and/or remote geographic areas.

Thus, library consortia can be seen as a way of improving business performance and patron satisfaction. It is also seen that the libraries around the world have known the benefits of working cooperatively for a long time and have formed consortia for purposes such as sharing cataloguing data, collection development and the acquisition of materials, and sharing the high costs of storage and preservation.

A survey of the literature indicates that consortia arrangements can be a 'win-win' situation for libraries, publishers and users alike (Phillips, 2001):

- Libraries gain greater bargaining power in contractual negotiations and, depending upon how the consortium is structured, may streamline processes in the selection, evaluation and acquisition of online resources. Cost savings at the individual institution level can be realized, providing additional purchasing power overall.
- For publishers a consortium provides a single point of negotiation and the potential for greater take-up of their products when attractive packages are offered. Standard licenses benefit publishers as well as libraries and, under some models, publishers gain consolidated ordering, renewals and payment. Consortia agreements sometimes also bring publishers new customers, which may ultimately increase their revenue.
- Users may get benefited more convenient for access to more titles. This is especially the case if improved bibliographic control can be achieved. The combined resources of consortium members are more likely to be able to achieve this than individual libraries working on their own to catalogue titles.

Thus, the consortia have become an accepted means for many libraries to provide more and better resources for users for the same or lower cost. They have emerged as effective in squeezing somewhat better deals out of publishers for electronic licenses, thereby increasing access and reducing per-use costs of information. They have demonstrated that demand rises with decreasing prices in the digital world. All about them have been discussed in previous chapters. Now, some important library consortia working at international level and national levels are discussed.

10.1. LIBRARY CONSORTIA AT INTERNATIONAL LEVEL

One of the first USA academic Consortia was the Triangle Research Libraries Network, formed in 1933. However, the first Consortium in the State of Illinois was founded in 1965 that was known as ILLINET, the Illinois Library and Information Network, which had a foundation of 18 Libraries that supplied services to over 500 public libraries (Weech, 2002). In fact, the consortia became so prolific in the USA, they have to-publish a Directory of Academic Library consortia as early as 1972.

Though, there are numerous very successful types of consortia amongst public libraries, but in the area of e-services, there is found a range of inconsistencies. For example, in the USA co-operation is extensive, with some of the most successful being the Internet Public Library (http://www.ipl.org) and the Librarian Index to the Internet (http://lii.org/). However, it is also found that in Europe funding for projects from the European Commission is often dependent upon co-operation, and when the project is completed the partnerships fell apart. Dobbie (2002) found that Switzerland, Denmark and Belgium have excellent networks of consortia, but other countries were struggling to develop co-operative e-services. On the other hand, Australia is shown to be innovative and a model for the establishment of cooperative Digital Collections.

Internationally, there are numerous examples of formal/informal co-operative groups and consortia that are very successful. Though, the International Coalition of Library Consortia (ICOLC) first met informally as the Consortium of Consortia (COC) in 1997, but it continues to be an informal, self-organized group comprising of nearly 200 library consortia from around the world (Feather, 2015). Coalition serves primarily higher education institutions by facilitating discussion among consortia on issues of common interest.

One of the largest Consortia in the world is OhioLink that itself is a consortium of 90 Ohio college and university libraries, plus the State Library of Ohio which work together to provide Ohio students, faculty and researchers with the information they need for teaching and research. It is serving to more than 600,000 students, faculty, and staff, and its membership includes 16 public/research universities, 23 community/technical colleges, 51 independent colleges and the State Library of Ohio. Sanville (1999, 2001) states that libraries can overcome the inherent limitations of the print medium, the entrenched and limiting economic practices of vendors to individual institutions, and even they may be imposed, self-limiting, collection development mentality of information rationing that pervades our community. Consortium can set the evolution of our industry on a new and better long-term course by radically changing the value equation of information delivered per dollar / rupee spent.

Further, the use of new technologies in libraries to cope with the collection related problems gave a steep rise in the formation of various library consortia after 1960s round the globe. Later, a number of library consortia appeared in Asia, Europe, North America, South America, Africa and Australia which have membership of an International Coalition of Library Consortia (ICOLC). A brief gist of library consortia activities in some of the important countries of the world is given below.

10.1.1. Library Consortia in United States

Library consortia in the United States arose from a need for sharing when resources or funding for those resources were scarce. This is as true today as it was over 100 years ago when the first American consortia were formed. They continue to be a growing and important part of the library profession. However, Triangle Research Libraries Network, established in 1933, is considered as earliest library consortium in the United States. Later, Library associations such as Association of Research Libraries (ARL), the Research Libraries Group (RLG), and the Centre for Research Libraries (CRL) and Online Computer Library Centre (OCLC) have developed and elaborated national level consortia arrangements in United States, which, in turn, led to the development of regional level library consortia. A study commissioned by United States Office of Education states that more than 125 academic library consortia were existed in 1972, ninety percent of which were formed in the 1960s. In 1994, VIVA, the Virtual Library of Virginia, was came into existence followed by GALILEO, the California Digital Library that were established in 1995 and in 1997 respectively.

Other consortia initiatives came into existence during the same period include Committee on Institutional Cooperation (CIC), which is an academic consortium of ten universities of United States, Illinois Library and Information Network (ILLINET); Pennsylvania Academic Library Consortium (PALC) and State-wide California Electronic Library Consortium (SCELC), etc. Guzzy (2010) has reviewed 15 academic library consortia of United States such as: “CARLI (Consortium of Academic and Research Libraries in Illinois)”, “Carolina Consortium (CC)”, “Community College Library Consortium (CCLC)”, “Iowa Community College Online Consortium (ICCPC)”,

"Kansas Regents Library Database Consortium (KRLDC)", "Library Deans and Directors Group of the State University and Community College System of the Tennessee Board of Regents (TBR Library Deans and Directors Group)", "LOUIS (The Louisiana Library Network)", "MOBIUS (Consortium of Libraries in Missouri)", "NILRC (Network of Illinois Learning Resources in Community Colleges)", "Orbis Cascade Alliance—Oregon/Washington", "SUNY Connect (State University of New York)", "VALE (Virtual Academic Library Environment of New Jersey)", "WALDO (Westchester Academic Library Directors Organization)", "WISPALS Library Consortium (Wisconsin Project for Automated Libraries)", "Wyoming Community College Library Consortium", "Washington Research Library Consortium" (Payne, 1998). According to Minearo (2009), there were around 1500 consortia tying colleges and universities in the United States in 2009.

10.1.2. Library Consortia in United Kingdom (UK)

The term 'co-operatives' is used popularly than the term 'consortia' in the United Kingdom (UK). There are two popular models in UK with regard to electronic resource sharing, namely:

- Library Purchasing consortia, and
- Access Schemes

However, the national level collaborative venture in the UK includes Consortium of University Research Libraries (CURL) that was established in 1982, the Standing Conference of National and University Libraries (SCONUL), UK Libraries Plus (UKLP), the British Library, the Library Association and the Council of Polytechnic Librarians.

While regional level library consortia initiative includes Access to Libraries in North amptonshire (ALIS), Access to Libraries for Learning (ALL) for the Sheffield College and Sheffield libraries, ATLIS (Access to Libraries in Swansea). Bley (2000) mentions that the main organization for the purchase/subscription of electronic resources in the UK is the Joint Information Systems Committee (JISC) which is working with various societies and agencies. JISC initiated the National Electronic Site License Initiative (NESLI) to achieve attractive pricing models for electronic content. The main aim of NESLI is to make the full-text electronic resources available to universities in UK at a discounted rate.

Besides, there are numerous regional academic library consortia that play a vital role, complementing the roles and functions of the national organizations such as the SUPC (Southern Universities Purchasing Consortium) (1974), M25 Consortium (1993) (Ball and Pye, 2000), CALIM (the Consortium of Academic Libraries in Manchester), SCURL, The London Libraries Consortium (2004), and the Collaborative Academic Store for Scotland (CASS), etc.

10.1.3. Library Consortia in South Africa

Academic library consortia in South Africa are indeed beasts whose time has come at last, although whether they constitute a second coming for our profession or our end users remains to be seen. They can probably be described as a group of diverse entities, rough and as yet unsure of their destination (Darch, Rapp and Underwood, 1999). However, library consortia in South Africa are categorized by its objectives and governing and structures (Thomas and Fourie, 2006). In each case, the higher education consortium acts as a legal body, while the library consortium is a committee of the institutional parent body.

Cape Library Cooperative (CALICO), established in 1992, was considered as the first formal library consortium in South Africa. The Gauteng and Environs Library Consortium (GAELIC), established in April 1996, is the largest academic library consortium in South Africa.

Further, during the period from 1992 to 1998, five academic library consortia came into existence, namely, the CALICO (Cape Libraries Co-operative, 1992); GAELIC (Gauteng and Environs Library Consortium, 1996); FRELICO (Free State Library Co-operative, 1996); SEALS (South Eastern Academic Library System, 1987); EASEL (Eastern Seaboard Libraries, 1997) and CATNIP. But from 1998 to 2003, these consortia further consolidated their roles, responsibilities and increased the number of member institutes.

10.1.4. Library Consortia in Australia

Australian Library and Information System was developed in very systematic manner. CAVAL (known as CAVAL Ltd.) is the first of its library consortia which was formed in 1978 for providing shared services to the information and library sectors throughput Australia. Commonwealth Scientific and Industrial Research Organization-the CSIRO has 50 member libraries and provides consortium facility to all science and research related activities of Australia. Council of Australian University Librarians-the CAUL facilitates access to electronic resources to research scholars, faculty and students of the universities in Australia. NSLA- the National & State Libraries Australasia E-Resources Consortium was established in 2002.

Later, the Australian Academic and Research Library Network (AARLIN) a consortium of Australian university libraries emerged from a Council of Australian University Librarians (CAUL) planning workshop in 1999 and later was adopted as one of the strategic objectives of CAUL. Twenty of the thirty-eight Australian universities and the National Library of Australia are active participants in the project and have contributed funds. AARLIN project has established cooperative arrangements between the institutions involved for the direction and management of the project (Parker, Gow and Lim, 2002). It provides a collaborative research information infrastructure to its member institutes. It also helps to streamline information access and maximize e-resource discovery and dissemination and provide a web-portal for these services.

JANUS that works as an Australian equivalent to NESLI of UK, is funded by federal government to develop a business model for an integrated, collaborative approach to electronic collections. It provides integrated access to research information and supports national collaborative purchasing in each designated field.

10.1.5. Library Consortia in China

Library consortia in China emerged in the 1980s as the need to strengthen cooperation among libraries. Initial efforts were limited to the sharing of collection information via printed bibliographies or catalogue cards. Cooperation was later extended to the areas of inter-library lending and cooperative cataloging in small scale, and occasionally to coordinated acquisitions (Dong and Zou, 2009). However, at large scale, library consortia in China were first achieved in the late 1990s and they have developed rapidly since 2002. Today, in China, most of the library consortia are identified by: type, such as academic, public, or special library; geographical proximity; and administrative division.

China Academic Library and Information System (CALIS), established in 1998 by the Ministry of Education (MoE), turn out to be most important endeavour in China. It is funded by central government and consists of 13 information centers and 70 member libraries (Dai, Chen and Zhang, 2000). It aims to promote and improve resource sharing among academic libraries, reduce the expenses for participating libraries, and support the development of higher education in China. Its long-term goal is to build the largest academic digital library in China, and to construct, integrate, preserve, and distribute digital resources to all the universities and colleges in China.

A few other most successful library consortia are the National Science and Technology Library (NSTL) and the Science Library System; CALIS the university library system at the national level and the SHELIB in Shanghai; JALIS in Jiangsu Province; TJDL in Tianjin; and the Hong Kong Academic Library Link at the regional level (Chen, 2013). Besides, the JULAC that is initiated by the university librarians in Hong Kong has some support from the government through bodies charged with the oversight of the universities (Perushek and Douglas, 2014).

10.1.6. Library Consortia in Other Parts of the World

It is seen that the world is witnessing increase in cooperative activities especially for sharing electronic resources and the economic motivation still keeps on driving the formation and establishment of library consortia (Satyanarayana, Krishnan and Arora, 2004). A few important initiations by USA, UK, South Africa, Australia and China have already been discussed earlier.

Some other important development in library consortia worldwide include: FinELib in Finland (Hormia-Poutanen, 2002), Anatolian University Libraries Consortium (ANKOS) in Turkey (http://www.ankos.org.tr), Consortium of Academic Libraries in Manchester (CALIM) established in 1992, TEBNET in Taiwan, ThaiL in Thiland, LCoNZ in New Zealand 2004, Novanet in Canada (Marshall,1999), Spanish Library Consortium in 1996, CBUS (1999), BugGalicia and CBUA in (2001), BUCLE (2002), National Electronic Information Consortium (NEICON) and Science Library Advanced Network (RUSLANet) in Russia. Besides, Coordinamento Interuniversitario Basi dati & Editoria in Rete (CIBER) and Italian National Forum on Electronic Information Resources (INFER) in Italy (Gargiulo, 2003), Nigerian University Libraries Consortium (NULIC) in Nigeria (Okeagu and Okeagu, 2008), SWALINET etc. are also there which are working in different parts of the world.

Now have a look on some important of them in details (mainly based on Patil, 2014) including USA and UK etc:

10.1.7. CARLI (Consortium of Academic and Research Libraries in Illinois)

CARLI, the Consortium of Academic and Research Libraries in Illinois, was formed in July 2005 to serve the consortia needs of academic and research libraries in Illinois. However, there had been consortia existing in Illinois since the 1980s prior to the formation of CARLI.

Fig. 10.1. Snapshot of CARLI
(*Source*: https://www.carli.illinois.edu)

These were:

- Illinois Cooperative Collection Management Program (ICCMP), formed in 1986, provided statewide collection studies and grants.
- Illinois Digital Academic Library (IDAL), formed in 1999, provided centralized electronic resource licensing.
- Illinois Library Computer Systems Organization (ILCSO), formed in 1980, provided the shared integrated library system Illinet Online which later became I-Share.

CARLI took birth as a result of consolidation of these three consortia. Its mission is to create and maintain a rich, supportive, and diverse knowledge environment to facilitate teaching, learning, and research through the sharing of collections, expertise, and programs.

(i) Membership : CARLI serves 8.5 lakh students and thousands of faculty and staff covering almost 94 percent of the higher education clientele in Illinois. It has 145 libraries as its members. Any institution that is recognized by Illinois Board of Higher Education (IBHE) and a member of Illinois Library and Information Network (ILLINET) can join CARLI but those institutions that do not meet the above criteria may also be considered for the membership of the consortium.

There are two kinds of members - governing members and affiliate members. Governing members are eligible for all services and can participate in all programmes whereas affiliate members can avail most services and programmes. Thus, the difference is due to the facilities in terms of services provided and programmes available to them.

(ii) Services : The following services are provided by CARLI:

(a) ***E-Resource Programmme*** **:** Participating libraries are provided access to a large number of e-resources in a consortium mode enhancing the collections of individual libraries. It not only increases the access to resources for libraries but also provides access to collections of lasting value. CARLI has arrangements with EBSCO, Sage, Springer, etc. whose databases are provided free to all members. Besides these, CARLI helps its members by providing access to other databases on discount.

(b) ***I-Share*** **:** I-Share database is the union catalogue of all participating libraries which contains 11.5 million unique bibliographical records and 36 million item records. These pertain to 82 CARLI I - Share member institutions. I- Share also acts as an OPAC also for individual libraries.

(c) ***Document Delivery*** **:** I-Share libraries allow users to borrow documents form other libraries. Libraries are assigned user id which can be quoted to borrow documents from other libraries. Libraries participating in the I-Share programme have to pay a fee. This goes towards paying the vendor of the Voyager software that is used for I-Share.

Besides, CARLI organizes training programmes for the staff of participating libraries. It also conducts training programmes for the users. Webinars are also conducted on the topics related to e-resources for their effective and efficient utilization.

10.1.8. CONCERT (Consortium on Core Electronic Resources in Taiwan)

CONCERT, Consortium on Core Electronic Resources in Taiwan, was set up in 1990 to take advantage of the growing popularity of web-based full-text documents. Its Science and Technology Policy Research and Information Center (STPI) tries its best to fully exploit the economies from group-purchase and resource sharing as the coordinator of CONCERT. It has leased 22 international database systems, partly funded by the Ministry of Education and National Applied Research Laboratories.

(i) Objectives : The main objectives of CONCERT include the following:

- To enhance sci-tech policy research and establish knowledge bank;
- To work on major themes that include critical national issues; and
- To establish national integrated information service mechanism.

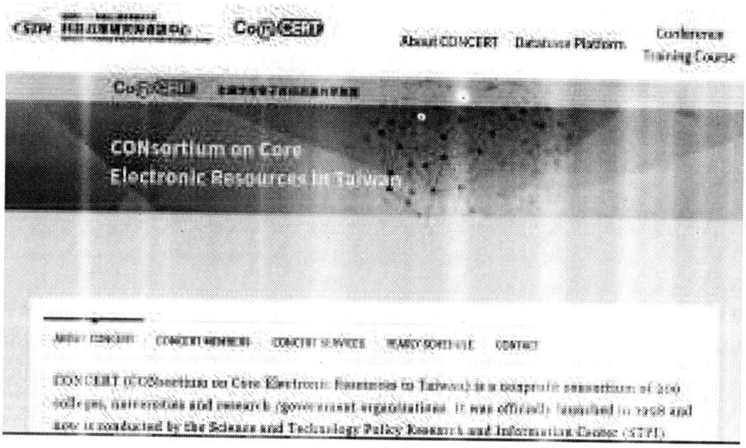

Fig. 10.2. Snapshot of CONCERT
(*Source* : http://concert.stpi.narl.org.tw/abouteng)

(ii) Features of CONCERT : The following are some of the salient features of CONCERT:

- It is developing and integrating national information resources and introducing international information resources to foster the domestic research through information service databases like CONCERT, ILL, etc.
- It is providing critical insights for governmental policy decision-makers by undertaking policy research of S&T development and value-added analysis, establishing the monitor system of manpower allocation in the S&T industry as well as performing information & communication security endorsed by the Executive Yuan of ROC.
- It is serving as a major dissemination gateway of knowledge innovation in support of cutting-edge technology research by taking part in nation-based nanotechnology programme, performing patent analysis, and offering technology transfer interface, and bringing about economic benefits as a result.
- It is accelerating bilateral & multi-lateral

collaboration by participating in the information activities worldwide, and introducing research accomplishments throughout nations as so to upgrade image.

Besides, it has international cooperation with other organizations not just a means to acquire international resources but also has opened more channels to disseminate the information about the national S&T activities and performance to the international arena. It provides access to over 100 databases to about 230 members. There are two types of members- full or core members, which are 9 at present and affiliate members which are 220. CONCERT members cover 70 nationals as well as private universities, 51 Sci-Tech universities, 36 colleges, 15 junior colleges, 30 R&D organizations and 18 government organizations.

10.1.9. SANLIC (South African National Library and Information Consortium)

Fig. 10.3. Snapshot of SANLIC
(*Source* : https://sanlic.org.za)

SANLIC, the South African National Library and Information Consortium, which is a consortium of higher education and research libraries in South Africa works with a mission to provide high quality research materials to participating institutions at cost-effective rates. Its mission is to "facilitate, on a nonprofit basis, affordable access to scholarly electronic information in support of the learning, teaching and research activities of its members".

This is achieved mainly through collective negotiations with publishers and aggregators. It also promotes the use of high-quality, open access electronic information resources. In addition, SANLIC carries out a wide range of activities aimed at providing its members the following services related to its mission:

- Electronic information resources site licensing
- Evaluation and management of electronic information resources
- Marketing and promotion of electronic information resources
- Training
- Advice
- General assistance and support, and
- Communication, liaison and lobbying

Besides, it also publishes regularly its newsletter 'SCANLiCTALK' informing its clientele about its activities and resources.

10.1.10. CURL (Consortium of University Research Libraries)

CURL, the Consortium of University Research Libraries, is a Consortium of University Research Libraries in UK. Several activities of CURL are funded by the JISC. CURL helps the member institutions to build distributed and hybrid research library in their institutions with an aim to help the researchers all over the world:

- to search, locate and request resources of all kinds

in different formats, easily and quickly from their desktops;

- have quick and easy access to an increasing amount of electronic resources - both born-digital and digitized;
- have physical access to manuscripts, archives or printed items that have not been digitized and cannot be moved, wherever these are held; and
- have other printed items from outside their own institutions delivered to them efficiently.

CURL's mission is to increase the ability of research libraries to share resources for the benefit of the local, national and international research community. The total membership of CURL has grown to 28 libraries in UK including 22 university libraries, as well as the British Library, the National Library of Scotland and the National Library of Wales.

CURL's services and related projects may include the following:

(i) Online Databases : CURL database consists of bibliographic records of documents available in members' libraries as well as the data from other sources, such as the Library of Congress. The records are stored in UKMARC which can be accessed via telnet or Z39.50 clients. However, the database is available to non-members of CURL on charged services. The database currently consists of more than 38 million records of good quality, which is growing constantly. CURL also has established bibliographic standards for contributors and records are flagged to indicate standard. The service is open to any non-profit organization.

(ii) COPAC (http://copac.ac.uk/) : Copac is a union catalogue that is funded by the JISC. It provides free access to the merged online catalogues of members of the CURL. There are over 30 million records on COPAC representing the merged holdings of 26 CURL member institutions, including the British Library and National Library of Scotland, plus special collections from a small number of non-CURL libraries. The remaining CURL libraries' catalogues are also being loaded. COPAC web site contains service information and support materials.

(iii) Archives Hub (http://www.archiveshub.ac.uk/) : Archives Hub is a collaborative service, which provides a single point of access to descriptions of archive collections held in universities and colleges throughout the United Kingdom. Over 60 institutions are contributing high-quality information to the hub, which covers over 20,000 archives. The website is free to use and contains information relevant to a wide range of research areas. The service is funded by the Joint Information Systems Committee (JISC) and is overseen by CURL. The service at the University of Manchester runs as MIMAS and development work on the Archives Hub software is undertaken by the Cheshire Development Team at the University of Liverpool.

(iv) Britain in Print (http://www.britaininprint.net/) : Britain in Print project, funded by the Heritage Lottery Fund, is a collaborative venture led by Edinburgh University Library which involves participation of ten CURL libraries including the Edinburgh Royal College of Physicians and the Mitchell Library in Glasgow. Britain in Print project that was launched in 2003 provides free access to information about the rich collections of early British books which are held in twenty-one of the nation's most important libraries.

Besides, the CURL-CoFoR (http://www.cocorees.ac.uk/) is also there that is a new CURL initiative which is set up to provide its members and other research libraries with practical tools, such as the templates, guidelines and recommendations, for collaborative acquisition and retention. It also gives special attention to techniques for serial deduplication and to the mapping of relationships between research activity and library provision.

10.1.11. EIFL (Electronic Information for Libraries)

EIFL, the Electronic Information for Libraries, is a not-for-profit organization based in Europe which provides access to knowledge through a global network to developing and countries in transition in Africa, Asia, Europe and Latin America. Just, starting with providing access to e-journals libraries in Central and Eastern Europe in 1999, it has spread wings enabling access to knowledge for learning, teaching, research and sustainable development into 60 countries.

Fig. 10.4. Snapshot of EIFL
(*Source* : https://www.eifl.net)

EIFL provides the following programmes:

(i) EIFL-Licensing : EIFL negotiates with the publishers to provide access to scholarly material for research and education on discount rates. It provides consortia access to libraries in more than 60 countries. E-resources ranging from scholarly journals, e-books to bibliographic databases from more than 25 vendors are available for use. It also trains local librarians in the licensing and management of the e-resources.

(ii) EIFL-OA - Open Access : EIFL is a strong advocate of open access. It helps the institutions to build and sustain open access repositories.

Besides, EIFL helps libraries to install and use free and open source software. It also provides training to professionals to use open source software.

10.1.12. ICOLC (International Coalition of Library Consortia)

ICOLC, the International Coalition of Library Consortiais a Consortium of Consortia. Launched informally in 1997 in St. Louis, Missouri, it comprises over 200 library consortia across the world and the Coalition represents thousands of member libraries worldwide (Feather, 2015). The Coalition serves primarily to higher education institutions by facilitating discussion among consortia on issues of common interest.

ICOLC performs the following activities to accomplish the tasks:

- It conducts meetings twice a year generally in March/April in North America and September/October in Europe to keep participating consortia informed about new electronic information resources, pricing practices of electronic providers and vendors, and other issues of importance to Directors and Governing Boards of consortia.

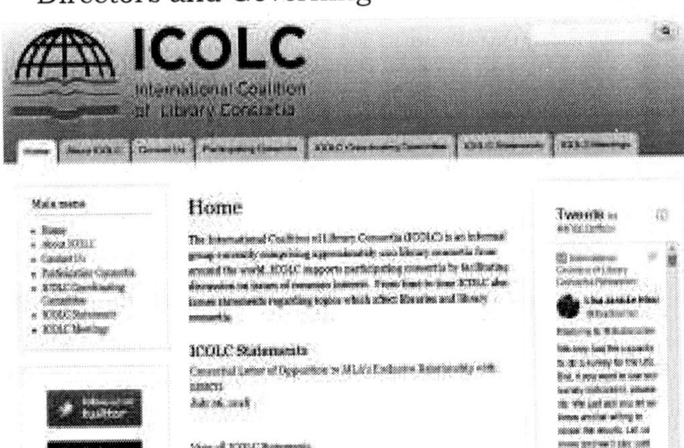

Fig. 10.5. Snapshot of ICOLC
(*Source* : https://icolc.net)

- The Coalition meets with the members of information provider community, providing a forum for them to discuss their offerings and to engage in dialog with consortial leaders about issues of mutual concern.

Besides, it also maintains list servs and web pages for the benefit of its members.

10.1.13. CALIS (China Academic Library Consortium)

CALIS, the China Academic Library Consortium, is a nationwide academic library consortium of China which is funded primarily by the Chinese government. Its details are as follow:

(i) Structure and Management of CALIS : It is an alliance formed by member libraries on a voluntary basis to facilitate resource sharing in pursuit of common interests. However, CALIS differs from library consortia in the United States in that it is a national network. It resembles with multistate consortia in the United States with respect to geographic distribution of member libraries, but it is like tightly knit or even centrally funded statewide ones in terms of management.

CALIS members are distributed in twenty-seven provinces, cities and autonomous regions in China, making an entirely centralized management difficult. Thus, after surveying some of the major library consortia in the United States, Europe and Russia, CALIS adopted an organizational mode characterized by a combination of both centralized and localized management—that is, a three-tiered structure. CALIS has established a coordination and management network comprising one national administrative center, which also serves as the North Regional Center, five national information centers and seven regional information centers. Its thirteen centers are maintained by full-time staff members provided by the libraries in which these centers are located. The National Administrative Center (located in Peking University)—overseen by officials from the concerned office at the Ministry of Education and the Presidents of Peking and Tsinghua Universities and advised by an advisory committee consisting of experts from major member libraries—is responsible for the construction and management of CALIS, which also makes policies and regulations, and prepares resource-sharing agreements.

Each of five national information centers under the guidance of the National Administrative Center, are responsible for building and maintaining an information system in one of five general areas—humanities, social science, and science; engineering and technology; agriculture and forestry; medicine; and national defense—in coordination with regional centers and member libraries. The host libraries where these centers are located possess relatively abundant collections in their respective areas. These centers, which are intended to be information bases that cover all major disciplines of science, are responsible for importing databases for sharing and constructing resource-sharing networks among member libraries and for providing searching and document delivery services to member libraries.

Further, depending on their location, academic libraries in China are divided into eight groups, with each forming a regional library consortium. Each regional consortium is overseen by a regional management center, except for the consortium in the north, which is directly managed by the national management center. The regional centers not only participate in nationwide projects in coordination with the national centers and other regional centers, but they also are responsible for promoting cooperation among libraries in their particular regions.

(ii) Funding : The development and operation of CALIS has been funded in large part by the Chinese government, but its future expansion and operation of the system is expected to rely in large part on other sources of funds.

Besides, government grants, local matching funds are given by the province or city that desires to have a regional center in supplementation to the government funds for the construction of its local center. Member library funds are also there primarily derived from the university budgets, which are used to purchase electronic resources and cover the expenses incurred from the use of the CALIS service software platforms.

(iii) Principles for Cooperation among Members : The successful operation of a library consortium clearly depends on good working relationships among members and between members and the consortium. All members are required to adhere to a set of principles in dealing with these relationships at CALIS. These principles are known as the CALIS Principles for Cooperation among Members and they include:

- Common interests of CALIS are above those of individual member libraries.
- Member libraries should not cooperate at the expense of the interests of others.
- CALIS provides services to member libraries for no profit.
- Member libraries are all equal and enjoy the same privileges.
- Larger member libraries are obliged to make more contributions.

It is seen when CALIS was established it had sixty-one member libraries from major universities participating in "Project 211." Later, as many other major universities were interested in joining the alliance, the number of CALIS members has reached to seventy. CALIS at the present, serves to about 700,000 students.

(iv) Union Catalogues : This is database currently contain 500,000 bibliographic records of the Chinese and Western language books and periodicals in all member libraries.

(v) Dissertation Abstracts and Conference Proceedings : This database now contains abstracts of doctoral dissertations and proceedings of national and international conferences collected from more than thirty member libraries.

(vi) Current Chinese Periodicals : This database contains contents and indexes of current Chinese periodicals from about thirty member libraries.

(vii) Key Disciplines Databases : CALIS has sponsored the development of twenty-five discipline-specific databases by member libraries. Each of these data-bases contains about 50,000 to 100,000 records.

However, the first three classes of databases are prepared in the USMARC, UNIMARC, or CCF format for the ease of use by patrons and cataloguing staff and in data exchange. Clients from member libraries may perform a Web-based search of the above databases. Most of them contain secondary documents and abstracts, and access CALIS online resources using browsers. Besides, Inter-Library Loan System is also there which is developed on the basis of ISO10160/10161 protocol, and consists of ILL protocol machines and client terminals which are in member libraries and are interconnected to form a CALIS Inter-Library Loan Network. It has also developed an OPAC system where the patrons may visit the system using common browsers, search all CALIS databases, and send search results directly to the CALIS inter-library loan service. Besides, the patrons also may access an ILL server through Web/ILL, tracking the status of submitted inter-library loan requests, inquiring about fees, and so on.

10.2. LIBRARY CONSORTIA IN INDIA

The growth of library network and consortia in India can be traced to the initiatives taken by NISSAT in the year 1986. CALIBNET was the first that was established in 1986 followed by the DELNET in 1988 with initial funding from the NISSAT. Other library networks initiated in India are Pune Library Network (PUNENET, established in 1992), Madras Library Network, (MALIBNET, established in 1993), Ahmedabad Library Network (ADINET, established in 1993), Bombay Library Network (BONET, established in 1994), Mysore Library Network (MYLIBNET, established in 1994), etc. However, the establishment of the INFLIBNET by the University Grants Commission (UGC) in 1991 as a national-level network can be considered as a major turning point in the evolution of library networks in India. Observing importance of the network, it was awarded as an Inter-University Centre of UGC in 1996. Majority of the university libraries got automated with the help of INFLIBNET Centre.

DRDO E-journal Service (DRDO Consortium) (Moorthy, 2009); Consortium for E-Resources in Agriculture (Visakhi, 2009, Chandrashekharan, 2012), and FORSA Consortium, RGUHS-HELINET, DeLCON (http://delcon.gov.in) and ERMED (http://www.nmlermed.in/) are major library consortia initiatives in India. Some important library consortia are discussed in brief here (based on Singh and Bhaskar Rao, 2008; Krishnamurthy, 2009; Moorthy, 2009; Visakhi, 2009; Varaprasad and Madhusudhan, 2010; Sudhier, 2011 and Patil, 2014):

10.2.1. E-ShodhSindhu

E-shodhSindhu has been formed by merging INDEST-AICTE Library Consortium, UGC-INFONET Digital Library Consortium and N-LIST programme of INFLIBNET from April 2016. It is providing more than 16,000 core and peer-reviewed journals and a number of bibliographic, citation and factual databases in different disciplines from a large number of publishers and aggregators to its member institutions including centrally-funded technical institutions, universities and colleges that are covered under 12(B) and 2(f) Sections of the UGC Act.

UGC-INFONET Digital Library Consortium that was launched in December 2003 by A. P. J. Abdul Kalam, the then President of India. Consortium was providing differential access to more than 8,250 core and peer reviewed electronic journals and ten bibliographic databases from 29 publishers, scholarly societies, aggregators, and university presses to 219 universities that are covered under the core membership of the consortium and 214 institutes that are covered under associate membership programme. These e-resources covered almost all subject disciplines including arts, humanities, social sciences, physical sciences, chemical sciences, life sciences, computer sciences, mathematics and statistics etc.

Likewise, the Indian National Digital Library in Engineering Sciences and Technology (INDEST) Consortium was set-up by the Ministry of Human Resource Development (MHRD) in the year 2003 to provide access to selected electronic journals and databases to technical institutes including IISc, NTs, NITs, IIMs and a few other centrally-funded Government institutes. It provided differential access to 20,666 peer-reviewed journals and 10 bibliographical databases to 65 core member institutes till December 2015.

Besides, *National Library and Information Services Infrastructure for Scholarly Content* (N-LIST) was the college component of INFLIBNET to provide access to e-resources to students, researchers and faculty from colleges and other beneficiary.

(i) Aims and Objectives : The main objective of the e-ShodhSindu is to provide access to qualitative electronic resources including full-text, bibliographic, factual and legal databases to academic institutions at a lower rate of subscription. However, other major aims and objectives of the e-ShodhSindhu are to:

- Develop a formidable collection of e-journals, e-journal archives and e-books on perpetual access basis;

- Monitor and promote usage of e-resources in member universities, colleges and technical institutions in India through awareness and training programmes;
- Negotiate rates of subscription for all e-resources required by all higher education institutions (HEIs) and offer them to all for subscription;
- Extend all services of e-ShodhSindhu to core as well as other institutions on subscription payment basis;
- Provide access to subscription-based scholarly information (e-books and e-journals) to core as well as associate members,
- Provide access to scholarly content available in open access through subject portals and subject gateways;
- Bridge digital divide and move towards an information-rich society;
- Take-up additional activities and services that require collaborative platform and are not being performed by existing consortia; and
- Move towards developing a National Electronic Library with electronic journals and electronic books as its major building blocks.

(ii) Membership : The membership of the Consortium, as on now, is available to all academic institutions including CFTIs (Centrally Funded Technical Institutes), Central Universities, Deemed Universities funded by UGC, state universities & colleges that are covered under 2(f) and 12(B) Sections of UGC Act. Other institutions including private universities, non-12(B) colleges etc. may also subscribe to e-resources on rates negotiated by the consortium on their own.

Fig. 10.6. Snap Shot of E-Shodhsindhu
(*Source* : https://www.inflibnet.ac.in/ess/)

All Academic Institutions are required to register on the Online e-Resource Requisition System (http://ess.inflibnet.ac.in/oes) using credentials provided to them by e-ShodhSindhu. Institutions that do not have login credential, may send their email request to eshodhsindhu@inflibnet.cic.in. e-Shodh Sindhu negotiates rate of subscriptions to resources and their publishers/agents and are available on the portal. Though, the institutions may subscribe to these resources based on the rates negotiated by e-ShodhSindhu and make payments directly to publishers from their own funds, but e-ShodhSindhu also subscribes selected e-resources for members who are eligible for central funding by UGC/MHRD/AICTE depending upon the availability of funds.

(iii) Subscribed Electronic Resources : Consortium subscribes to electronic resources in all major subject disciplines being taught in CFTIs, universities and colleges. It includes wide variety of materials including e-journals, bibliographic databases, factual databases, and legal databases, reviews published by scholarly societies, university presses, institutions, commercial publishers and aggregators.

e-ShodhSindhu Consortium offers differential access to more than 16,000 full-text journals from 13 publishers,

4 bibliographic databases to core member institutions. The college component of the consortium, called N-LIST, provides access to 6,500+ journals and 31,35000+ e-books to more than 3000 colleges under the N-LIST programme.

(iv) How to Access Electronic Resources : Consortium co-ordinates with the member institutions and publishers for seamless access to e-resources through static IP addresses of member institutes. In case of colleges registered under the N-LIST Programme, since most colleges do not have static IP addresses, access to e-resources to the registered colleges is provided through EZ-Proxy set-up at the INFLIBNET Centre and Shibboleth-based access for some resources. Authorized users from colleges can access e-resources and download articles by them directly from the publisher's website once they are duly authenticated as authorized users through EZ-Proxy deployed at the INFLIBNET Centre. The Consortium has developed an online interface for creation, updation and modification of valid users of the colleges by the respective college administrators.

Consortium attends to the problems faced by member institutions and liaise with publishers to resolve such problems. It also operates IN FED which uses SAML-based software and architecture to facilitate off-campus authentication of authorized users using internal identity and access management system of member organizations.

(v) Archives Purchased under E-ShodhSindhu : The e-ShodhSindhu has also purchased / subscribed to South Asia Archives (SAA) and World E-Book Library (WeL) on behalf of National Digital Library (NDL). World e-Book Library include 3 million (30,00,000) primary sources spanning past 1000 years of world history in more than 320 different languages. In addition, contemporary journal collections of WeL include scholarly journals and academic articles from every academic field. Its South Asia Archive contains more than 4.5 million pages spanning the period of 18th and mid-20th century from documents across the

Indian subcontinent, including India, Pakistan, Burma, Afghanistan and Bangladesh. The access to SAA and WeL is available to all the institutions covered under the eSS Consortium as well as institutions under other Government funded Consortium like CeRA, DelCON, NKRC-CSIR/DRDO, etc. Individuals may also access both these resources through the National Digital Library.

(vi) ILL Service using JGate Plus : J-Gate Plus is a virtual library of journal literature customized as a e-journals access gateway and database solution. It acts as a one-point access to journals subscribed currently under consortium as well as university libraries designated as Inter Library Loan (ILL) Centres beside open access journals. INFLIBNET has identified 26 potential universities as ILL Centres in the country to fulfil ILL requests from the users affiliated to institutions covered under the Consortium. JGate has facility to trigger e-mail request for articles to Inter Library Loan Centres as well as to INFLIBNET Centre.

(vii) Monitoring Usage Statistics through InfiStats : INFLIBNET Centre has developed a portal called InfiStats. for monitoring the usage statistics of various e-resources made accessible to the member institutions. InfiStats uses "Standardized Usage Statistics Harvesting Initiative (SUSHI)" Protocol (ANSI/N1S0 Standard No. Z39.93-2007) that defines an automated request and response model for harvesting of usage data for electronic resources using Web services framework. InfiStats portal imports the usage data from the publisher's website automatically and store it in a database on InfiStats. InfiStats interface provides title level COUNTER rcports to member institutions. The member institutions can also login to this portal for monitoring the usage of their respective e-resources.

It is already mentioned earlier that e-ShodhSindhu Consortium offers differential access to more than 16,000 full-text journals from 13 publishers, 4 bibliographic databases and many more to core member institutions. However, the details of negotiated resources are available at https://ess.inflibnet.ac.in/oes/.

10.2.2. FORSA (Forum for Resource Sharing in Astronomy/ Astrophysics)

FORSA, the Forum for Resource Sharing in Astronomy/ Astrophysics was formed because of the efforts of the librarians working in institutes where astronomy and astrophysics was one of the major research areas in the early 1980s when they felt the need to establish a forum among the libraries to enable sharing of resources due to the following reasons (FORSA, 2012):

- Very few institutes in the country were involved in research in astronomy and astrophysics;
- Considerable interaction already existed between astronomers of institutes doing research in astronomy and astrophysics;
- No library can be self-sufficient in the resources, and access to the holdings of the member libraries would help in minimizing duplication; and
- Information resources should be used to the mutual advantage of the members as well as for optimum use.

Thus, based on the proposed plans made by the members of Forum, the first meeting of the Forum for Resource Sharing in Astronomy/Astrophysics (FORSA) was arranged on July 29, 1981, at Raman Research Institute, Bangalore, where the emphasis was placed on obtaining detailed information related to literature in Astronomy and Astrophysics for speedier dissemination of information. Thus, FORSA was formed on 29thJuly 1981.

(i) Objectives : The objectives of FORSA are to:

- Develop collection in IT environment;
- Facilitate e-access to journals and books;
- Participate actively in resource sharing, ILL;

- Provide document delivery by fax, e-mail, speed post, courier, etc.;
- Merge database of library holdings (books/ journals) and facilitate access to merged database;
- Digitize the archival materials of the institutes and making available on website for access by all;
- Facilitate access to website of each institute's library;
- Participate actively in consortia plans for sharing e-journals, e-books and other databases with various publishers and academic societies publications and joining existing consortia where forum members are benefited;
- Come forward for open access and to develop institutional repositories; and
- Welcome new members of institutes where astronomy is one of the subjects and library has collection pertaining to the subject.

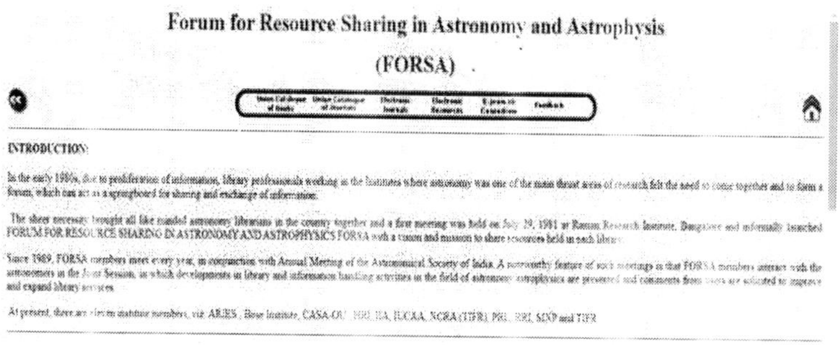

Fig. 10.7. Snapshot of FORSA
(*Source* : http://www.rri.res.in/htmls/library/forsa.html)

(ii) Members : FORSA is an example of the Open Consortium category. It is an open model having participant institutes affiliated to different government departments. This is a model where professionals willingly come forward and support consortia formation. Currently FORSA has 12 members and it works towards the goals and services which the founder members have started. Its member libraries include:

- Aryabhatta Research Institute of Observational Sciences (ARIES), Manora Peak, Nainital.
- Bose Institute, Kolkata.
- Harish- Chandra Institute, Allahabad.
- Indian Institute of Astrophysics (IIA), Bangalore.
- Inter-University Centre for Astronomy and Astrophysics (IUCAA), Pune.
- National Centre for Radio Astrophysics (NCRA), Pune.
- Nizamiah Observatory, Department of Astronomy, Osmania University, Hyderabad.
- Physical Research Laboratory (PRL), Ahmedabad.
- Raman Research Institute (RRI), Bangalore.
- S.N.Bose National Centre for Basic Sciences, Kolkata.
- Saha Institute of Nuclear Physics, Kolkata, and
- Tata Institute of Fundamental Research (TIFR), Mumbai.

(iii) Funding : The funding is decentralized where each institute has to pay its share depending upon resources subscribed. The bills are raised separately and payment has to be made out of its library budget or fund created exclusively for consortium subscription.

(iv) Services : All the participating libraries are well equipped with recourses and share them for mutual benefit. They provide the following services:

- Access to OPAC.
- Access to online journals.
- Inter library loan, and
- Document Delivery by e-mail, speed post, courier and fax.

(v) Workshops and Conferences : FORSA organizes workshops and conferences on emerging areas. Some such programmes were organized on KOHA and DSpace. A meeting is arranged every year along with the Annual Meeting of the Astronomical Society of India.

(vi) Involvement of Large Libraries : FORSA has a medium to big libraries, viz. TIFR, IIAP, RRI, BI, and PRL with wide range of collections not only in astronomy but also strong collection in the fields of physics, mathematics and computer science. No doubt, these libraries have demonstrated a remarkable spirit of cooperation before formation of FORSA.

(vii) Governance : FORSA is an informal group with no legal sanctity. Coordinator has to sign licensing document on behalf of all participants. FORSA activities are governed by Coordinator, assisted by all participating libraries, in respect of resource selection, negotiations. MoU is taken from all members for commitment, contribution and sharing e-resources.

Besides, the consortium subscribed both paper and electronic format through supplier. In 2002, consortium tried for Kluwer journals but PRL could not join it. Since 2003, PRL is part of the consortium for Kluwer journals. FORSA is subscribing to 25 e-journals to their users with the payment of 12.5 percent over the print subscription. This consortium has successfully negotiated with publishers of Nature to provide access to its eversion at a price of almost 1/3 of the list price. In 2004, this group has extended its membership to Physics and Maths libraries in the country who have common interests to carry forward the aim of FORSA and its activities.

10.2.3. National Knowledge Resource Centre (NKRC)

National Knowledge Resource Consortium (NKRC), established in the year 2009, is a network of libraries and information centers of 39 CSIR and 24 DST institutes. It aims to provide electronic access to international Science & Technology journals to CSIR Science & Technical personnel, thereby strengthening the facilities for pooling, sharing and electronically accessing the CSIR information resources in a cost-effective manner, and also for nucleating the culture of electronic access with a view to catalyzing the evolution of digital libraries. It provides access to more than 5,000 e-journals, patents, standards, citations and bibliographic databases. It also provides access to large number of open access resources in science and technology.

Fig. 10.8. Snapshot of NKRC
(*Source* : http://nkrc.niscair.res.in/)

NKRC's origin goes back to the year 2001 as CSIR E-journal Consortium, when the CSIR Network project with NISCAIR set up the Electronic Journals Consortium to provide access to 1200 journals of Elsevier Science to all its users. Over a period of time, the consortium not only grew interms of the number of resources but also in terms of the number of users as more like-minded institutes evinced interest to join the consortium. Council of Scientific and Industrial Research (CSIR) which has thirty-nine constituent laboratories together was subscribing to over 4,000 scholarly and research journals at a cost about Rs. 25 crores every year. The collection of print editions creates an annual depository of 5,00,000 plus printed articles spread across the labs in stand-alone manner. The fifth meeting of the Heads of CSIR

Laboratories and Information Centres held at RRL in Trivandrum in February 2001in order to enhance the accessibility, use and increase the resource base of world S&T literature, had recommended that a Consortium for access to e-journals be set up.

Consequently, Director General, CSIR set up a Study Group to collect and compile information on the journals presently subscribed by the CSIR laboratories, including CSIR Headquarter and also to study the feasibility and economic viability of CSIR laboratories subscribing to identified journals on-line on a consortium basis and devise a system for the management of the consortium, and equitable sharing of the expenditure thereof.

Thus, based on the recommendations made by study group, the CSIR accepted the recommendations and decided to set up a consortium, 'CSIR E - Journals Consortium' for electronic access to journals. However, it became NKRC in the year 2009 by merging 39 labs of CSIR and 24 labs of DST.

(i) Objectives : The main objectives of the consortium are:

- To provide staff the electronic access to world S&T literature to strengthen the facilities for pooling, sharing and electronically accessing the CSIR information resources;
- To provide access to world S&T literature to CSIR labs and DST labs; and
- To nucleate the culture of electronic access with a view to catalyze the evolution of digital libraries.

(ii) Activities of Consortium : The broad activities envisaged to be involved in carrying out the project include: identification of vendors; invitation of proposals; negotiation; signing of agreement; enabling access; training; payment to vendors; monitoring; usage statistics; analysis and reports.

(iii) Funding : The Consortium is wholly funded by CSIR and DST to NISCAIR, which handles all NKRC activities, a CSIR Institution located in Delhi.

(iv) Involvement of Larger Libraries : All CSIR and DST Labs' KRCs are well established both with resources and infrastructure. Notable CSIR Labs are - NAL, NCL, PRL, CDRI, RRLT, NIO, and DST Labs are - RRI, IIAP, JNCASR, BI, SNBNCBS, WIHG, IIG, BSIP, ARIES, etc.

(v) Governance : There is Coordination Committee with representatives from lead institutes who negotiate with publishers on selected e-resources. NISCAIR takes care of overall responsibility of NKRC activities. Each institute has a Nodal Officer (NO) to monitor access, usage of resources provided. Besides, nodal officers can also proposee-resources based on recommendations of users at each institute, which are normally taken at NKRC's Coordination Committee Meetings, keeping in view wide usage amongst participating libraries.

NKRC facilitates access to 5,000+ e-journals in all major publishers, patents, standards, citation and bibliographic databases, namely Web of Science, Derwent Innovation Index, ASTM International Standards. NKRC is also a single point entity that provides its users with access to a multitude of open access resources a part from licensed resources. The consortium envisions emerging as a leader to serve the R&D sector with much needed information to strengthen the research and development system in the country.

Thus, the consortium provides an opportunity for CSIR labs to have access to 5000 international reputed e-journals beside DST labs.

10.2.4. IIM Consortium

Indian Institutes of Managements are the premier national business management education institutions set up by the Government of India, which are governed by independent Board of Governors. The major objective of the institutions is to train young graduates to become professional managers. The IIMs are available at 13 places in Ahmedabad, Bangalore, Calcutta, Lucknow, Kozhikode, Indore, Shillong, Tiruchirappalli, Raipur, Udaipur, Rohtak, Ranchi and Kashipur.

The concept of IIM Library Consortium was floated a few years back when the librarians of all the IIMs had been interacting extensively in the year 2000 on the possible resource sharing of the CD-ROMs/Digital Databases being regularly subscribed to by them. Thus, a pilot study was conducted in this regard on the CD-ROMs/Digital Databases being currently subscribed to by the various IIMs and it was found that:

- ABI/Inform (Abstracts), ABI/Inform (Full-Text - Business Periodicals Ondisk - BPO) are being subscribed to by IIMA, IIMB, and IIMC respectively,
- Business Source Elite (BSE), the full-text journal service of EBSCO, is being subscribed to by IIMA, IIMI, and IIMK, and
- EconLit (Silver Platter) is received at IIMA and IIMK, and EconLit (Ovid) at IIMI.

Thus, the librarians of IIMs discussed and deliberated in one of their meetings that it is the right time for all IIMs to jointly approach publishers for journals and databases of common interest for better services and prices. Hence, they decided:

- While doing this exercise, the information resources of any of the institute(s) should not be affected in any manner, and shall ensure quality improvement and revenue saving to each institute.
- They may approach publishers of CD-ROM Databases to begin with, as Consortia, for better pricing and services.
- Eventually, other digital databases and journals shall

also be covered by the Consortia programme.

- The proposal of IIM Library Consortium seeks the authorization and guidance of the Heads of all the IIMs, to proceed further.

Fig. 10.9. Snapshot of IIM Consortium
(*Source* : http://www.iimlibrariesconsortium.ac.in/)

Based on the above, four of IIMs placed orders for databases such as BSE and Econlit and the rest two IIMs placed orders for ABI/Inform. Subsequently, the Directors of all IIMs in one of their meetings held in August 2001 approved the formation of IIM Library Consortium and encouraged the librarians to actively participate for mutual benefit.

(i) Objectives : The objectives of the IIM Consortia are to:

- ensure among the IIMs, optimum utilization and enhancement of the resources;
- minimize the expenditure by consortia-based subscriptions to the commonly subscribed databases and journals;
- approach publishers of CD-ROM databases to begin with as a consortium for better pricing and services; and
- cover other digital databases and journals by the programme.

(ii) Funding : Consortium budget is shared by all participating institutions.

(iii) Involvement of Larger Libraries : All IIMs have strong collection of resources both in print and electronic form and exchange of information is dealt with amongst IIMs libraries very strongly.

(iv) Governance : One of the members of the consortium has to take complete responsibility of making payment and getting agreements signed by all the members. The Steering Committee consisting of all participants identifies and selects resources for further ordering etc.

(v) Resources Available through Consortium : In the case of journals, all the IIMs put together subscribes to over 2550 scholarly titles. Having convinced on the dire need for journals consortia, major publishers such as Elsevier, Kluwer, Wiley, Blackwell and MCB University Press were approached and they all represented in the second meet which was held at IIM Bangalore in 2001. The end result has been highly praiseworthy, that over 740 e-journals IIMs are able to get online access, across all the IIMs, by paying a nominal additional amount.

The present information resource base of the IIM Consortium is as: Blackwell Hss Collection; Capitaline; Nexis.com+Corporate Information; ISI Emerging Markets; Kluwer Online; Talyor & Francis and John Wiley.

10.2.5. CeRA (Consortium for e-Resources in Agriculture)

Consortium for e-Resources in Agriculture (CeRA) was formed in November 2007 at the Indian Agriculture Research Institute (IARI), Pusa, New Delhi to provide access to information in agriculture particularly the e-resources to researchers, teachers and scientists, students, extension workers, policy planners and administrators in the National Agricultural System (NARS).It was funded by the National Agricultural

Innovation Project (NAIP).

(i) Objectives : The objectives of CeRA are to:

- Upscale the existing R&D information resource base of ICAR institutions/ universities comparable to world's leading institutions/organizations.
- Subscribe e-journals and create e-access culture among scientists/ teachers in ICAR institutes/ agricultural universities.
- Assess the impact of CeRA on the level of research publications measured through NAAS id and Science Citation Index.

(ii) Organizational Structure of CeRA : CeRA activities are governed by Steering, Monitoring and Negotiation and Working Committees and well supported by the Project Implementation Unit, NAIP. CeRA headquarters acts as an interface between all researchers in member institutes towards implementation of objectives of the consortium. CeRA members have the access of on-line journals through IP authentication, which provides a fool-proof system of security and also avoids memorizing user ID, password, publishers' URLs, etc.

(iii) Membership : The members of CeRA comprise of ICAR institutes and state agriculture universities. At present the membership is 147.

(iv) Services : The following services are being provided by this consortium.

- **Online Access:** Members are provided IP authenticated online access to full-text articles in more than 2900 journals in agricultural sciences. These comprise those subscribed by the consortium, by the participating libraries and the open access journals.
- **Document Delivery :** Members are provided access to full-text of journal articles not subscribed by CeRA but subscribed by individual libraries through

Document Delivery Request System, the DDRS.

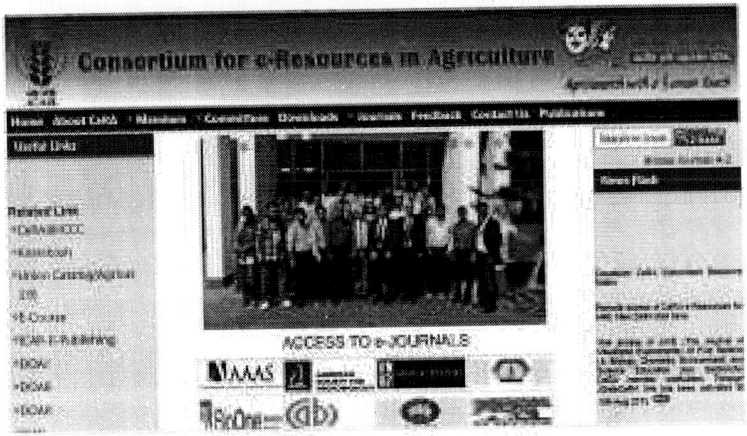

Fig. 10.10. Snapshot of CeRA Consortium
(*Source* : http://cera.iari.res.in/index.php/en/)

(v) Training : Training programmes are held regularly for members in different institutions under NARS to enable the use of resources and services in CeRA. They are also helped in their day today use of services through online help and chat with the experts in consortium.

(vi) Funding : The consortium gets its centralized funding from ICAR.

(vii) Governance : The overall governance CeRA rests with Steering Committee which deals with the policy issues and also plays an advisory role. The Negotiation, Monitoring Committees deal with negotiation with publishers and monitors progress of activities, and Working Committee deals with current activities.

However, IARI Library is considered as National Agricultural Library, which is biggest in Asia, caters major agricultural information requirements in the country.

10.2.6. TIFR Libraries Consortium

Tata Institute of Fundamental Research, the TIFR is one of the leading research institutes in the country, which is considered as the cradle of Indian science. Its library was established in the institute that has grown into a stature as one of the best managed scientific libraries in the country with specialization in core collection on physics, mathematics and nuclear sciences. However, the subject area coverage was further extended in the fields of biological sciences and radio astronomy by establishing NCBS, Bangalore and NCRA, Pune respectively. TIFR Libraries Consortium that was formed in the year 2000, which exploited model offered by Springer for multisite licensing and cross sharing of content among all libraries working under the umbrella of TIFR, is the first limited, purposeful and successful consortia - model. Eventually, many centers and field stations were established and subject fields were widened for inclusion in the expanded consortium.

Besides TIFR, there are six centers and six field stations and second campus in Hyderabad which has been established recently. All these together constituteas the members of TIFR Libraries Consortium. They are:

TIFR Main Campus is at Mumbai, and its 2nd Campus is at Hyderabad. Further, other centers are: HBCSE, Mumbai; NCRA, Pune; CML, Pune; NCBS, Bangalore; CAM, Bangalore. Besides, Field Stations are: HEGRO, Pachmarhi; GMRT, Khodad; GL, Gauribidanur; BF, Hyderabad; and CRL, Ooty; RAC, Ooty.

(i) Core Programmes : With expanding nature of the institutes and their information requirements, every attempt was made to subscribe to e-resources through consortium which are multidisciplinary in nature and with wide scope and coverage. TIFR Libraries Consortium has entered into negotiation with the Web of Science, MathSciNet, ACS Journals, AIP Journals, APS Journals, Elsevier Journals Back files, EMS Journals, Euclid Prime Journals, IOP Science, Oxford Journals Science Archive, Springer E-Books, Springer LINK, Springer Journals Archive, Taylor & Francis Journals(Physics & Mathematics), Walter d'Gruyter Mathematics Journals,

Wiley Journals (selected journals), Wiley Journals Archive and World Scientific Journals etc.

Subsequently, it has increased the co-operation and now there are several consortia-based subscriptions to electronic resources made available keeping in view the various research programs pursued by TIFR and its centers. Apart from these, TIFR and centre libraries are the members of Department of Atomic Energy (DAE) Consortium for the resources of Elsevier Science Direct which includes resources of Cell Press. This is a major initiative from DAE to facilitate access to large number of e-resources from Science Direct (Dattatraya and Sami, 2014).

(ii) Funding : The main library of TIFR is the source of main funding and consortium activities are handled by the TIFR Library.

(iii) Involvement of Large Libraries : TIFR's main library is the source of providing access to information. In addition, each center and field stations have excellent core collection; for example, in the fields of radio astronomy (NCRA, Pune), and biological sciences (NCBS, Bangalore).

(iv) Governance : TIFR Library Committee and its librarian as the Member Secretary/Coordinator for the Consortium select the resources for all libraries keeping in view recommendations from Centers/Field Stations. Negotiations are done and consortium deals are realized as per the need of all participants. However, the bills received are settled at the headquarters of TIFR, Mumbai.

10.2.7. DAE Consortium

The Department of Atomic Energy (DAE) initiated its consortium activities for institutions under its umbrella and signed up with Elsevier's Science Direct in 2002. There are 36 DAE affiliated institutions including TIFR, BARC and SAMEER. Thus, the consortium caters the needs of

36 DAE Institutions including TIFR, BARC and SAMEER.

(i) Core Programmmes : Consortium has agreement with five publishers and provides access to over 2000 e-journals to all its participants. The major publishers covered are: Elsevier for ScienceDirect, Springer and MathSciNet, etc.

(ii) Funding : The Department of Atomic Energy, Government of India, Mumbai.

(iii) Involvement of Large Libraries : TIFR, BARC and IGCAR are leading institutes in the consortium having excellent core collection in the areas of physics, mathematics, nuclear sciences and engineering sciences.

DAE Consortium is governed by BARC/TIFR, Mumbai.

10.2.8. ISI Library Consortium

Indian Statistical Institute that was founded on 17th December 1931 by Professor P.C. Mahalanobis in Kolkata, is an institute for research and higher education in statistics and allied fields. The institute was granted the status of an institute of National importance by an Act of Parliament in 1959, which is an autonomous institution under the Ministry of Statistics and Programme Implementation, Government of India. The Institute's headquarteris in Kolkata, and has two major centers at Delhi and Bangalore, where libraries are well equipped to cater information needs of their faculty, students and research workers. ISI Library was able to form two consortia - one in 1999 with a single resource - MathSciNet and other one which was implemented in 2003 with various publishers.

The participating libraries include Headquarter Library and Center's libraries at Delhi and Bangalore. For MathSciNet, there are over 18 members come under the consortium.

(i) Core Programmes : MathSciNet Consortium is

the core programme for which the idea was mooted during 1999 in a Library Committee Meeting held at ISI Library, in presence of Member Coordinator of National Board of Higher Mathematics (NBHM), DAE, Government of India. It was decided to have MathSciNet database and agreement was signed on 29th November 1999. By this agreement, the AMS grants a license of access to database on the Web. The ISI is also functioning as the Eastern Regional Center of NBHM. ISI Library is funded partly by NBHM grant for MathSciNet database along with its print version - Mathematical Review. More than 18 members have joined this consortium, covering eastern part of the country. Since then, this consortium is successfully working.

ISI Library Consortium has another step in forming the consortium with other publishers that was initiated and implemented in 2003. ScienceDirect Consortium of ISI Libraries comprising of Headquarter and its two centers was moved and license agreement was signed in March 2003, thereby getting access to 1500 titles with full-text. In 2003, consortia-based subscription was entered with EconLit Database, the electronic version of Journal of Economic Literature, published by American Economic Association. The access to this database was also extended to few other members, which was continued till 2005. Springer Verlag publisher's journals were added (78 titles) in the consortium during 2004.

ISI Library has also become a member of INDEST-AICTE Consortium (now e-shodhSindhu) for subscription of IEEEs Electronic Library (IEL) and also formed a consortium agreement with SpringerLink for three members. Efforts are on for license agreement with various publishers.

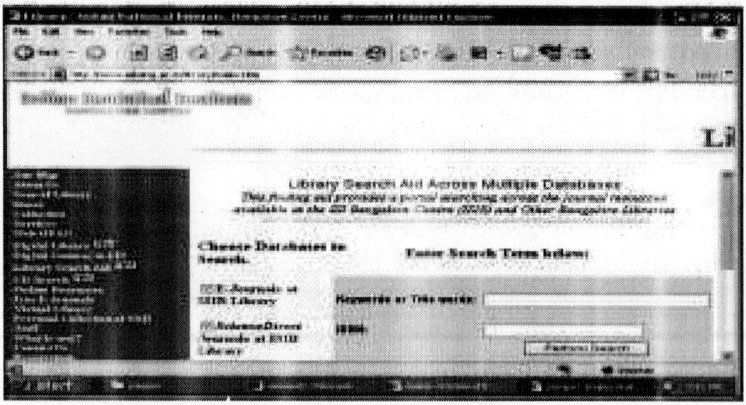

Fig. 10.11. Snapshot of ISI Library Consortium
(*Source* : Krishnamurthy, 2009)

(ii) Funding : Funding is provided by Headquarter of ISI and partly by NBHM for MathSciNet.

(iii) Involvement of Large Libraries : ISI Headquarter and its two centers' library collection and consortium resources together cater the information requirements of all researchers of ISI and other concerned members.

It is governed by a library committee at headquarter which takes care of selection, approval, ordering, payment, etc. keeping in view 3 centers requirements. However, the ISI Library handles consortium activities.

10.2.9. MCIT Library Consortium

Ministry of Communication and Information Technology comprises of four departments, viz. Department of Information Technology (DIT), Department of Telecommunication (DOT), Department of Posts (DOP) and Telecom Regulatory Authority of India (TRAI). Each Department has a number of PSUs, organizations and autonomous bodies which total number is 18 and all the organizations have their own Library & Documentation Centers to meet out the information needs of their officials.

Thus, a consortium for above libraries that is known as MCIT Library Consortium was started in 2005 where which NIC played a key role in the formation of the consortium. The Consortium is to provide resource sharing among the institutes/organizations under Ministry of Communication and Information Technology— and subscription to e-resources at consortium platform to reduce the cost and increase usage so as to increase the productivity of the S&T Professionals of the R&D set ups under the Ministry (Upadhyay and Mishra, 2008).

(i) Members : 18 members are participating in this consortium.

(ii) Core Programmes : Subscription of common e-resources, Union Catalogue of Print Documents and resource sharing. It provides the access to electronic resources to all participating libraries.

Fig. 10.12. Snapshot of MCIT Library Consortium (*Source* : http://mcitconsortium.nic.in)

(iii) Resources available through Consortium : IEEE Electronic Library; ACM Digital Library; International Standards online; Computer Science Collection from Elsevier Science, JCCC Gateway, EBSCO Database, e-books from John Wiley, Microsoft Press and OCLC, USA are some of the resources being subscribed under this consortium.

(iv) Funding : Centralized funding is arranged.

(v) Involvement of Large Libraries : NIC, DIT, CDAC, and CDOT.

It is governed by Department of Information Technology, Government of India. A Consortium Committee is constituted for governance and making the consortium effective. C-DOT is maintaining the bank account and fund on behalf of MCIT Consortium.

10.2.10. Electronic Resources in Medicine (ERMED) Consortium

ERMED Consortium, an initiative taken by the Director General of Health Services (DGHS), Government of India was started in 2008 to develop nationwide electronic access to information resources in the field of medicine for delivering effective health care for all. The authorities provide financial support required for the purchase of electronic journals to government medical colleges and the institutions. However, the payment per site is charged for e-resources purchased by the consortiumfor private medical colleges and institutions.

At present, there are 72 members including ICMR Institutes, DGHS Institutes/Centers, AIIMS and NTR Health University.

(i) Core programmes : NML started ERMED consortium in 2008 with 40 members including 28 ICMR+10 DGHS + AIIMS + NTR Health University, Andhra Pradesh. It provided electronic journals from 5 publishers, which contained 1515 medical journals. ERMED invested Rs. 2.6 Crore for electronic journals in 2008. In 2009, the ERMED members increased from 40 to 72 Government Medical Colleges/Institutes across the country. NML paid Rs. 7.55 crore for Government Medical Colleges/Institutes. The letter for self-payment was also sent to some Private Medical Colleges/Institutes.

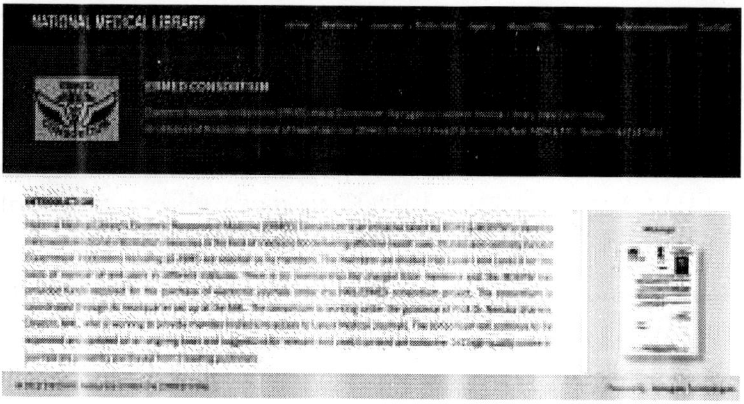

Fig. 10.13. Snapshot of ERMED Consortium (*Source* : http://www.ermed.in/)

ERMED is providing over 2742 journals since March 2012 from 1065 journal publishers, which include 932 open access journals, 770 consortia-based journals, 946 Proquest journals and 54 Gale journals. Among this 1031 journals are subscribed by ERMED and 284 are subscribing by cross sharing. Even though ERMED gives more focus on medical journals, there are some journals from other subject also such as: Engineering (43), Arts and humanities (38), Agriculture (33), Business, Economy & Management (16),Chemistry (41), Engineering (43), Earth science (6), Environmental science(50), General and Multidisciplinary (12), Information Technology (11), Law(8), Library & Information Science (7), Mathematics (8), Material Science &Metallurgy (6), Physics (12), and Social Science (124) but naturally Health Science (2096) and Life Science (386) journals.

ERMED resources can be searched and browsed through its versatile search platform at www.nmlermed.in.

(ii) Funding : The funding is centralized.

(iii) Involvement of Large Libraries : ICMR Institutes; DGHS Institutes/Centers; and AIIMS.

ERMED consortium is coordinated through its headquarters set up at National Medical Library (NML), Delhi.

10.2.11. JCCC@ICMR & ICMR Consortium

Indian Council of Medical Research, an apex body in India for the formulation of biomedical research that was founded in 1911, is one of the oldest medical research bodies in the world. Council promotes biomedical research in the country through intramurals as well as extramural research.

Intramural research is carried out by the Council's various institutes (30 number): which include permanent research institutes/centers which are devoted to the research in specific discipline of biomedicine; and regional medical research centers which take regional health problems into consideration.

While, *extramural research* is promoted by ICMR through: establishing centers for advanced research in different areas around existing expertise and infrastructure in related medical colleges/universities and research institutes across the country; task forces which are target oriented, time specified and follows certain specific methodology; and open ended research on the basis of application for grant-in aid received from scientists in non-ICMR Research Institutes, Medical Colleges and Universities, etc.

There exist libraries and information centers attached to each institute to cater information requirements but due to proliferation of information and electronic products, there was an urgent need to integrate vast network of institutes in order to provide required information. Thus, ICMR looked into JCCC for efficient resource sharing and optimization of subscribed journals. It also has undertaken various activities to help to address the challenges of digital technology to researchers and initiated two types of consortia - JCCC@ICMR, which covers all ICMR subscribed journals and full-text of free open access journals; and ICMR E-Consortium, which provides full-text of subscribed e-journals.

(i) Participating Libraries : ICMR's network of 30 Institutes' libraries and information centers.

(ii) Core Programmes : Its core programmes include the following:

(a) ***JCCC@ICMR :*** JCCC@ICMR was launched on 27th July 2004 and it is catering the needs of ICMR's libraries. It is providing a single point access to around 1680 journals out of which 858 titles are subscribed by 30 institutes and 197 open access (free) biomedical journals. It provides a common platform for all the members to have an access regarding the availability of journals. It also facilitates for getting an article from other libraries through JCCC platform.

(b) ***ICMR E-Consortia* :** ICMR E-Consortia was launched in 2007 which initially subscribed a few journals in a consortia mode for all ICMR Institutes, where researchers could have the access of subscribed journals at their desk-top. Journals subscribed with archives are: Nature, Science, Lancet, NEJM and BMJ.

(iii) Funding : ICMR is getting monetary support from Ministry of Health and Family Welfare, Government of India.

(iv) Involvement of Large Libraries : ICMR has 30 research institutes/centers spread across the country. Each library has developed core collection synchronizing their areas of specialization. In addition, consortia of JCCC@ICMR and ICMR E-Consortium has added a great fillip to supplement access to more information.

ICMR Headquarters' Publication and Information Division handles all activities related to JCCC@ICMR and ICMR E-Consortia.

10.2.12. DRDO E-Journals Consortium

Defense Research and Development Organization

(DRDO) is the largest government- funded research and development organization in India with a chain of over 53 laboratories and establishments spread across the country. Each establishment has its own library collection in the concerned area of specialization with limited library budget. Keeping in view the scenario of national/ international developments in forming consortia, DESIDOC, a constituent establishment of DRDO took initiation in forming consortium, with the objectives of providing DRDO S & T personnel global access to scientific and technical literature and to meet the users' ever-growing demands. Thus, the DRDO e-journal consortium came into being during 2007 and its service came into effect from January 2009 (Moorthy, 2009).

(i) Resources available through Consortium : DRDO e-Journal Service came into being with effect from 01 January 2009 covering 448 titles from 7publishers, namely ACM Digital Library (47 journals, magazines, transactions, etc.), ACS (36), AIAA (7), Elsevier Science Direct (195 titles), IEE+IEEE (157 titles plus conferences, standards), Jane's (5), and Science (1). However, due to the limitation of sites available for accessing titles of ACM (5), AIAA (10), Jane's (30),Science (13), and Elsevier Science Direct (access to 195 titles, 8 sites and access to their own subscribed titles in 34 other labs), a content browsing service was felt necessary. J-Gate Custom Content for Consortium(JCCC) Service was added to facilitate access to contents of all the journal titles subscribed by 20 major DRDO labs. JCCC service helps in obtaining a legal copy, by post, of an article required by a user in a laboratory not subscribing the title but is available in another laboratory.

(ii) Funding : Centralized funding is received from DRDO. However, the DESIDOC is implementing agency.

(iii) Involvement of Larger Libraries : Besides DESIDOC, many of DRDO labs have independent library & information centers with collection in their areas of specialization. However, the consortium has added better access to more information. This is consortium is being operated through DESIDOC under a Monitoring Committee comprising of members from DRDO and its constituent units. A Review Committee takes care of formulating policies, and negotiation with publishers. DESIDOC handles subscription to resources on behalf of all labs.

10.2.13. DeLCON DBT-Electronic Library Consortium

The Department of Biotechnology (DBT), Ministry of Science and Technology, Government of India has launched its Electronic Library Consortium (DeLCON) in January 2009 in order to meet out the growing needs of R & D information requirements. DeLCON has been set-up to promote the use of electronic databases and text access to journals by the research and academic community in the country (Lal, 2012).

Currently, there are about 34 institutions who participate in the DeLCON actively.

(i) Core Programmes : Around 917 selective journals from 20 leading publishers and a database - SCOPUS are covered under DeLCON. These are all accessible by the DeLCON consortium members through DeLCON Portal. The resources subscribed under consortium include: AAAS, AACR, ACS, ARs, ASBMB, ASM, Cold Spring, T&F, LWW, Marry Ann Liebert, Natur, OUP, Springer, SGM, SFH, Wiley-Blackwell, Elsevier, ASPB, ASI and SCOPUS Database.

(ii) Involvement of Larger Libraries : All major DBT Institutions' libraries have core collection in the areas of their specialization, which support strongly consortium services and activities.

Fig. 10.14. Snapshot of DeLCON DBT-Electronic Library Consortium (*Source* : http://delcon.gov.in)

Operation and management of DeLCON activities are handled by National Brain Research Centre, Gurgaon.

10.2.14. SNDT Women's University LISA Consortium

SNDT University has taken a lead in forming a Consortium for Library and Information Science Abstracts published by CSA. However, five university libraries have joined the consortium, which is a minimum number required to go for consortium subscription.

(i) Core Programmes : This database currently abstracts and indexes over 440 periodicals from more than 68 countries and in more than 20 different languages. Subject coverage includes all aspects of librarianship, library users, information retrieval and more.

(ii) Funding : Funding is met by all participating libraries at the deep discounted rates.

(iii) Involvement of Larger Libraries : Five university libraries are participating in the LISA Consortium.

However, SNDT University Library handles all activities of the consortium.

10.2.15. HELINET Consortium

HELINET, the Health Science Library and Information Network, an outstanding initiative by Rajiv Gandhi University of Health Sciences (RGUHS) has set a new benchmark in health science education in India concerning access to information. It was started in 2003 as a collaborative effort to network 25+ medical colleges in the state for promoting e-journal access and resource sharing (Health Science Library and Information Network, 2012).

Its mission is to network all the Health Science libraries for minimizing the cost of acquisition and maintenance of learning resources and maximizing their utilization among the faculty, students and researchers in the health science colleges and institutions.

HELINET has expanded its access to 709 journals from 200+ publishers. AMA (American Medical Association), BMJ (British Medical Journal), Annual Reviews, Blackwell, CVMosby, Elsevier, Lippincott, Ovid, Springer, George Thieme Verlag, Taylor & Francis, and WB Saunders etc.

SUMMARY

Thus, it is seen that the current age of library consortia proves to be the best form of library cooperation locally, regionally, nationally and internationally. It is one of the emerging phenomena for libraries to provide information to their users with an edge over the normal routes of accessibility. The library consortia through its strength of the number of institutions, offers vigorous business opportunities to the electronic publishers which can attract the best possible price and terms of agreements.

Various library consortia working world wide and in India of course, have been discussed in this chapter. But there is an urgent drive to pay attention for induction and the motivation of the library communities towards the technology driven opportunities and to orient with the challenges of the current environment. The consortia are a thing of past that has flourished to its fullest in developed nations. However, they are gaining momentum in the developing countries also like India and in future more and more consortia would emerge to serve their members with more information and with modem techniques and tools.

BIBLIOGRAPHICAL REFERENCES

Ball, D. and Pye, J. (2000). Library Purchasing Consortia: the UK Periodicals Supply Market. Learned Publishing, 13(1): 25–35.

Bley, R. (2000). NESLI: A Successful National Consortium. Library Consortium Management, 2(1): 18-28.

Chandrashekharan, H. (2012). CeRA - The E-Journal Consortium for National Agricultural Research System. Current Science, 102(6): 847-851.

Chen, Shunzhong. (2013). Promoting Resource Sharing through Consortia: A Case Study of Shanghai Library. Interlending & Document Supply, 41(2): 59-61.

Dai, L., Ling, C. and Zhang, H. (2000). China Academic Library and Information System: An Academic Library Consortium in China. Information Technology and Libraries, 19(2): 66-70.

Darch, C. Rapp, J. and Underwood, P. (1999). Academic Library Consortia in Contemporary South Africa. Library Consortium Management: An International Journal, 1 (1-2): 23-32.

Dattatraya, A. and Sami, L.K. (2014). Access to E-Resources: TIFR Libraries' Consortia Approach. Asian Journal of Information Science and Technology, 4 (1): 5 – 10.

Dobbie, A. (2002). Co-Operation versus Competition in the Development of E-Services in Libraries, Bertelsmann Foundation, Gutersloh.

Dong, Elaine Xiaofen and Zou, Tim Jiping (2009). Library Consortia in China. University Libraries Faculty Publications and Presentations. 17. Available at: http://scholarworks.uark.edu/libpub/17.

Feather, C. (2015). The International Coalition of Library Consortia: Origins, Contributions and Path Forward. Insights 28 (3): 89–93.

FORSA (2012). Forum for Resource Sharing in Astronomy & Astrophysics Consortium (FORSA). Available at: http://legacy.icolc.net/FORSA.html.

Gargiulo, P. (2003). Electronic Journals and Users: CIBER Experience. Available at: http://eprints.rclis.org/4477/2/Electronic_Journalslast.pdf.

Guzzy, Judith E. (2010). U.S. Academic Library Consortia: A Review. Sabbatical Projects. Paper 2. Available at: http://scholarspace.jccc.edu/sabbatical_projects/2.

Health Science Library and Information Network. (2012). Available at: http://jgate-lielinet.infomiindia.co.in/.

Hormia-Poutanen, K. (1999). Developing the National Electronic Library in Finland. NordInfo-Nytt, 22(2): 17–24.

Krishnamurthy, M. (2009). Accessing of E-Journals: A Consortia Approach. Available at: https://www.isical.ac.in/~serial/consortia/CBSOR-09.pdf.

Lal, D.D. (2012). Consortia Based Electronic Information Resource Sharing in Department of Biotechnology Institutes. Annals of Library & Information Studies, 59: 181-186.

Lowe, D. and Feighan, D. (1999). Saving a Buck and Avoiding the Muck: Consortium Models in Database Delivery: the Australian Experience. Available at: http://www.csu.edu.au/special/online99/proceedings99/302.

Marshall, P. (1999). Novanet, Inc.-Nova Scotia, Canada. Information Technology and Libraries, 18 (3): 130-134.

Minearo, R. (2009). Academic Consortia. Available at; http://www.highereducationconsortia.com/HECSummer2009CooperationUpClose.html.

Moorthy, A.L. (2009). DRDO E-Journals Consortium. DESIDOC Journal of Library & Information Technology, 29 (5): 18-23.

Okeagu, G. and Okeagu, B. (2008). Networking and Resource Sharing in Library and Information Services: the Case for Consortium Building. Information, Society and Justice Journal, 1(2): 255-262.

Parker, D., Gow, E. and Lim, E. (2002). AARLIN: Seamless Information Delivery to Researchers. In: Gaining Insight from Research Information: Proceedings of 6th International

Conference on Current Research Information Systems. Kassel University Press. Kassel. Available at: http://www.uni-kassel.de/CRIS20002/files/pdf/Parker.pdf.

Patil, Y.M. (2014). Consortium Approach to Resources Sharing in an E-Environment. Scientific Publishers (India), Jodhpur.

Payne, Lizanne. (1998). The Washington Research Library Consortium: A Real Organization for a Virtual Library. Information Technology and Libraries, 17(1): 13-18.

Perushek, D.E. and Douglas, A. (2014). Culture, Politics and University Library Consortia in China and the US: A Comparative Introduction to CALIS, GWLA and JULAC. Library Management, 35 (8/9): 594-606.

Phillips, Margaret. (2001). Moving Towards Public Access to Online Information Resources in Australia. In Proceedings of the Information Online 2001. Available at: http://conferences.aliaorg.au/online2001/papers/digital.issues. iiicJtitml.

Sanville, T. (1999). Use Levels and New Models for Consortial Purchasing of Electronic Journals. Library Consortium Management, 1 (3-4): 47-58.

Sanville, T. (2001). Use of Electronic Journals in OhioLink'S Electronic Journal Center. 67th IFLA Council and General Conference held during August 16-25, 2001. Available at: http://origin-archive.ifla.org/IV/ifla67/papers/118-141e.pdf.

Satyanarayana, N.V., Krishnan, S. and Arora, J. (2004). Library Consortia and Resource Sharing Initiatives in India: A White Paper. Rajiv Gandhi University of Health Sciences, Bangalore.

Singh, K. and Bhaskar Rao, V. (2008). An Overview of the Library Consortia in India. PLANNER-2008 Paper. Available at: http://ir.inflibnet.ac.in:8080/ir/ bitstream/1944/1124/1/10.pdf.

Sudhier, K.G. (2011). E-Journal Consortia and Indian Consortia Initiatives: An Overview. PEARL- A Journal of Library and Information Science, 5 (2): 39-49.

Thomas, G. and Fourie, I. (2006). Academic Library Consortia in South Africa: Where We Come From and Where We are Heading? The Journal of Academic Librarianship, 32 (4): 432-438.

Upadhyay, P. K. and Mishra, R. (2008). Consortium of Ministry of Communication and IT Library & Information Systems for Resource Sharing and Creating a Common Digital Library. Information Age, 2 (2): 8-10.

Varaprasad, S.J.D. and Madhusudhan, S. (2010). E-Journal Consortium: Is It a Success Story Always. DESIDOC Journal of Library & Information Technology, 30 (2): 92-96.

Visakhi, P. (2009). Consortium for e-Resources in Agriculture. DESIDOC Journal of Library & Information Technology, 29 (5): 24-30.

Weech, T. (2002). Back to the Future - When Resource Sharing seemed to Work: the Rise and Fall of Successful Consortia. Interlending and Document Supply, 30 (2): 80-86.

Further Readings (Only Books)

Ahmad, N. (2017). Next Generation Library System. Manakin Press Pvt. Limited, New Delhi.

Chaudhary, S.K. (2014). Library Networking. APH Publishing Corporation, New Delhi.

Elguindi, A. and Schmidt, K. (2012). Electronic Resource Management: Practical Perspectives in a New Technical Services Model. Chandos Publishing, Oxford.

Frederick, Donna E. (2016). Managing E Book Metadata in Academic Libraries. Chandos Publishing, Oxford.

Fresnido, Ana Maria Balenbin and Yap, J.M. (2014). Academic Library Consortia in the Philippines: Hanging in the Balance. Emerald Publishing Group, Bingley.

Hodgson, C. (2002). The RFP Writer's Guide to Standards for Library Systems. National Information Standards Organization Bethesda, Maryland.

Horton, Valerie and Pronevitz, Greg (Eds.) (2014) Library Consortia: Models for Collaboration and Sustainability. ALA, Chicago (USA).

Johnson, P. (2018). Fundamentals of Collection Development and Management. American Library Association, Chicago (USA).

Nazir, Tawfeeq (Ed.) (2018). Library Science and Administration: Concepts, Methodologies, Tools and Applications. Information Resources Management Association (USA).

Patra, N. K. (2017). Digital Disruption and Electronic Resource Management in Libraries. Chandos Publishing, Oxford.

Praveen, N. (2018). Library Consortia: A Complete Guide. Lambert Academic Publishing, Germany.

Ramanan, T. and Jayasuriya, S. (2012). Library Consortium: Resource Sharing among University Libraries in Sri Lanka. Lambert Academic Publishing, Germany.

Vyas, M. (2017). Pharmaceutical Library Consortium: Need of the Current Time. Laxmi Book Publication, Solapur.

Yep, J.M., Perez, M.J.V., Ayson, M.C.I. and Entico, G.J.E.L. (Eds.) (2015). Special Library Administration, Standardization and Technological Information. IGI Global, Hershey, Pennsylvania.

Index